LMS LOCOMOTIVE REVIEW

No. 1 – PASSENGER TENDER ENGINES
inherited from the former L&NWR

by
R. J. ESSERY & PETER DAVIS

CONTENTS

WILD SWAN PUBLICATIONS

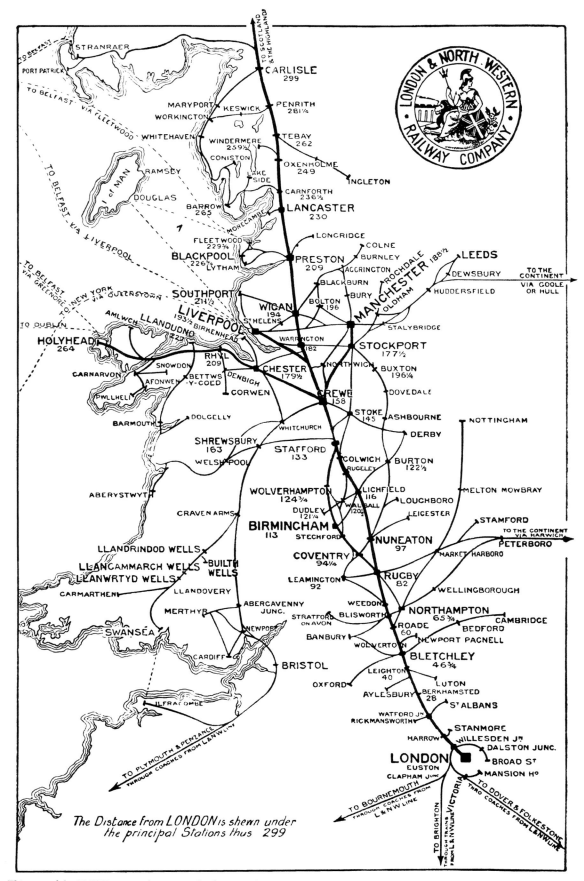

This map of the LNWR was on the reverse side of a menu dated 5th July 1909 where there is also a delightful picture of the dining room in the Queen's Hotel, Birmingham. For the record, lunch was 2s 6d. The map shows the extent of the LNWR system with what today is known as the West Coast Mainline, almost a straight line from London Euston to Carlisle for Scotland and the Highlands – truly the Premier Way.

FOREWORD

The question of what the LMS inherited from the constituent and subsidiary companies has often been considered in regular planning meetings for the *LMS Journal*. As far as we could see, the subject is not one to have commanded much attention from other authors and begs the question, what did the LMS inherit, how good was it and how long did it last before the new company replaced these assets?

This question could be directed to a variety of subjects ranging from fixed structures, signalling, livery, locomotives and rolling stock and even company identity, but we have chosen to begin our investigation with the largest constituent company of the LMS, the London & North Western Railway and to deal with its stock of locomotives. Self styled 'The Premier Line', it was formed in 1846 by the amalgamation of the London & Birmingham, Grand Junction (an 1845 amalgamation of itself with the Liverpool & Manchester and several minor Lancashire companies) and Manchester & Birmingham Railways. When considering the L&NWR prior to the 1923 grouping, we must also consider the North London Railway, a line that was incorporated by an Act of 26th August 1846 as the East and West India Docks and Birmingham Junction Railway. In December 1908, an agreement to last twenty-one years was entered into between the North London and London & North Western Railway Companies to the effect that the North London would continue to exist as a separate corporation, but their senior officers would be retired and their places taken by the corresponding officers from the L&NWR.

There was also the Lancashire & Yorkshire Railway Company, the origins of which lay in a number of small lines that came together in 1847 assuming the title Lancashire & Yorkshire Railway. Terms for amalgamation were agreed between the L&NW and L&Y in December 1921 and from 1st January 1922 the combined system was operated as one railway. For the purpose of this work, the locomotives of the Lancashire & Yorkshire Railway are excluded, but the locomotive stock of the North London Railway are included.

Although it is not possible or even desirable to ignore the pre-1923 history, it is not intended to delve into the various aspects of LNWR locomotive history so beloved by some writers. The question of the suitability of Webb's designs, in particular his compounds, will not form part of this work; indeed the publisher and I take the view that the LMS inherited all manner of mechanical items from the constituent and subsidiary companies and, that the quality varied, but they became LMS stock, and the purpose of these books is to record, as objectively as possible, what it was and how it fared during the years that followed. Therefore, in many respects, this is a 'broad brush' approach and no attempt has been made to include every minor detail that affected every class of locomotives. Nevertheless, this illustrated survey has taken many pages, so we have divided it into three manageable volumes, the first covering passenger tender classes, the second the tank engine classes, and the third the goods tender engines.

The information in this work has been compiled from a number of sources, the majority of them secondary, and when crosschecking it became clear that not all the dates and facts quoted were identical. While every effort has been made to crosscheck them, the lack of prime source material means that information given may be at variance with other published works on the subject. There are many ways of interpreting historical fact and we hope this work will be seen as accurate and comprehensive and add to our knowledge of the story of LNWR locomotives during the post-1923 period.

The final point is addressed to those readers who are also railway modellers. Experience as editor and publisher of both *LMS Journal* and *Midland Record* has shown us that many readers use these titles as a source of reference and information for modelling projects, so accurate detail information is important to them, therefore we will try to be mindful of their needs.

ACKNOWLEDGEMENTS

We would like to thank Peter Chatham, Simon Fountain, David Hunt, John Jennison and Graham Warburton, for their advice about certain aspects covered; Jim Jones for allowing me to quote from his notebook of personal railway experiences, and Peter Davis, whose contribution was immense and without which the work may never have been completed, so I invited him to be joint author on the project.

Bob Essery

© Wild Swan Publications Ltd. and R. J. Essery & P. Davis
ISBN 978 1 908763 03 7

Designed by Paul Karau
Printed by Amadeus Press, Cleckheaton

Published by
WILD SWAN PUBLICATIONS LTD.
1-3 Hagbourne Road, Didcot, Oxon, OX11 8DP

INTRODUCTION AND SUMMARY

On 4th August 1914 when war was declared, the British railways were taken over by the Government under the Regulation of Forces Act 1871 and administered by the Railway Executive Committee. This arrangement continued during the immediate postwar years until 15th August 1921 when the Government relinquished control, and four days later, on 19th August 1921, The Railways Act 1921 was given Royal Assent. This paved the way for the grouping of the British railway system to take place. Readers may find it helpful if we begin with a brief note about what happened.

THE REORGANISATION OF THE BRITISH RAILWAY SYSTEM

The railways in Great Britain were to be formed into groups, and a number of options were considered before the final scheme was adopted. The First Schedule of the 1921 Act gave particulars of the 'constituent' and 'subsidiary' companies to form each group. Before 1st January 1923, the constituent companies in any group were allowed to submit to the Minister of Transport an agreed amalgamation scheme, and the amalgamated companies could also submit agreed schemes for the absorption of the subsidiary companies in their groups. Failing agreement, schemes for amalgamation and absorption were to be settled by the amalgamation tribunal set up under the Act.

AMALGAMATION AND ABSORPTION SCHEMES

Under the terms of the Act, both amalgamation and absorption schemes could, with the consent of the proprietors, provide for the payment of compensation for loss of office to directors of constituent and subsidiary companies respectively, and they also had to contain provisions as to the management of superannuation, and other funds. The date tentatively fixed for the completion of the grouping of the British railway companies was 1st July 1923, with the amalgamations of constituent companies preceding the absorption of subsidiary companies. Agreed amalgamation or absorption schemes had to be submitted to the stock and debenture holders concerned before being referred to the tribunal. No stamp duty was to be paid in respect of any amalgamation or absorption scheme. In the event of postponement later than 1st July 1923, in the case of any group, during the period of postponement the undertakings concerned 'may, and shall if the amalgamation tribunal so direct, be used, worked, managed, maintained and repaired as one joint undertaking'. It was also stated that the net receipts should be distributed as agreed or as might be decided by the tribunal and that preliminary amalgamation and absorption schemes might be submitted.

A major amalgamation of two companies that were to become part of the LMS took place on 1st January 1922 when the London & North Western and Lancashire & Yorkshire Railway companies amalgamated, with the title of London & North Western Railway. The locomotive stock of the two constituent companies continued to be numbered in two separate series and, for operating purposes, the old L&NWR was referred to as Division 'A' and the L&Y as Division 'B'. This arrangement continued after 1923 until the Company's operating divisions were reorganized, as described later.

On 1st January 1923 the locomotive stock of the L&NWR Division 'A' comprised 2,305 tender locomotives and 1,206 tank engines; L&NWR 'B' Division stock amounted to an additional 1,654 locomotives (981 tender and 673 tank engines). However, within the 'A' Division total there were 109 ex-North London Railway locomotives together with fifty 2–8–0s of Great Central Railway design that had been purchased from the Government. Later, the 'A' Division became the LMS Western Division and the 'B' Division became the Central Division, and the subject of these changes is covered at page 7. Several authors have written previously about Midland Railway domination of early LMS locomotive affairs, stating that the LMS was flooded with Midland designs and often suggesting that they were not really suitable for the work they had to perform. Whilst there may be some truth in certain statements, they usually overlook a few simple facts. First, the economics of running a huge concern like the LMS made standardisation a sensible course of action, and within the constraints of the various loading gauges, weight limitations, etc, Midland designs were probably the easiest to adapt to suit all constituents. Secondly, Midland locomotives were undeniably the most economical types when it came to repair costs, and the most economical in day-to-day running were also to be found in the Midland ranks. Thirdly, Midland boilers, whilst not world-beating, were good steam raisers that lasted well and were economical in maintenance terms. Lastly in this necessarily short treatise, the frames on Midland engines lasted far better than most of their counterparts, which in part may have been due to the Midland's method of working often lighter loadings than on the LNWR for passenger trains and double heading many heavy goods and mineral trains, and details such as buffers and springs were much more robust than some others, particularly those of the L&NWR. In this category was also the valve gear which, whilst not being of the much-vaunted long-lap type, was notably robust and maintained its events far better between scheduled repairs than that produced elsewhere. Even that well-known hater of all things emanating from Derby, E. S. Cox, admitted as much. The advantages of long-lap valves were anyway not as clear-cut as some commentators would have us believe and whilst not wishing to turn this work into a treatise on valve gear design, one short discussion will suffice to illustrate the point.

When the LMS Standard 7F 0–8–0 was compared with the ex-L&NWR G2 on Toton – Brent coal trains, the initial results showed a 30% reduction in coal consumption in favour of the newer engine and this was hailed as proof of the superiority of its modern long-lap valve gear. However, a closer look at the results reveals that the water consumption, and hence steam usage, was only $5\frac{1}{2}$% better and that the vast majority of the reduced coal consumption was due to the greater efficiency of the 7F's boiler. When it is realised that the basic efficiency of the later engine's steam circuit was improved by higher working pressure and superheat temperature as well as its six-ring piston valves suffering less steam leakage, the efficiency of the G2's short-lap valves and cylinders was virtually the same.

Simply put, the ability of sufficient steam to enter the cylinders is governed by the size of the port opening and the time the valve is open; at high speeds the short-travel engine will possibly be at a disadvantage due to throttling, or 'wire drawing', but at low speeds this is not a significant factor. Hence, for a goods engine slogging along at 17 mph or so, which was the norm for mineral trains, the ability of steam to enter the cylinders in sufficient quantity will be the same for short-lap valves at long cut-off and long-travel valves at short cut-off. In this context it is interesting to note that the Achilles heel of the 7F was said to be its axleboxes, which is not really surprising if we take into account the probability that driving a long-lap engine usually involves using shorter cut-offs for a given speed and load, which will result in more pronounced oscillations in torque per revolution and hence more stress on axleboxes. This is particularly damaging on inside-cylinder engines where size for size the axleboxes are more heavily loaded than on their outside-cylindered counterparts anyway; the LMS wasn't the only railway to experience problems with inside-cylinder, long-lap locomotives.

As it turned out, the large saving in coal consumption recorded in the Toton – Brent trials was not realised in long-term service and the short-valve travel G2 outlasted its more 'modern' long-travel 7F counterpart. There are many more arguments that can be put forward concerning the benefits or otherwise of long-lap valves involving increased likelihood of slipping at low speeds, wear on valve gear, increased vibration, higher maintenance costs, etc, but they are too involved to go into here. Suffice it to state that the subject is far from clear-cut in favour of such gear in all instances and the men who made the decisions about what to build were not idiots. It is laughable to suggest, as some commentators have done, that those who were appointed to high-ranking positions within the largest joint-stock organisation in the world at that time, and which was run by hard-headed businessmen, didn't know what they were about when it came to providing motive power for the Company.

Prior to the Midland Railway renumbering its locomotive stock in 1907, almost without exception all major British railway companies used systems that at first sight were rather haphazard.

A necessity in any business is the listing of assets. However attractive the naming of objects may have been in the past, when it came to cataloguing the many aspects of a business of the size of the LNWR, numerical lists were essential. The assets to be listed were best grouped under two separate headings – *static* and *kinematic*. In the former, used for relatively permanent objects like stations, bridges and engine sheds, or for simple consecutive recording of orders, contracts and the like, numbers once assigned would remained unaltered. The number became an attribute of the subject – Bridge No. 140, for example, was always the aqueduct just to the south of Shugborough Tunnel.

In the kinematic catalogue, on the other hand, the subject was an attribute of the catalogue number. Most often used to list items of rolling stock, there was no permanent link between catalogue number and subject. Locomotive No. 140, for example, was any one of four completely different machines at different times in the company's history, each of which themselves also carried different numbers at various times.

The financial accounting and stock control methods of the LNWR were derived from those of the Liverpool shipowners, the dominant group of directors in the newly amalgamated company. Simple in concept, they led directly to the LNWR locomotive numbering system. The other British railway companies employed similar methods but many later adopted numbering schemes based on operating needs rather than those of the accountants.

The two categories of charging assets are well known. All locomotives built for new railways were, in common with the lines themselves, charged to capital account; that is they were paid for out of money subscribed by shareholders. Once the lines were up and running, all repairs and replacements were charged to revenue account; in other words, they were paid for out of the money earned in the operation of the railway. Locomotives, when worn out or obsolete, would be replaced by new ones and charged to the revenue account. As such they would, as far as the accountants were concerned, become the engines they had replaced. Hence they would take the numbers of the old engines.

Whenever a small company was absorbed into the LNWR, its capital would be added to that of the parent company and so its locomotive stock had to use new numbers in the capital list. An exception occurred where lines were vested jointly in two or more companies and the locomotive stock shared between those companies. In a case like that of the Birkenhead Railway, for example, whose capital remained intact when it was shared between the GWR and the LNWR, the absorbed engines were given vacant numbers in the 'normal' capital list without extending it. Conversely, when the company's lines were doubled or quadrupled in order to deal with growing traffic, or new lines built, thus generating new traffic, new locomotives would also be provided from capital and so extend the capital or 'nominal' list.

As production methods improved, it became economic to order new engines in batches rather than individually, and those charged to revenue would have to be found places in the nominal list, sometimes at the expense of engines no longer capable of front line work but, nevertheless, still useful. The latter were therefore usually placed on a 'duplicate' list, although rarely they may become part of the 'ballast' (later known as service) stock. This was non-revenue-earning stock used exclusively by the company in the maintenance of its infrastructure.

Different railways chose different methods of denoting their duplicate stock. Some kept the same number but added the suffix 'A' or 'B' or used the prefix '0', while others reserved a special block of numbers, with or without letters, for their duplicate engines. The LNWR came in the latter category.

In 1907, on the Midland Railway, all this was changed and the system that was introduced provided the basis for the future LMS renumbering schemes. Midland Railway locomotives were numbered in three series, 1–1099 passenger tender locomotives. 1100- 2199 tank engines and 2200 upwards freight tender engines. Generally the system was retained until the grouping; the division of engines into passenger and freight power classes came later and with the exception of the '2000 Class,' the passenger tank engines preceded the freight tank engines in the block of numbers reserved for tank engines.

Railway enthusiasts and those who were responsible for operating the railways often look at matters in a different way. For example, minute detail variations, which often excite enthusiasts, remain unnoticed by railwaymen; one personal experience will serve to make this point. One day I found that 'our engine', which we had to prepare, was an LMS 'Jubilee' Class 4-6-0. My driver knew it as a '5X'; 'Jubilee' meant nothing to him, and furthermore it was a named engine which was rather rare for Saltley Shed. This was the first time, that I had ever fired a 'namer', to use a spotter's term. In an excited frame of mind, I drew all this to the driver's attention and all that he said was, "Really, it is just so much extra weight to carry", referring to the small nameplate. It is doubtful if he even noticed it, but if he had, it meant nothing, it did not affect the mechanical working of the engine in any way. Therefore, it should be realised that attitudes varied and this becomes apparent when we consider what happened after the grouping.

Prior to the Whyte notation being adopted as a method for categorising locomotive wheel arrangements, rather unwieldy descriptions were used; however, the old terms were long lived. Reproduced at *Fig 1* is the index of an L&NWR locomotive engine diagram book. My copy is not entirely complete; the original was loose-leaf and there is no cover, which may have been dated, but the book was in use after 1923. Note page 4A, "6'6" Six Coupled 'Claughton' Class 5'5" Dia Boiler", a rebuild carried out in 1928. The inclusion of the North London locomotives was to be expected, but there were two pages for the Knott End Section engines, and this rather confirms that the book was prepared after the 1923 grouping and they were included in this L&NWR document. All the old L&NWR locomotive descriptions were still in use well after 1923 and the Whyte notations, which date from the Edwardian years, were not used. Therefore it is not surprising that the new LMS classifications, largely based upon Midland Railway practice, did not entirely follow L&NWR practice.

LMS CLASSIFICATION OF INHERITED STOCK
In order to set out how the LMS classified the L&NWR locomotive stock, the earliest document in my possession that deals with the subject is dated September 1923 (*Fig 2*). It summarises the new LMS number series for L&NWR engines, which also includes the locomotives of the Wirral Railway, but no Wirral Railway locomotive diagrams are known to me and they were not in the L&NWR diagram book. However, as mentioned, the Knott End Railway engine diagrams were included, even though these locomotives were allocated new LMS numbers in the series that was designated for locomotives from the old Lancashire & Yorkshire Railway.

Finally, we have the all-important Classification, or Motive Power Classification as it is shown on the 1929 document (*Fig 3*). The origin of these classification numbers lay in the Midland Railway practice of classifying passenger engines. This began in the closing years of the 19th Century and is

INDEX.

Page	CLASSES OF ENGINES.
1.	7-0" Four Coupled Simple "Renown" Class.
2.	7-0" Four Coupled Compound "Alfred the Great" Class.
3.	7-0" Four Coupled Compound "Jubilee" Class.
4.	6-6" Six Coupled "Claughton" Class.
5.	6-6" Four Coupled "George V" Class.
5A.	6-6" Four Coupled "Precursor" Class converted to "George V" (Piston Valves).
6.	6-6" Four Coupled "Precursor" Class.
6A.	6-6" Four Coupled "Precursor" Class (Flat Valves) Superheated.
7.	6-6" Four Coupled Straight Link.
8.	6-0" Six Coupled "Prince of Wales" Class.
9.	6-0" Six Coupled "Prince of Wales" Class (Walschaert's Valve Motion).
10.	6-0" Six Coupled "Experiment" Class.
11.	6-0" Four Coupled Side Tank.
12.	6-0" Four Coupled Straight Link.
13.	5-6" Six Coupled Side Tank.
14.	5-6" Four Coupled Side Tank.
15.	5-0" Six Coupled Side Tank. (18" Cyls)
16.	4-6" Four Coupled Side Tank. (8 Wheels).
17.	4-6" Four Coupled Side Tank. (6 Wheels).
18.	5-0" Six Coupled Goods (19" Cyls).
19.	5-0" Six Coupled Goods (18" Cyls).
20.	5-0" Six Coupled Special D.X.
21.	4-3" Eight Coupled "G2" Class. (Superheated)
22.	4-3" Eight Coupled "G1" Class. (Superheated)
22A.	4-3" Eight Coupled G2A Class. (Superheated)
23.	4-3" Eight Coupled Side Tank. (Superheated)
24.	4-3" Eight Coupled Shunter.
25.	4-3" Eight Coupled "G" Class.
26.	4-3" Eight Coupled Coal Class "D".
27.	4-3" Eight Coupled "C" & "C" Classes.
28.	4-3" Eight Coupled Compound Coal Class "B".
29.	4-3" Eight Coupled Compound Coal Class "E".
30.	4-3" Eight Coupled Compound Coal Class "F" Class.
31.	4-3" Six Coupled Coal.
32.	4-3" Six Coupled Coal Side Tank.
33.	4-3" Six Coupled Saddle Tank.
34.	4-3" Six Coupled Special Tank.
35.	4-3" Four Coupled Shunter.
36.	4-0" Four Coupled Crane Engine.
37.	4-0" Four Coupled Shunter.
38.	2-6" Four Coupled Shunter.
39.	4-8" Eight Coupled Consolidation Engine "MM" Class.
40.	5-5" Four Coupled Outside Cyl Bogie tank Eng. "1 to 10" Class.
41.	5-11" Four Coupled Inside Cyl. Bogie Tank. Eng. "51" Class.
42.	4-4" Six Coupled Side Tank Goods. (Outside Cyls) "75" Class.
43.	3-10" Four Coupled Steam Crane No 29 A.
44.	4-6" Six Coupled Side Tank. No 1747 Knott End Section.
45.	3-9" Six Coupled Side Tank. No 1732 Knott End Section.
4A.	6-6" Six Coupled Claughton Class 5-5" Dia Boiler.

Fig. 1. This is the first page of the locomotive diagram book and whilst some of the descriptions may be unusual, this is what was in use from 1923. The diagrams have been used in the class chapters.

LONDON MIDLAND AND SCOTTISH RAILWAY COMPANY.

Engine Re-numbering for London & North Western and Wirral Engines.

SUMMARY OF LOCOMOTIVE STOCK.†

Classi-fication.	New Engine Numbers.	Type.	Railway.	Remarks.
PASSENGER TENDER ENGINES.				
1	5000—5109	2—4—0	L. & N.W.	Straight Link.
2	5110—5117		L. & N.W.	Jubilee.
2	5118—5130		L. & N.W.	Alfred the Great.
2	5131—5186		L. & N.W.	Renown.
3	5187—5266	4—4—0	L. & N.W.	Precursor Sat'd.
3	5270—5319		L. & N.W.	Precursor Supt
3	5320—5409		L. & N.W.	George V.
3	5450—5554		L. & N.W.	Experiment.
4	5600—5844	4—6—0	L. & N.W.	Prince of Wales
5	5900—6029		L. & N.W.	Claughton.
PASSENGER TANK ENGINES.				
1	6400—6419	0—4—2	L. & N.W.	4' 3" Shunter.
1	6420—6434	2—4—0	L. & N.W.	4' 6" four coupled Side Tank.
1	6435—6512	4—4—0	L. & N.W.	North London.
1	6515—6600		L. & N.W.	4' 6" four coupled Side Tank.
1	6601—6757	2—4—2	L. & N.W.	5' 6" four coupled Side Tank.
1*	6758—6762		W.	
1*	6770—6776	0—4—4	W.	
3	6780—6829	4—4—2	L. & N.W.	6' 0" four coupled Side Tank.
1	6830		W.	
1	6850—6851	4—4—4	W.	
2	6860—6936	0—6—2	L. & N.W.	5' 0" six coupled Side Tank, 18" cylinders.
3	6948—6949	0—6—4	W.	
4	6950—6996	4—6—2	L. & N.W.	5' 6" six coupled Side Tank.
GOODS TANK ENGINES.				
	7200—7205	0—4—0	L. & N.W.	4' 0" four coupled Shunter.
	7206—7216		L. & N.W.	
	7217	0—4—2	L. & N.W.	North London Crane Engine.
2	7220—7457		L. & N.W.	4' 3" Special Tank.
2	7458—7502	0—6—0	L. & N.W.	4' 3" Saddle Tank.
2	7503—7532		L. & N.W.	North London.
2	7550—7841	0—6—2	L. & N.W.	4' 3" six coupled coal side tank.
5	7870—7899	0—8—2	L. & N.W.	4' 3" eight coupled shunter.
5	7930—7959	0—8—4	L M S	
GOODS TENDER ENGINES.				
1	8000—8087		L. & N.W.	Special DX.
2	8088—8314	0—6—0	L. & N.W.	4' 3" Coal.
1	8315—8327		L. & N.W.	5' 0" Goods. 17" cylinders.
2	8330—8624		L. & N.W.	5' 0" Goods. 18" cylinders.
4	8700—8869	4—6—0	L. & N.W.	19" Goods.
3	8900—8952		L. & N.W.	B class.
4	8953—8967		L. & N.W.	C class.
4	8968—9001		L. & N.W.	C1 class.
4	9002—9064	0—8—0	L. & N.W.	D class.
4	9065—9153		L. & N.W.	G class.
4	9154—9394		L. & N.W.	G1 class.
5	9395—9454		L. & N.W.	G2 class.
3	9600—9615	2—8—0	L. & N.W.	E and F classes.
5	9616—9645		L. & N.W.	R.O.D.

* Engines 6762 and 6776 are 2 class.

† This summary and attached list refers to the stock at September, 1923.
Details of subsequent alterations will be issued periodically.

Fig. 2. This list was published in September 1923 and gives the new LMS stock numbers for the LNWR and Wirral Railway stock. It is interesting to note that the stock of the old L&Y, which had been part of the LNWR since January 1923, is not included.

LONDON MIDLAND AND SCOTTISH RAILWAY COMPANY.

SUMMARY OF LOCOMOTIVE STOCK.

Derby, October 5th, 1929.

Engine Numbers.	Type.					Motive Power Classification.	Origin of Locomotive.
4997-4999	2—6—0 — 0—6—2 Freight Tank					Not Classified.	Garratt.
5000-5104	2—4—0 Passenger Tender			...		1	L.N.W. Straight Links.
5110-5186	4—4—0	,,	,,		...	2	L.N.W. " Renown."
5187-5319	,,	,,	,,	,,	...	3	L.N.W. " Precursor."
5320-5409	,,	,,	,,	,,	...	3	L.N.W. " George V."
5413	,,	,,	,,	,,	...	3	N.S. " G " Class.
5450-5554	4—6—0	,,	,,	,,	...	3	L.N.W. " Experiment."
5600-5845	,,	,,	,,	,,	...	4	L.N.W. " Prince of Wales."
5900-6029	,,	,,	,,	,,	...	5 & 5x	L.N.W. " Claughton."

The Class 5x Engines are as follows :—5906, 5908, 5910, 5927, 5946, 5948, 5953, 5957, 5962, 5970, 5972, 5975, 5986, 5993, 5999, 6004, 6013, 6017, 6023, 6029.

Engine Numbers.	Type.					Motive Power Classification.	Origin of Locomotive.
6100-6149	4—6—0 Passenger Tender			...		6	L.M.S. Standard " Royal Scot."
6422-6434	2—4—0	,,	Tank		...	1	L.N.W.
6518-6757	2—4—2	,,	,,		...	1	L.N.W.
6762	,,	,,	,,		...	2	Wirral. Purchased originally from L. & Y.
6780-6829	4—4—2	,,	,,		...	3	L.N.W. " Precursor " Tank.
6864-6936	0—6—2	,,	,,		...	2	L.N.W.
6950-6996	4—6—2	,,	,,		...	4	L.N.W.
7100-7149	0—6—0 Freight Tank ...				...	3	L.M.S. Standard.
7207-7216	0—4—0	,,	,,	...	...	Not Classified.	L.N.W.
7217	0—4—2	,,	,,		...	,,	N.L. Crane.
7220-7455	0—6—0	,,	,,	...	...	2	L.N.W. Special Tank.
7460-7502	,,	,,	,,	...	...	2	L.N.W. Saddle Tank.
7503-7532	,,	,,	,,	...	...	2	L.N.W. (N.L.).
7550-7841	0—6—2	,,	,,	...	...	2	L.N.W.
7850-7869	0—4—2	,,	,,	...	...	1	L.N.W.
7870-7899	0—8—2	,,	,,	...	...	6	L.N.W.
7930-7959	0—8—4	,,	,,	...	...	7	L.M.S. (L.N.W. Type).
8029-8084	0—6—0 Freight Tender...				...	1	L.N.W. Special " DX."
8088-8313	,,	,,	,,	...	...	2	L.N.W. Coal.
8315-8327	,,	,,	,,	...	...	1	L.N.W. 5′ 0″—17″ Cylinders
8330-8364	,,	,,	,,	...	...	2	L.N.W. 5′ 0″—18″ Cylinders.
8366	,,	,,	,,	...	...	1	L.N.W. 5′ 0″—17″ Cylinders.
8367-8624	,,	,,	,,	...	...	2	L.N.W. 5′ 0″—18″ Cylinders.
8650-8664	,,	,,	,,	...	...	1	N.S. Class " E."
8668 & 8669	,,	,,	,,	...	...	2	N.S. " 100."
8673-8678	,,	,,	,,	...	...	2	N.S. " 159."
8681-8688	,,	,,	,,	...	...	3	N.S. " H."
8700-8869	4—6—0	,,	,,	...	...	4	L.N.W. 19″ Goods.
8901-8954	0—8—0	,,	,,	...	...	6	L.N.W. " G1."
8957-8961	,,	,,	,,	...	...	4	L.N.W. " C."
8962	,,	,,	,,	...	...	6	L.N.W. " G1."
8963	,,	,,	,,	...	...	4	L.N.W. " C."
8964-8966	,,	,,	,,	...	...	6	L.N.W. " G1."
8969-8999	,,	,,	,,	...	...	3	L.N.W. " C1."
9002-9394	,,	,,	,,	...	...	5 & 6	L.N.W. " D," " G " and " G1."

The Class 5 Engines are as follows :—9002, 9003, 9009, 9010, 9013-9015, 9017, 9028, 9035, 9038-9040, 9045, 9047-9052, 9055, 9056, 9061, 9062, 9063, 9068-9070, 9072, 9077, 9078, 9080, 9081, 9086, 9088-9090, 9095-9098, 9102, 9105-9110, 9113, 9117-9120, 9123, 9126-9130, 9134, 9136, 9138, 9141, 9143, 9145-9148, 9150, 9152.

Engine Numbers.	Type.					Motive Power Classification.	Origin of Locomotive.
9395-9454	0—8—0 Freight Tender...				...	7	L.N.W. " G2."
9500-9584	,,	,,	,,	,,	...	7	L.M.S. Standard.
9600-9615	0—8—0	,,	,,	...	...	6	L.N.W. " G1."
9616-9665	2—8—0	,,	,,	...	...	7	M.M.

Fig. 3. This document summarises the LMS locomotive stock between 5000 and 9665 as at 5th October 1929. Note that the suffix 'P' for passenger and 'F' for freight engines has not been used and that the 'Precursors' are shown as Class 3 and not 2 as they should have been.

described in greater detail in *Midland Record* 21 (see page 46 of the Special issue). By 1905 the Midland Railway had classified its goods engines as power class 1, 2 or 3, the higher number being the most powerful. However, in 1911 the new goods engines, known subsequently as Class 4F, entered service and these remained the most powerful goods engines owned by the Company.

The system was simple; the motive power classification number provided the operating staff with all the information they required. It made no difference what the driving wheel diameter was, or if the engine was saturated or superheated. The loading book gave all the details of loads that various power classes were allowed to pull over given sections of line, depending upon the class of train being hauled, and a separate book gave the point-to-point timings that made it clear how long it should take any class of train to travel over each section of line. There was a third published reference, 'Lines over which Locomotives are Permitted to Run'; this was necessary because not every locomotive was allowed to run over every line and it was important that those responsible for diagramming locomotives were aware of the various restrictions that applied.

For example, a mineral train running between point A and B was allowed X minutes and the only variable factor was the weight of train that could be hauled, with a Class 2 pulling a heavier train than a Class 1 engine, and a Class 3 a heavier train than a Class 2, but all being expected to cover the distance in the same period of time. In presenting this simple illustration, factors such as maximum length of train over a section have not been taken into account. Sometimes it was not possible to fully utilise the more powerful locomotives' haulage capacity because of length of train restrictions, usually based upon length of lie-byes should a train need to be shunted off the main line to allow a faster train to overtake. In 1928 the LMS introduced the use of a suffix to the power classification number, P for Passenger and F for Freight; later MT was introduced for locomotives described as Mixed Traffic and X if the power classification was between two levels, e.g. 5X, which applied to locomotives that were more powerful than Class 5 but not as powerful as Class 6. However, enginemen usually referred to the locomotives by power class number only. For example, Class 4 (not 4F), or Class 8 (not 8F) generally ignoring the F, P or MT.

The LNWR, having followed the Midland lead by instituting Centralised Goods Traffic Control from 1912 onwards, in 1915–6 introduced a similar locomotive classification system to that of the MR. There was a similar Loading Book, part of the Appendix, giving train tonnages for each class of engine. However, whereas the MR classification system began low and finished high, the LNWR did the opposite – the highest power was Class 1, which is illogical as well as inflexible (what do you call a new more powerful engine than your existing Class 1 without re-classifying the whole fleet?), which is the main reason why the LMS didn't adopt it. The classification system for passenger traffic had been introduced in 1913 but without class numbers. There were five categories of passenger traffic and six classes of goods engine on the LNWR.

In the sections that follow we have made use of a number of the LNWR locomotive diagrams; there are two reasons for doing this. Firstly, they are reproductions of the diagrams used by the Company and therefore historically important, and secondly, they present the basic information about the various types of locomotives that were inherited by the LMS. This information could have been presented in tabular form but it was considered that the use of the original diagrams is preferable. It should be noted that in the past, many writers have used certain class descriptions that do not appear in either of the official documents referred to above. Where it is felt that the use of these descriptions may be helpful, they have been included in the text, but generally we have used information and descriptions that appear in LMS documents.

EARLY LMS POLICY FOR CONSTRUCTION

Construction of locomotives to constituent company designs continued after 1923 and although it is usually seen as the perpetuation of only Midland Railway designs which became LMS Standard classes, there were exceptions. Four 0–6–2Ts were built at Stoke in 1923, one before and three after the terms of amalgamation were agreed with the NSR. A number of 4–6–0s of LYR design were ordered by the LNWR in 1922 and completed during 1923–25; the work also included ten 4–6–4Ts based upon the tender locomotives. In Scotland, twenty Caledonian Railway 4–6–0s were built at St Rollox in 1925 and Nasmyth, Wilson, built ten CR 0–4–4Ts in 1925. As far as the LNWR were concerned, a new design of thirty 0–8–4 freight tank engines was built in 1923. These are shown on the 1923 list as LMS and in the 1929 list as LMS (L.N.W. Type), and there was also the final example of the 'Prince of Wales' class that entered service in 1924. With the exception of the Midland Railway classes adopted as LMS Standard classes, the final locomotives to be constructed to what were in effect pre-1923 designs were developments of the 1909-design LT&SR 4–4–2Ts. Three batches of these were built between 1923–27 and a fourth batch of ten in 1930. Rebuilding and reboilering certain classes continued for many years and some locomotives built before 1923 were renumbered prior to Nationalisation. Details of what happened to the old LNWR classes after 1923 are given in the relevant sections.

At this point in the story of what happened to the locomotive stock of the LNWR, it is necessary to consider in detail the management structure and decisions about new construction. For many years this aspect of the history of the LMS has either been ignored or, in my view, misrepresented, so by providing this information a clearer picture will emerge about how the Company's locomotive stock was managed.

So how was LMS locomotive policy decided during the formative years of the Company? To answer that question we must go back to the first informal meeting of LMS directors that was held on 15th December 1922, when 23 of the allotted 28 directors attended, with the Hon. C.N. Lawrence from the LNWR taking the chair. At this time the ex-CR and NSR directors had yet to be appointed. The meeting decided that the Company would be run via nine Committees, each representing a portion of the Company's activities, one of which was the Rolling Stock Committee whose terms of reference were: 'To take charge of all matters connected with rolling stock, including the construction, purchase and repair of engines, carriages, wagons, road vehicles and electric plant and power stations, and the supervision of the Company's workshops connected therewith. To supervise generally all matters relating to mechanical plant'. The first members of this committee were: J. Bruce Ismay and George Macpherson (both ex-LNWR), W. L. Hitchens, Joseph H. Kaye and G. R. T. Taylor (all ex-LYR), Sir Alan Garrett Anderson, Alfred Harold Wiggin and Douglas Vickers MP (all MR) the latter as Chairman.

It was usual for all Committees to meet either the day before or on the morning of a Board meeting. In addition to the members of the various Committees, it was not unusual to have the relevant heads of Departments present, which, in the case of the Rolling Stock Committee, would be the CME together with the Carriage and Wagon Superintendent, dependent upon the agenda.

Policy was generally originated at committee level following a presentation by one or more heads of department and discussion by the members of the committee who, if they approved, would refer the matter to other committees who may have had an interest in the subject, and when the new policy was endorsed at this level it was then presented to the Board for their approval. The CME or other officers did not, as some authors have suggested, determine LMS locomotive policy without Board approval.

The first Chief Mechanical and Electrical Engineer of the LMS was George Hughes, LNWR-LYR and his senior officers are listed below. Although the Lancashire & Yorkshire Railway had amalgamated with the LNWR in 1922, I have shown those who were ex-LYR as LNWR-LYR.

between November 1927 and November 1928 a further change was agreed and the divisional structure became Western (the old 'A' Division), Midland, Central (the old 'B' Division) and Northern. Although this was largely a change of title, there were some boundary changes, for example the old Midland lines in South Wales became part of the Western Division.

COMMITTEES

Commencing on 1st January 1924, the make-up of all the Committees was revised to take into account the appointment of ex-CR and NSR Directors with the Rolling Stock Committee as follows: The Hon. Arthur H. Holland Hibbert, George Macpherson (both ex-LNWR), G. R. T. Taylor (ex-LYR), Sir Allan Garrett Anderson, KBE, Douglas Vickers, Alfred Harold Wiggin (all ex-MR), Albert E. Pullar (ex-HR), Capt. James Hamilton Houldsworth (ex-CR), Major Frank H. Wedgewood (ex-NSR).

The Chairman of the LMS, The Hon. Charles Napier Lawrence, and his two deputies, Sir Guy Granet ex-MR and Edward Brocklehurst Fielden ex-LYR, were ex officio members of all committees.

Following the experience of the first year, at the Board meeting held on 27th March 1924 it was agreed to revise the Committees, and as a result the Locomotive and Electrical Committee was divided and a separate Carriage and Wagon

Name and pre/1923 Company	Pre-1923 Designation	LMS Designation
Sir Henry Fowler KBE, CBE, JP, LLD, DSc, Wh.Sc, M.Inst.C.E, M.I.Mech.E, M.Inst.T. (MR)	CME (MR).	Deputy CME & Mechanical Engineer Midland Division.
H.E.Obrien DSO (LNWR – L&Y)	Electrical Engineer. Horwich	Electrical Engineer.
Hewitt Pearson Montague Beames MICE, MIMechE, MILoco E. (LNWR)	Divisional Mechanical Eng. Crewe	Mechanical Engineer. Crewe
George. N.Shawcross MBE M.I.Mech.E (LNWR-LYR)	Divisional Mechanical Eng. Horwich	Mechanical Engineer. Horwich.
A.R.Trevithick CBE, MICE. M.Inst.C.E. (LNWR)	Divisional Carriage Superintendent. Wolverton	Divisional Carriage Superintendent. Wolverton.
W.W.H. Warneford OBE (LNWR)	Divisional Wagon Superintendent, Earlestown.	Divisional Wagon Superintendent. Earlestown.
Francis Edward Gobey OBE (LNWR – L&Y)	Divisional Carriage & Wagon Superintendent. Newton Heath	Divisional Carriage & Wagon Superintendent. Newton Heath

Other senior members of the Chief Mechanical & Electrical Engineers Department were:

J. A. Hookham, MICE, MIMechE (ex-NSR) – Mechanical Engineer (Stoke-on-Trent)
David L. Rutherford, MICE (ex-FR) – Mechanical Engineer (Barrow)
William Pickergill, CBE (ex-CR) – Mechanical Engineer (St. Rollox) Glasgow
Robert H. Whitelegg (ex-GSWR) – Mechanical Engineer (Kilmarnock).
David Chalmers Urie (ex-HR) – Mechanical Engineer (Inverness).

At first the LMS Railway was divided into three operating Divisions, Midland, Northern and Western, with the latter subdivided into 'A' and 'B'. The old LNWR was the 'A' Division and the old L&Y the 'B' Division, but sometime

Committee was formed, consisting of Ismay (LNWR), Taylor (LYR), Booth (MR) (Chairman), Vickers (MR), Wiggin (MR), Houldsworth (CR) and Wedgwood (NSR). The new Locomotive and Electrical Committee now consisted of the same members, with Vickers (MR) as chairman.

This was followed by the appointment on 30th June 1925 of Sir Josiah Stamp as President of the Company, and on 28th October 1926, to commence from 1st January 1927, by the appointment of four Vice Presidents, who were: – S. H. Hunt, CBE (ex-LNWR), J. Quirey, J. H. Follows, CBE and R. W. Reid, CBE (all ex-MR). It is interesting that none of these were Directors, but maybe they did know a thing or two on how to run a railway? Then came the retirement of H. G.

Burgess (ex-LNWR) the Company Secretary, on 31st March 1927, and as a result of these changes the management style of the LMS was to change for the duration of the Company.

There was now an overwhelming representation of men from the Midland Railway with Sir Guy Granet as Chairman of The Board (ex-Chairman of the MR), Sir Henry Fowler (ex-MR Chief Mechanical Engineer following the retirement of George Hughes from 15th November 1925), R.W. Reid (ex-MR Carriage and Wagon Superintendent), J. Quirey (ex-MR Accountant) and J. H. Follows (ex-MR General Superintendent). It would be unlikely for Mr Hunt (ex-LNWR Chief Goods Manager) to exercise much influence on such matters as locomotive policy. With the addition of the Secretary and Chief Legal Adviser, these five officers now formed the LMS Executive Committee.

Each Vice President took the place of the General Manager in relation to a group of Departments representing them on the Committee: one for the accountancy and service departments, one for works and ancillary undertakings (excluding hotels), and two for the Railway Traffic Operating and Commercial section of the LMS.

Therefore it may reasonably be assumed that during the first years of the LMS, things were not quite right in the way the Company was run and some 'fine tuning' was required; the standing committees had already been amended three times in less than eighteen months. The first Chairman, Lord Lawrence, resigned after one year in office, as indeed had the first General Manager, Sir Arthur Watson.

LOCOMOTIVE RENEWAL PROGRAMMES

In order to show how problems on the ex-LNWR lines were dealt with, it is necessary to quote from a letter from the CME, to the Chairman and Directors of the Locomotive & Electrical and Traffic Committee. Dated 27th April 1927, it set out the reason for including 100 Standard 0–6–0 Shunting Tank Engines in the 1927 Locomotive Building Programme.

'Referring to Locomotive and Electrical Committee Minute 355 and Traffic Committee Minute No. 1171 of the 15th December, 1926, we have now completed our investigations as to the necessity for a further supply of 0–6–0 Standard Goods Shunting Tank Engines, and ask for authority for 100 of these engines to be built for the following reasons.
1. Many of the old Shunting Tank Engines, particularly those on the L.N.W. section, are considerably above the average age and are so far worn that it would not be economical to repair them extensively; further, the former North London Section Passenger Tank Engines are also above the average age and in need of replacement and it is considered that the Standard Shunting Tank Engines fitted with screw reversing gear and carriage warming apparatus would be suitable for this Section.
2. There is a great demand for Standard type shunting engines for yard shunting and trip working to replace old and obsolete engines now used.'

Although most authors see William Stanier, whose service as CME of the London Midland & Scottish Railway in succession to E.J.H. Lemon commenced on 1st January 1932, as the man who changed the face of the locomotive stock of the Company, it is very clear from the above that from the formation of the LMS the problems of old locomotives that were 'time expired' and the need for standardisation, with a reduction of spares, in particular boilers, that had to be carried in stock, was recognised by those responsible for motive power and traffic working. Although the following report referred

to all the locomotive stock of the Company, its inclusion here provides a very clear picture of the problems of the day. The references that follow have been taken from various LMS Committee minutes that are held at the National Archive mostly under the Rail 418 and Rail 422 reference numbers. Both the spelling and where possible the original format has been retained although to assist the reader follow the events some 'clarification text' has been added by the author.

Locomotive Renewal Programme 1932. New Work Order 2557. 28th October 1931

Submitted report from the Chief General Superintendent and Chief Mechanical Engineer (with covering note from the Chairman) in regard to the Locomotive Stock Position, and the proposed Locomotive Renewal Programme for 1932.

The locomotive position at 31st December 1930 was fully reported to the Traffic Committee on the 25th March, 1931.

It was specified that as a result of improved shop output of repairs and the infusion of larger types, about 270 locomotives should be withdrawn and broken up. At the same time it was stated that decreased use due to trade depression should be met by storing locomotives.

250 locomotives have been definitely earmarked for breaking up, of which 91 have actually been broken up and the remaining 153 will be definitely broken up by 31st December 1931.

Steam engine mileage has decreased by 5% in 1931, compared with 1930, and the number of stored locomotives has increased from 430 at 31st December 1930, to 704 at 19th September 1931.

Further improvements have been effected in the shop output of repairs in 1931, resulting in a further reduction in the numbers of engines under and awaiting repair, as under:–

	Total Stock	No. under & awaiting repair	Percentage of total stock
31st December, 1927	10,214	897	8.78%
31st December 1930 (including 450 stored)	9,319	377	4.05%
19th September 1931 (including 704 stored)	9,245	295	3.17%

Reference was also made in the report to the question of greater mileage and hours used per locomotive day. Experiments in this direction are still going on, and a report will be submitted as soon as the matter has reached a definite stage, but throughout 1931 there has been an improvement in the number of miles and hours per locomotive in use.

1931 Programme

With regard to the 1931 Programme, Traffic Committee Minute No. 2678, dated 25th March 1931, authorised the building of 181 new locomotives in the place of 183 displaced locomotives and 2 rail motors.

89 of the new locomotives had been completed at 19th September 1931, and it is estimated that the whole of the 181 will be completed at Crewe by April 1932, and Derby by July 1932.

73 of the 183 displaced locomotives have up to now been broken up, 67 more will be broken up between now and December 1931, and the remaining 45 will be broken up in the early part of 1932, in any case not later than the date of the completion of the new locomotives. Breaking up is dependent upon exhausting the residual useful life of individual locomotives.

1932 Programme

Having regard to the financial position and considerations of the developments in other forms of traction, it is recommended that a short term building programme should be authorised to cover the period from the completion of the 1931 programme (Crewe in April, 1932 and Derby in July, 1932) to December 1932. This will also bring the completion of the programme into line with the Company's financial year and the next programme will relate to output in the calendar year 1933.

The present programme will conform to the objective of the long term programme in the standardisation of stock to about 19 separate types and the elimination of old and uneconomic types. It is recommended, with the approval of the Executive, that 75 locomotives of the following types be built in the Company's Shops at Crewe and Derby, viz:—

Tender Engines		No.
Passenger superheated	4–4–0	20
Freight superheated	0–8–0	20
Mixed Freight superheated	2–6–0	10

Tank Engines		
Passenger superheated	2–6–4	10
Passenger superheated	2–6–2	10
Freight superheated	0–4–0	5
	Total	75

172 locomotives, as shewn below, will be displaced and broken up, viz:—

Tender Engines		
Passenger	38	
Freight	58	
Tank Engines		
Passenger	37	
Freight	59	
	Total	172

The total estimated cost of the 75 new locomotives is £344,354 and the estimated replacement cost of the 172 locomotives to be displaced and broken up is £594,050.

A reduction in capital cost of £249,676.

In consequence of the disappearance of 5 separate old and uneconomic types, materials in stock will become obsolete as under:—

Value standing in Stores Stock Account	£8,040
Less Scrap Value	£1,628
Loss due to obsolescence.	£6,412

The estimated charge to the Renewal Fund will be as follows:—

Cost of 75 new locomotives	£344,354
Loss due to obsolescence of materials	£6,412
	£350,766
Less Scrap value of 172 displaced locomotives	£46,592
Total Charge to Renewal Fund	£304,174

The annual Renewal Provision made in the 1930 accounts for a full year was £1,047,500.

The adjustment of Capital Account will be left over until the economic stock position is more defined.

The costs are based on the experience of the latest finished orders and generally represent the prices of materials and cost of labour in 1929 and 1930. Prices of materials and rates of wages are at present less than 1929 and 1930 but having regard to the uncertainty as to Commodity prices in 1932 the costs have not been revised. Statistical information is embodied in the report shewing the comparative summarised effects of the proposed 1932 programme bringing out the decrease in numbers of stock, weight, tractive power, annual mileage, replacement cost of the locomotives to be built as compared with those displaced; also the increase in average weight, tractive power, and annual mileage in the case of the proposed new locomotives, as compared with those to be displaced.

At January 1923, there were 393 different types of locomotives; at December 1930, the number had been reduced to 273, and the scrapping of the 250 locomotives with the 1931 building programme further reduced the number to 256, and the proposed 1932 programme will further reduce the number to 252. The number of superheated locomotives at January 1923, was 1,870, equal to 18% of the total stock, at December 1930, 3,518 equal to 38%, at the end of the 1931 programme 3,649 equal to 40% and at the end of the proposed 1932 programme will be 3,700 equal to 41%.

The average age adjusted by weight of the 172 displaced locomotives is 39.057 years compared with the average theoretical life of 38.924 years, on which the annual renewal provisions for the particular locomotives have been based since the early amalgamation figure of 33⅓ years was corrected to a life for each type.

The report also contains comparative statistics of Locomotive Stock before and after the proposed 1932 programme.

The movements in stock up to the end of the 1932 programme reflect the aggregate changes in the qualitative and quantitive demands due to traffic variations by the closing of branch lines, improved shop organisation, intensive user, improved design of Locomotives and other causes.

Costs of repairs, and coal consumption have been taken from the records of expenditure incurred on individual locomotives forming the classes concerned for the four years 1927, 1928, 1929 and 1930, excepting in the case of two classes of new engines for which no actual costs are available and these have been estimated on the basis of actual costs of locomotives of the nearest type.

The comparative costs per engine mile of the proposed new locomotives and those to be displaced are as follows:—

	New Locomotives Pence	Displaced Locomotives Pence	Increase (+) or Decrease (−) Pence		%
Tender Locomotives					
Repairs (Shops & Sheds)	4.58	4.96	−.38	=	7.66
Renewal Provision	0.69	0.92	−.23	=	25.00
Coal at 20/- per ton	6.18	6.50	−.32	=	4.92
TOTAL	11.45	12.38	−.93	=	7.51
Tank Locomotives					
Repairs (Shops & Sheds)	3.71	3.78	−.07	=	1.85
Renewal Provision	0.45	0.53	−.08	=	15.09
Coal at 20/- per ton	5.35	4.71	+.64	=	13.59
	9.51	9.02	.49		5.43

The estimated annual savings based on engine miles without adjustment for increased power are as follows:—

REPAIRS, RENEWALS AND COAL CONSUMPTION

		£
Tender Locomotives		
1,513,065 engine miles at decreased cost of .93d. per mile		5,863
Tank Locomotives		
799,660 engine miles at increased cost of .49d. per mile		1,633
		4,230

	£	£
Interest 5½% on £249,676 decreased cost of new and displaced locomotives.	13,732	
Less 5½% on £6,412 in respect of obsolescent materials.	355	13,379
TOTAL		£17,609

The average weight, Tractive Power and mileage capacities of the new locomotives are in each case greater than those of the displaced locomotives. Average Tractive Power will be increased by 23% in the case of Tender locomotives and 37% in the case of Tank Locomotives.

The increased capacity is due to the liberation of the older types of locomotives now due for heavy repairs, for which by the closing of branch lines and other changes in the nature of work, the demand has ceased to exist.

The provision of the new standard locomotives of increased capacity will result in the saving of double heading and improved engine workings and punctuality of trains.

Costs per engine mile do not move precisely in relation to Tractive Power but some adjustment is required to allow for the quality of work for which the new standardised locomotives are designed as represented by the increased Tractive Power of 23% and 37% of the Tender and Tank locomotives respectively

The comparative unit costs per engine mile equated by Tractive Power, are as follows:—

	New Locomotives Pence	Displaced Locomotives Pence	Increase (+) or Decrease Pence	%
Tender Locomotives				
Repairs and Renewals	0.21863	0.29869	−0.08006	= 26.80
Coal Consumption	0.25541	0.33018	−0.07477	= 22.65
TOTAL	0.47404	0.62887	−0.15483	= 24.62
Tank Locomotives				
Repairs and Renewals	0.21863	0.29869	0.08006	= 26.80
Coal Consumption	0.25757	0.30973	0.05216	= 16.84
TOTAL	0.45785	0.59315	0.13530	= 22.81

In other words, the cost of traction will for these units be decreased by over 20%.

The estimated total annual savings adjusted for increased capacity in respect of the proposed construction and breaking up will be as follows:–

REPAIRS, RENEWALS AND COAL CONSUMPTION

Tender Locomotives   £
36,610,120,740 Tractive Power Miles @ 0.15483d.
per 1,000   23,618

Tank Locomotives
16,609,737,860 Tractive Power Miles @ 0.13530d.
per 1, 000   9,364
                                                                                32,982

Interest
Decreased cost of new locomotives compared with replacement
cost of displaced locomotives £249,676 @ 5 ½%   13,752
Less increased cost due to obsolescent stock of
materials at a net value of £6,412 @ 5½%   £353
                                                                                13,379

Total Estimated Decreased Annual Cost   £46,361

The shops at Crewe and Derby are at present manned for the construction of 75 and 50 large locomotives per annum respectively involving the employment of about 1,500 men, on day shifts of 5 day weeks. The number of men employed in the Chief Mechanical Engineer's Shops and the number of new locomotives completed by the Company and Contractors respectively in recent years were:–

	Chief Mechanical Engineer's Shops		Contractors
	Staff	Built	Built
1927	20,500	166	219
1928	19,800	172	167
1929	17,400	194	31
1930	17,700	153	34
1931	13,700	126	—
1932 (Proposed)		130	—

The staff figures are equated by time and the number on the books at 1st January, 1931, was 20,850 and at 5th September, 1931, was 16,396.

If the proposed programme is authorised the new work will commence as the work under the 1931 programme is completed and the latter position is now being reached in some sections of work.

The continuity so attained will result in economic costs of renewals and repairs by the balancing of output and the spread of overhead expenses.

In the absence or delay of authorisation serious displacement of labour will immediately ensue, resulting in dismissals of up to about 1,500 men between now and the end of the 1931 programme.

The approximate allocation of the expenditure of £344,354 for the 75 new locomotives is as follows:–

	£	%
Wages (to be paid to Company's employees)	106,750	= 31
Materials to be purchased (including a portion of the steel to be manufactured at Crewe from purchased pig iron etc)	151,516	= 44
	258,266	= 75
Overhead expenses	86,088	= 25
TOTAL	£344,354	

Approved, and
Referred to the Board.

By including this lengthy document I have placed on record the proposed policy as set out by senior management to manage the locomotive stock and over the years to improve 'productivity'. Finally, it should be noted this was agreed prior to the arrival of William Stanier as the Chief Mechanical Engineer and rather proves that he did not create the policy but rather that he implemented what had already been agreed.

RENUMBERING POLICY AND LOCOMOTIVE LIVERY

During the course of my research I have never found anything to say how or why the LMS adopted the system used for renumbering the locomotive stock following the grouping in 1923. The earliest document that has come to light is at *Fig. 2*, which is an undated list summarising the stock of the London & North Western and Wirral Railways at September 1923. Although at that time the locomotive stock of the old Lancashire & Yorkshire Railway had been amalgamated into the L&NWR, it is not included in the list.

On the other hand, the decision about the painting styles for carriages and locomotives is documented in the minutes of the LMS Rolling Stock & Locomotive & Electrical Committee and is reproduced below. What is probably surprising is that the question of carriage stock colours was decided first, and when this was agreed, the Committee turned their attention to locomotives. However, passengers travelled in carriages and they were in public view rather more than the locomotive at the head of the train, which no doubt was the reason why carriages determined the colour of the locomotives. We begin with carriages.

Painting of London Midland and Scottish Company's Passenger Stock

26th April 1923. Rolling Stock Committee Minute 39

The General Manager reported that the question of the colour or colours to be adopted as the standard for the passenger stock of the Company, should be determined at an early date. The number of passenger vehicles belonging to the Companies now forming the London Midland and Scottish Group was 27,364, of which 9,735 were painted the North Western colours, 9,281 Midland colours, and 6,763 L&Y colours.

Having regard to the fact that the greater number of coaches were in the colours of the first two named companies, he had endeavoured to compare the practice in regard to the painting of their stock, both in regard to the first treatment and subsequent maintenance, and he explained that the former Midland Company used eighteen coats of paint and varnish as the first treatment compared with thirteen in the case of the former L&NW Company, and in respect of the subsequent maintenance, the Midland Company re-varnished every fifteen months and repainted every five years, whilst the North Western Company repainted every four years, no re-varnishing being undertaken in the intervening period.

A true comparison of the cost was extremely difficult owing to the difference in practice, but from the figures which had been submitted to him, it would appear that to adopt the Midland practice would cost an additional sum of £56,524 per annum compared with the North Western practice. A further factor to be considered was the appearance of the stock, not only when turned out of the Shops but after having been in the service for some time and with a view to enabling the Committee to judge, he had arranged for five coaches to be on view at Euston this week as follows:—

(1) A North Western coach painted and fitted exactly in the North Western style.
(2) A Midland coach in the Midland style.
(3) A North Western coach which has been in traffic and which is about due to be sent into the shops for renovation.
(4) A Midland coach in the same condition.
(5) A coach of the same type painted outside white upper and crimson lake base, and inside trimmed with blue and the fittings walnut.

And he suggested that the Committee should inspect them with a view to deciding the colour or colours to be adopted, and also the inside fittings of the coaches.

At this date the nine members of the Rolling Stock Committee, who were all Directors of the Company, were Mr D. Vickers, Chairman, Sir Alan G. Anderson and Mr D. Wiggins (ex-Midland) and Sir Thomas Royden, Messrs Hitchen, Ismay, Kaye, Macpherson and Taylor (ex-LNWR) and following their inspection they decided to adopt the colours of the old Midland Railway. So three ex-Midland and six ex-LNWR Directors decided to adopt Midland colours for coaching stock, which rather makes a mockery of the oft-quoted statement about the Midlandisation of the LMS by ex-Midland men following the grouping.

After deciding upon the colours for coaching stock, the question of locomotive colour was dealt with later in the year and begins with reference to Minute 53 of the Rolling Stock Committee meeting on 31st May 1923, 'Painting the Company's Engines', that was sent with a letter dated 8th June 1923 from Mr Hughes to the Rolling Stock Committee Chairman. After consideration by the Committee, the decision was made and can be summarised thus:—

Painting the Company's Engines
The Chairman reported that the Committee, appointed by Minute 119 of the last Meeting of the Board to consider the question of the colour of the coaching stock, had decided to recommend the adoption of the old Midland crimson lake colour, and it was necessary to come to some decision in regard to the locomotives.

After consideration it was ordered, that in future, the passenger engines be painted in the crimson lake colour, following the decision in respect of the coaching stock, and that the freight engines be painted black without the lining which has hitherto been adopted. Ordered also that the Company's engines be not named in future, but those engines which already bear a name, continue as hitherto.

That was the end of the debate and the decision was made. This instruction was later confirmed in a letter dated 5th December 1923 from the Horwich Drawing office and the relevant extracts are given below.

. . . the following details to be carried out on all engines re-painted on and after a date to be fixed later.

1) Coat of Arms. All engines to have the Company's Coat of Arms placed on the panel plate, or bunker side in the case of tank engines.
2) LMS Initials. All goods engines to have the letters LMS without stops, placed on the panel plates in a position corresponding to that occupied by the Coat of Arms on the passenger engines.
3) Engine numbers. The number of the engine to be placed on the tender, or on the tank sides in the case of tank engines, in large figures, transfers in two sizes available.
4) Engine Numbers on Smokebox Doors. The number of the engine to be placed on the smokebox door in the form of a cast iron plate.
5) Builders Name Plate. The Builders plate, if an outside builder, to be retained. For a railway built engine, or an outside maker's engine rebuilt plate, a small oval brass plate to be fixed to the driving splashers of tender engines and in the most suitable corresponding position on tank engines.
6) Tank Capacity plate. All tenders (or tanks in the case of tank engines) to bear a brass plate giving the capacity of the tender (or tank) in gallons. This plate to be fixed onto the back of the tender or bunker. Any existing number plates on tenders may remain.
7) Engine Classification Numbers. The engines classification number to be placed on the cab side, in a conspicuous position about the height of the driver's head; all engines to bear classification numbers.
8) The date of painting inside of the cab is immaterial.
9) Plate for Driver's Name. This maybe left over until asked for.
10) Shed numbers. Present practice to continue for the moment.

This directive, which was approved on 10th December 1923 came into immediate effect, but until the new coat of arms became available, new and repainted red engines were also given the small letters 'LMS' on the cab or bunker side as appropriate. Although not mentioned in the specification, the buffer beams were to be painted vermilion.

Renumbering
There are references to observation of renumbered and repainted locomotives in the November and December 1923 editions of the *Railway Magazine* and the subject of locomotive renumbering for all the LMS constituent and subsidiary companies is covered in some depth in the January and February 1924 editions of that title, but in this book we will consider only the locomotives of the old LNW and North London Railways. Therefore, in the absence of a firm date when the renumbering was agreed, I can only suggest that it was probably about July before a final decision was made and the renumbering instructions were issued, which means that a number of locomotives taken into LMS stock on 1st January 1923 were withdrawn before being allocated an LMS stock number.

There is an interesting note in the *SLS Journal* Volume 29 about the LMS renumbering and the fact that numbers allotted to some engines did not follow the locomotives in date order of building, with some older engines being interspersed between the numbers of locomotives of the same class that were built later. The examples given were 'Special DX Goods', 'Special Tanks' and 'Coal engines'. Whilst this may be of interest to students of LNWR locomotive history, the starting point for this work is what the LMS inherited and not why these anomalies occurred. Clearly there was some confusion and those responsible for setting out the renumbering programme made mistakes.

Those of us who are old enough to remember the renumbering of stock following Nationalisation in 1948 may recall that it was about February before the first signs of renumbering were seen. In my case the old LMS number was prefixed 'M', but the official details were not made public until the May/June edition of the *Railway Magazine* and in other railway publications. The 1948 renumbering was far less complicated than the one undertaken in 1923, so in the circumstances the timetable given above is not unreasonable. In addition to the renumbering, a system of power classification was also introduced, but we will begin with the renumbering by simplifying the document reproduced at page 4 (*Fig 2*).

Western Division Passenger tender engines were allocated the number block 5000–6399, Passenger tank engines 6400–7199, Freight tank engines 7200–7999, and Freight tender engines 8000–9999. Departmental Engines were not numbered.

The LMS decided to follow a sequence of wheel types, although the LNWR did not always have examples of them. However, they have all been listed below.

Passenger tender engines: 2–4–0, 0–4–2, 4–2–2, 4–4–0, 4–4–2, 4–6–0.
Passenger tank engines: 0–4–2, 2–4–0, 4–4–0, 2–4–2, 0–4–4, 4–4–2, 4–4–4, 0–6–2, 0–6–4, 4–6–2, 4–6–4.
Freight tank engines: 0–4–0, 0–4–2, 0–4–4, 0–6–0, 0–6–2, 2–6–0, 2–6–2, 0–8–0, 0–8–2, 0–8–4.
Freight tender engines: 0–4–0, 0–4–2, 0–6–0, 2–6–0, 4–6–0, 0–8–0, 2–8–0.

Where there was more than one class with the same wheel arrangement, the least powerful came first, or where there was more than one class of the same power, then the oldest class took precedence.

Following Nationalisation in 1948, the LMS locomotive stock was renumbered and while the majority of surviving LNWR locomotives saw their LMS stock number increased by 40000, others were renumbered and allocated new stock numbers in the 58xxx series; details are given in the various class sections.

In addition to renumbering, as previously mentioned, the LMS also adopted the Midland Railway system of power classification. All passenger and goods engines were allocated power class numbers from 1–5, but later new LMS locomotives and rebuilds of the 'Claughtons' saw additional classifications introduced. We should also not overlook that some engines were not classified; they were small freight tank engines. In 1928 there was a further change, 'P' was added to the power classification for passenger engines and 'F' for goods or, as they were also described, freight engines. In addition, as already mentioned, a new code, 'X' for a power output that was between 5 and 6 came into use, namely '5XP'.

Although shortly after the grouping a number of locomotives entered traffic carrying full LNWR lined-out livery, they also carried the letters 'LMS' executed in sans-serif characters together with the LNWR cast numberplate. Some of the new 0–8–4Ts entered traffic in LMS red carrying small letters 'LMS' on the side of the tank. Renumbering of L&NWR locomotives was rather slow. Clearly nothing could be done until the new numbering system had been agreed, but there were also examples of locomotives with the LNWR numberplate removed and a stencilled LMS stock number in its place. There were a few examples of locomotives fitted with tender side panels that displayed the new LMS number. Probably the first LNWR locomotive to receive a full LMS

repaint was a 'Claughton' No. 5971 *Croxeth*, as recorded in the November 1923 *Railway Magazine*, with reliable sources suggesting the locomotive was ex-works in July 1923.

The apparent slow progress made at Crewe with renumbering the old LNWR locomotive stock can be explained by the fact that from about mid-1924 until early 1926 renumbering ceased while the reconstruction of the works was underway, although some renumbering was undertaken at various locomotive sheds by removing the cast numberplate and painting the new LMS number where the plate had been attached. The LMS would have issued detailed lists showing both the old and new number, so there would not have been any confusion at engine shed or locomotive works level. My problem is the secondary sources that I have consulted, at times, give conflicting information, and in the absence of any prime sources that confirm what was or was not renumbered, I have tried to reconcile this conflicting evidence, but I cannot be certain there are not any mistakes in the sections that state what locomotives did or did not carry an LMS stock number. If any readers do find errors, I will endeavour to publish the corrections in Part Two.

This provides the opportunity to briefly explain what was happening at Crewe, and an extract from Minute 599 from the Locomotive & Electrical Committee, dated 29th March 1928, in the form of a report submitted by Mr Beames, Mechanical Engineer, Crewe will suffice. He said that so far as the reconstruction of the Erecting Shops was concerned, some deviation from the approved plan was desirable and would reduce costs. The reorganisation had taken three years to complete and it was anticipated it would enable a saving of £100,000 per annum to be made. The actual expenditure would not exceed £410,000, compared with the authorised amount of £427,151 recorded by Minute 92 of the Locomotive & Electrical Committee of 25th February 1925. However, whilst stressing the economies to be made and the reduction in the number of locomotives awaiting repairs, no mention of painting appears in his report.

What it did mean was that for the first few years of the LMS many old LNWR locomotives were allocated LMS stock numbers but they were not carried before the locomotives were withdrawn. Others ran for several years before they were renumbered. Many years ago the late David Jenkinson and I spent a number of years researching the livery carried by LMS locomotives, and the livery codes, created entirely by David, have stood the test of time, so I felt that we should use these in this book. To assist readers, the codes are set out at page 16. Readers who are interested in the story of locomotive liveries and size of numerals and insignia are referred to *Locomotive Liveries of the LMS, vols. 1&2* by Jenkinson & Essery, as given in the sources and further reading section at the back of the book.

Tender changing applied to all LNW classes and when the tender displayed one number and the smokebox another it was rather confusing, which led to a change of policy.

On 15th December 1927 the CME at Derby wrote 'It has now been decided that the engine numbers are not to be placed on the tenders, but that they shall be put on the engine cab panels, and the letters LMS on the tenders'. Until that date the only LMS tenders to carry distinctive numbers of their own were those from the Lancashire & Yorkshire Railway

'Claughton' class No. 2511 Croxteth *was the first locomotive to come out of Crewe Works in the correct LMS livery, painted red with 18-inch numerals on the side of the tender, small LMS letters on the side of the cab, and a smokebox door numberplate. This style with the separate letters on the side of the cab was shortlived and, as soon as the coat of arms transfer became available, the use of individual letters on passenger engines ceased and a transfer in the form of a yellow bordered red panel, at first with concave corners and then with round corners, was applied to goods engines.*
COLLECTION R.J. ESSERY

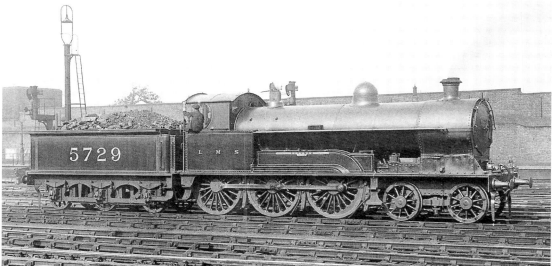

LMS No. 5729 was built as LNWR No. 1290 in July 1919 and named Lucknow *in July 1922. The LMS stock number was applied in February 1924, as seen in this picture. In August 1934 it was renumbered as 25729 and less than a year later, in February 1935, it was withdrawn.*
COLLECTION R.J. ESSERY

Here we see 'Superheated Precursor' No. 302 Greyhound *as LMS No. 5304. Built in July 1905, it was rebuilt with superheater, piston valves and 20½ inch cylinders in July 1917, one of sixty-four that were rebuilt in a programme that started in 1913. By the grouping, forty-three had been rebuilt and when they were renumbered, being the equivalent to the 'George the Fifth' class, the LMS allocated the number series 5276–5319 to them. However, the work continued and between March 1923 and November 1926 a further twenty-one were rebuilt, but since most had been allocated LMS stock numbers within the number series 5187 to 5266, the tidy pattern of numbers was lost. This picture was taken between January 1927 when the LMS stock number was applied and August 1936 when it was renumbered as 25304, running with this number until January 1947 when it was withdrawn from service.*
REAL PHOTOGRAPHS

This drawing appears to illustrate a proposal to provide a dedicated 1/8in steel plate panel for each tender engine number which could be bolted onto any suitable tender in order to match the engine. Someone realised that this would be far too expensive so a similar scheme was experimentally put into practice by bolting a frame made of 'T' section upper and lower rails and five vertical strips, into which individual plates could be slid in and out. This is almost the same as the device used by the GWR on smokeboxes to show the Train Reporting Number. Once tenders had been fitted with the holding frames, all that would be required were lots of panels showing numbers 1 to 0.

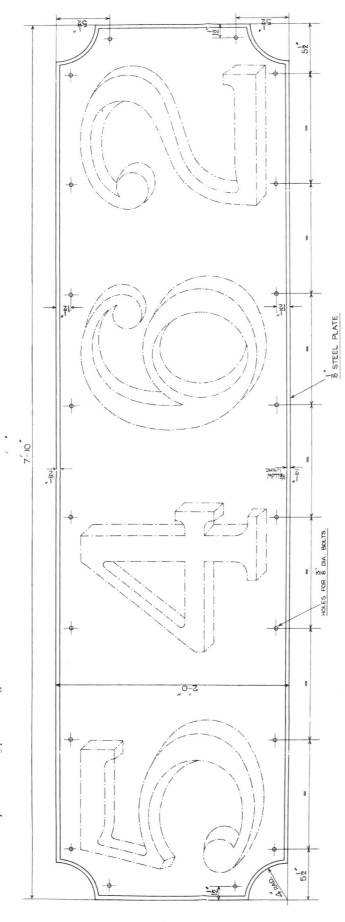

Derby drawing D54048 of 18th October 1923 entitled 'PANEL PLATE FOR NUMBERS WESTERN DIVISION A TENDERS'.

The two pictures that show No. 5788 were taken after the locomotive, built in November 1921 as LNWR No. 270, had been renumbered by the LMS in February 1924 and fitted with the number panel on the side of the tender. Unfortunately, I do not know how long it was carried and how many if any other locomotives were fitted with this device. The rear view of the tender was taken at Aston Shed on 26th June 1927 but unlike the broadside view, there does not appear to be anything on the cabside panel.

T. S. STEEL COLLECTION

We have included another picture of No. 5788 which shows that when the locomotive was renumbered a smokebox door numberplate was fitted. Oil reservoirs began to be fitted above the boiler handrail from 1922. The three pictures provide an 'all round view' of a 'Prince of Wales' class 4–6–0 which is covered from page 95.

COLLECTION T.S. STEEL

and the LNWR. The latter had followed, for sensible economic reasons, a deliberate policy of tender changing because at general repair a tender took less time in shops than a locomotive and therefore, provided the engine was given a suitable tender, it did not have to be the same one with which it arrived. The ex-Midland Railway tenders carried the stock number of the locomotive to which they were usually attached, but no tender number. Among the drawbacks to this system was that if an engine needed a different tender for any reason, it either had to be renumbered or the ensemble ran for a time with one number on the smokebox plate of the locomotive and a different number on the tender.

On 24th January 1928 the CME's Department at Derby issued a list of 'Distinctive Numbers for Tenders' showing individual engine and tender pairings. The numbering system was based on water capacities, the smallest capacity tenders taking the lowest numbers, and all tenders were numbered in order of capacity irrespective of the company of origin, except that LNWR and L&YR tenders, which had cast number plates, retained their original numbers and did not form part of the scheme. Within each capacity group, the tenders were numbered in the same order as the numbers of the engines to which they were attached, usually in the order Midland Railway, North Staffordshire Railway, Caledonian Railway, Glasgow & South Western Railway, Highland Railway, Barrow (Furness Railway and Maryport & Carlisle Railway).

DETAIL VARIATIONS

It would be quite impossible to list all the detail modifications and changes that took place to LNWR locomotives under LMS and later British Railways ownership, but with modellers in mind, we felt that we should try to summarise some of the more important and visually obvious changes that were made, so that readers will be aware of what to look for. We have included a number of LNWR engine diagrams and must draw readers' attention to the fact that the wheel diameter as quoted was 'nominal' – this needs an explanation.

From the earliest days until the mid 1880s, wheel tyres on LNWR engines were $2\frac{1}{4}$in thick, at first wrought iron and from 1859 of Bessemer steel. Tyres rolled at Crewe from about 1885 onwards were 3in thick for all carrying and tender wheels and driving wheels of 6ft diameter and above, and $2\frac{3}{4}$in for drivers below 6ft. The theory was that larger-wheeled engines ran higher mileages, hence the extra 'meat' on the tyres giving a similar life before scrapping of all types. Thus the officially quoted 'Nominal Diameter' was a lowest common denominator for the whole class, describing the actual diameter when the tyre was at scrapping limit (except for '7ft' where the tyres were more like 6ft 10in when scrapped). A '6ft 6in Straight Link' had new tyres 6ft 9in diameter and approximately 6ft 6in when scrapped. The wheel centre (or body) was 6ft 3in in diameter. From an unknown date, probably around 1900, 3in tyres were standardised for all diameter

LMS LOCOMOTIVE LIVERY CODES

Crimson Lake Livery variations

A1	Pre-1928 standard, 18in. figures,	LMS Coat of Arms
A2	Pre-1928 standard, 18in. figures,	Individual Letters 'LMS'
A3	Pre-1928 standard, 14in. figures,	LMS Coat of Arms
A4	Pre-1928 standard, 14in. figures,	Individual Letters 'LMS'
A5	Post-1927 standard, Gold/Black insignia,	10in. numerals
A6	Post-1927 standard, Gold/Black insignia,	12in. numerals
A7	Post-1927 standard, Gold/Black insignia,	14in. numerals (Midland pattern)
A8	Post-1927 standard, Straw/Black insignia,	10in. numerals (Midland pattern)
A9	Post-1927 standard, Straw/Black insignia,	12in. numerals
A10	Post-1927 standard, Straw/Black insignia,	14in. numerals (Standard pattern)
A11	Post-1927 standard, Gold/Red insignia,	12in. numerals
A12	Post-1927 standard, Gold/Red insignia,	1936 pattern
A13	Post-1927 standard, Yellow/Red insignia	10in. numerals
A14	Post-1927 standard, Yellow/Red insignia,	12in. numerals
A15	Post-1927 standard, Yellow/Red insignia,	12in. numerals (Midland pattern)

Lined Black Livery variations

B1	Lined Black livery, Horwich/St Rollox style	18in. Midland figures
B2	Post-1927 standard, Gold/Red insignia,	10in. numerals
B3	Post-1927 standard, Gold/Red insignia,	12in. numerals
B4	Post-1927 standard, Gold/Red insignia,	14in. numerals (Midland pattern)
B5	Post-1927 standard, Gold/Black insignia,	10in. numerals
B6	Post-1927 standard, Gold/Black insignia,	12in. numerals
B7	Post-1927 standard, Gold/Black insignia,	14in. numerals (Midland pattern)
B8	Post-1927 standard, Yellow/Red insignia,	10in. numerals
B9	Post-1927 standard, Yellow/Red insignia,	12in. numerals
B10	Post-1927 standard, Yellow/Red insignia,	14in. numerals (Midland pattern)
B11	Post-1927 standard, Gold/Red insignia,	1936 pattern
B12	1946 standard livery — full lining style	
B13	1946 standard livery — simpler original lining style	

Plain Black Livery variations

C1	Post-1928 standard, 18in. figures,	Standard cab/bunker panel
C2	Pre-1928 standard, 18in. figures,	Round cornered cab/bunker panel
C3	Pre-1928 standard, 18in. figures,	Individual Letters 'LMS'
C4	Pre-1928 standard, 14in. figures,	Standard cab/bunker panel
C5	Pre-1928 standard, 14in. figures,	Round cornered cab/bunker panel
C6	Pre-1928 standard, 14in. figures,	Individual Letters 'LMS'
C7	Crewe 'hybrid' style, 18in. figures,	LMS Coat of Arms
C8	Crewe 'hybrid' style, 14in. figures,	(Midland pattern), LMS Coat of Arms
C9	Crewe 'hybrid' style, 14in. figures,	(Standard pattern — straw), LMS Coat of Arms
C10	Crewe 'hybrid' style 18in. figures,	Individual Letters 'LMS'
C11	Crewe 'hybrid' style 14in. figures,	(Midland pattern), Individual Letters 'LMS'
C12	Crewe 'hybrid' style 14in. figures,	(Standard pattern), Individual Letters 'LMS'
C13	Post-1927 standard, Gold/Black insignia,	10in. numerals
C14	Post-1927 standard, Gold/Black insignia,	12in. numerals
C15	Post-1927 standard, Gold/Black insignia,	14in. numerals (Midland pattern)
C16	Post-1927 standard, Plain Straw insignia,	10in. numerals
C17	Post-1927 standard, Plain Straw insignia,	12in. numerals
C18	Post-1927 standard, Plain Straw insignia,	14in. numerals (Standard pattern)
C19	Post-1927 standard, Gold/Red insignia,	1936 pattern
C20	Post-1927 standard, Gold/Black insignia,	1936 pattern
C21	Post-1927 standard, Yellow/Red insignia,	10in. numerals
C22	Post-1927 standard, Yellow/Red insignia,	12in. numerals
C23	Post-1927 standard, Yellow/Red insignia,	14in. numerals (Midland pattern)
C24	Post-1927 standard, Plain Yellow insignia,	10in. numerals
C25	Post-1927 standard, Plain Yellow insignia,	12in. numerals
C26	Post-1927 standard, Plain Yellow insignia,	14in. numerals (Midland pattern)
C27	1946 standard insignia — smaller size	
C28	1946 standard insignia — larger size	

The livery codes above were created by the late David Jenkinson when he and I embarked upon the task of listing the various styles and combinations used by the company. During the course of our research, we visited Derby, where staff told us that transfers were the preferred method, whilst the following day at Crewe we were told it was quicker and more satisfactory to use paint!

wheels, the smaller centres being turned down by $\frac{1}{8}$in in order to maintain the same overall diameter with new tyres. The wheel centres of the '5ft 6in Side Tank' were, like those of the 'Precursor' 2–4–0, 5ft 3in as built – 5ft 8$\frac{1}{2}$in with new 2$\frac{3}{4}$in tyres – and 5ft 2$\frac{1}{2}$in when 3in tyres were fitted.

Boilers

Rebuilding saw many of the original LNWR round-top boilers replaced by Belpaire boilers; in addition, some round-top boilers show washout plugs; these were fitted to boilers built by the LMS. They were installed in the firebox outer-wrapper on a level with the crown of the inner firebox. The normal life of a locomotive boiler was about twenty years and most LNWR boilers were common to more than one class of locomotive. For example, the same boiler was common to the 'Coal Engines', 'Coal Tanks' and 'Special Tanks', 'Special DX' and '5ft 6in Tank'. Following the grouping, a boiler renewal programme began that included the purchase of boilers from 'the Trade'. Improvements to some boilers included the introduction of a single plate barrel that replaced the earlier three-plate design, while on the smokebox door the LNWR 5-spoke door wheel was often replaced by two handles. Renumbering saw the front numberplate applied to

We have used this front-end view of 'George V' No. 2291 Gibraltar, which became LMS 5356, to show the smokebox, the door of which was secured by a handle for positioning the dart, a 5-spoke threaded wheel for tightening the dart, and four 'dogs' on the rim of the door.   T. S. STEEL COLLECTION

This view of the front end of 19 inch Goods 4–6–0 No. 8729 has been included to show the difference between LNWR lamp sockets and LMS lamp holders. In the lower right picture are the LMS replacements and this picture of 8729 shows the LNWR socket.
T.S. STEEL COLLECTION

Photographed at Willesden on 13th June 1945, this is the front end of 0–8–0 No. 9041 carrying a 1A Willesden shed plate, but there was no front numberplate. LMS-style lamp holders can be seen and the smokebox door dart wheel had been replaced by a threaded handle. In this case the door had been left unfastened, presumably for fitters to deal with a 'blow'. The four 'dogs' had been moved clear of the door and the dart handle was not vertical.   H. C. CASSERLEY

the smokebox door, but not all ex LNWR locomotives carried them. Many were fitted to members of most classes in the early LMS days, but they were only really necessary on engines allocated to the Midland Division with its roundhouses. The Western Division had straight sheds. Crewe appears to have discontinued fitting new ones around 1928, but engines repaired at Derby had them fitted well into the 30s, judging by photographs. They were phased out gradually and while many ex-LNWR engines never carried them, others could be seen with them up until the outbreak of World War Two.

Safety valves

In 1923 LNWR locomotives were fitted with Ramsbottom-type safety valves, but on many locomotives these were replaced, to quote the *Railway Magazine* page 220, Volume LVI 1925, by, 'safety valves of Ross patent "pop" type.' Various descriptions have been used by authors to describe these safety valves and in this book we usually describe them as either

These pictures have been selected to show the difference between the original LNWR roof (top), and a roof that has been altered to conform to the composite or, as it was usually described, Midland loading gauge fitted to 9427. A drawing that shows both the LNWR and Midland gauges will be found at page 22.

These pictures show the front ends of two 4–4–0s, both fitted with LNWR taper shank buffers that were known as 'Cooke' buffers and described in the text opposite. They also show the original LNWR lamp socket type in use on No. 5116 and LMS type lamp holders that replaced them on No. 5454. Because of their base spigots it was not easy to store the LNWR lamps when they were not in use, they were turned sideways, which was fine when the lamps in use were lit, but in daylight and a distance away, it was not easy to see what the lamp codes were. The complete picture of No. 5116 will be found at page 45.

W. T. STUBBS

'pop' or Ross safety valves. This replacement programme did not include all ex-LNWR locomotive stock and many locomotives were withdrawn that were still fitted with Ramsbottom safety valves. The *Railway Magazine* illustrated an example of an 18inch Goods engine, which was not carrying its LMS stock number and continued by saying that 'other engines to which Belpaire boilers will be fitted as required are the 0–8–0 coal engines with 4ft 3in diameter wheels, the 4–6–0 'Prince of Wales' class and the 4–4–0 'George the Fifth' class.'

The first LNWR engine built with Ross valves was 'Claughton' No 1914 *Patriot* in May 1920. In 1924, Beames designed a range of Belpaire boilers with Ross valves, beginning with that for the 0–8–0s, to be interchangeable with the round-top type.

Locomotive Headlamps and Lamp Irons

No. 2222 *Sir Gilbert Claughton* was built with lamp brackets and a set of circular-bodied 'strap' lamps of the type used by the North Eastern Railway. While the nine engines completing the first batch had the usual lamp sockets, all the remaining 'Claughtons' had brackets and NER type lamps.

In 1923, Midland style locomotive headlamps became the LMS standard and on ex-LNWR locomotives this meant that lamp irons or, as they are sometimes known, lamp holders, were required. The LNWR standard was a lamp with a tapered peg for locating the lamp in the lamp socket, but when this was not used, the lamp was difficult to keep upright and enginemen used to store lamps not in use by propping them where they would be safe and between the handrail and the boiler close to the cab was a common solution whilst another way of storing 'peg' lamps when not required was to leave them in the socket but turned through 90 degrees so that the lenses didn't show forward. When the change from LNWR lamps to Midland style was made it meant that the lamps allocated to a locomotive had to be compatible to the fittings. However, the headlamps were included with the tools that were allocated to each locomotive so this change should not have caused any problems.

Buffers

During the LMS period, buffers were changed on many locomotives, and whilst reference to locomotive and tender buffers will be found in some of the photograph captions, a brief summary of buffers fitted to LNWR locomotives may be helpful. The oldest were the 'Webb' buffers and there were examples of the retention of these buffers, often with the wooden seating and 18 inch head on many engines and tenders from 1923 onwards whilst other locomotives were fitted with the LNWR taper-shank buffers with solid spindle. This buffer was made by Geo. Turton, Platts & Co and was also known as the 'Whale' buffer. A development of this buffer has a longer parallel section at the front of the body and is known as the 'Cooke' buffer, and from the early 1930s a further design, with a parallel body and square flange, usually referred to as a 'Stanier' buffer, was used.

These five pictures have been selected to show examples of buffers referred to in the text. This first one shows a Webb buffer with the wooden seating.

The Whale buffer, which was 1ft ½in long, had no parallel section. Max Dunn said they 'broke like carrots' in a rough shunt. Very few examples seem to have survived into LMS days.

The Cooke type of 1910 which was only 1ft 7½in long.

The 1917 Cooke design which was 1ft 8¼in long.

The parallel body buffer with a square flange that is often referred to as a Stanier buffer.

Ash hoppers, blowers and ejectors

Ash hoppers were fitted to a considerable number of locomotives designed by Webb and the idea was to allow ash from
the smokebox to drop to the ground via a chute. These were
removed from 1932 onwards. Ash blowers, or ejectors, to use
a more accurate description, were fitted to a number of classes
including the 'G1' and 'G2', 'Precursors' and 'George the
Fifth'. The ash ejectors were operated by rotation of the
blower handle; by manipulating the blower, it was possible to
stir up the ashes so that the combination of the steam blower
and blast from the engine when working ejected the ash
through the chimney. Unfortunately, this caused damage to
coaching stock and fires in woods and fields adjacent to the
railway. In 1930 the LMS began to remove them; the work
was authorised by DWO 2107 and a total of 1,764 engines
were to be dealt with. When the work was reported as
complete in 1937, it was recorded that the equipment had
been removed from an additional 266 engines, making the
total number of locomotives that had been fitted with this
device and still in service when the work of removing began
in 1930 as 2,030.

Cylinder lubrication

The LNWR sight-feed hydrostatic lubricator, fitted from
1889 onwards, worked the opposite way to the usual type
(e.g. Wakefield and Detroit) where the drops of oil rise from
the needle valve through a water-filled sight glass or chamber.
In the LNWR design, the oil syphoned from the top of the
body into branch pipes on either side through needle valves,
the drops passing through empty sight glasses into the delivery
pipes. They were mounted in the cab on the driver's side of
the spectacle plate. By the time of the grouping, the only
LNWR line engines fitted with Roscoe displacement lubricators mounted on the boiler back plate were the 'Straight
Link' classes ('Jumbos', '4ft 6in' and '5ft 6in' Tanks). As they
fed oil to the regulator mounted in the smokebox, their
function was only necessary when the regulator was open. In
1923 there were doubtless some old shunting engines, 'Special
Tanks' '4ft' and '2ft 6in Shunters', still with Roscoe displacement lubricators, but, as was the usual practice on all
railways, these were supplemented by Furness lubricators,
mounted either on the valve chest or cylinder covers, which
only supplied oil when the regulator was closed. Neither the

This picture was taken at Chester on 7th July 1921 on the footplate of LNWR No.1168 Cuckoo which became LMS No. 5102 in February 1926 and remained in service until it was scrapped in July 1931. The enginemen, in particular the driver, were leaning back in order to allow as much as possible of the firebox backplate to be in the photograph. Beginning at the top: the storm sheet had probably recently been in use as in dry weather it was stowed in one of the toolboxes – here it was furled. The driver's brake valve can be seen on the left above the Roscoe displacement lubricator for the regulator, and on the right the ejector steam valve can be seen immediately above the regulator handle. The regulator, in this case of the Webb smokebox type, was closed against the stop on the quadrant unlike the Ramsbottom type seen on the 'Super D' (in Vol 3) which had its own internal stop. On the left, a little lower down, the sight feed displacement lubricator for the pistons and valves is seen mounted on the cab front plate. On the boiler backplate we see (left to right), clack valve, firedoor handle, Webb water gauge with plungers (for testing water level and re-setting the ball valves following a burst glass), and toughened glass protector (introduced by Whale in 1904), fireman's side clack valve; lower down – reversing wheel (no locking lever on a 'Jumbo'), toothed rack for firedoor, can of cylinder oil on the 'coffee plate', and fireman's slacking pipe with knurled brass tap-wheel. Here both enginemen were wearing LNWR caps, and overalls, which were usually buttoned at the neck not elsewhere; however, the men on No. 231, see page 32, were wearing ties. Many men continued to wear their LNWR caps long after the LMS had issued them with new ones of the LMS design.

Midland nor the North Western hydrostatic lubricator was superior to the other; if indeed they were taken off the LNWR engines and replaced with Midland ones, it can only have been in the interest of standardisation and the reduction of stocks of spares.

Gauge Glasses

The dangerous arrangement whereby there was no protection for the enginemen if the boiler gauge glass burst had ceased many years before the LMS was formed, but after 1923 the Midland design was considered to be better and in a modified form it was used on ex-LNWR locomotives.

LNWR water gauges had separate try cocks, or 'buttons', as enginemen called them. During the post-1923 period, Midland-type gauges replaced some gauges, at first with unlinked handles, but later with linked handles, which overcame the problem of false readings. On the other hand, it was no longer possible to blow water back through the glass to clean the inside of the glass. So when a glass became too dirty to see through, the water gauge had to be dismantled to clean or replace it. In addition the LNWR gauge featured the diagonal black-striped backing plate, something that the Midland gauge lacked. From late 1932, standard LMS frames and protectors began to be fitted, which allowed blowing through by just opening the drain cock.

Blowdown valves

A manual blowdown valve was fitted to many LNWR boilers, but during the early 1930s the LMS was engaged in experiments to improve the treatment of water used in locomotive boilers, and in 1932, under NWO 2839, they were to be removed. In later years many ex-LNWR engines were fitted with LMS standard blowdown valves mounted on the right-hand side of the boiler backplate and operating whenever the regulator was opened.

Ancillary fittings

Although sandshields were generally removed before 1923, some were still fitted at the time of the grouping. From about 1919 the LNWR began to remove pyrometers and superheater dampers, but the work of removal was not completed by 1923, so some locomotives were still fitted with this equipment when they became LMS stock. In 1922, oil reservoirs to improve lubrication began to be fitted above the boiler handrails, and this work continued after the grouping. The LNWR cab profile was cut down on a number of locomotives to allow them to pass under the Composite or, as it is usually known, Midland loading gauge. In the sections describing the various classes we will refer to the more obvious changes that took place, in particular by use of photographs where possible, but we felt this general overview would be helpful for readers.

Motor trains

During the first decade of the 20th Century, many British railway companies were seeking to make economies and this was particularly true as far as branch lines were concerned. The most successful solution was the introduction of the Motor Train that the LNWR defined as, 'a small train, consisting of a detachable engine and one or more coaches, capable of being driven from the coach end.' The LNWR

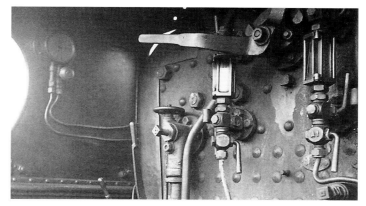

This cab interior view of a 'Super D' shows the LNWR two-handled regulator, while prominent in the picture are the two water gauges and the horizontal injector cone adjustment wheel and clack valve shutdown where the vertical wheel had been replaced with a square nut.   G.H. PLATT

A number of 'Coal Tanks' were fitted with a vacuum-controlled regulator that enabled the engine to work Motor Trains. In addition to the equipment on the side of the smokebox, a VCR-fitted engine had two brake vacuum pipes at each end. This was the Midland Railway design that was judged to be the most efficient of the various control systems used by the constituent companies of the LMS.   T. S. STEEL COLLECTION

The two pictures show an original LNWR cab (top) and an LNWR locomotive where the LNWR cab had been modified to composite gauge.

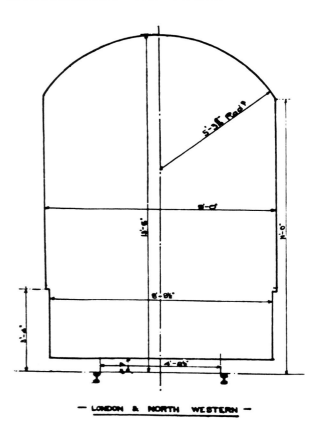

— LONDON & NORTH WESTERN —

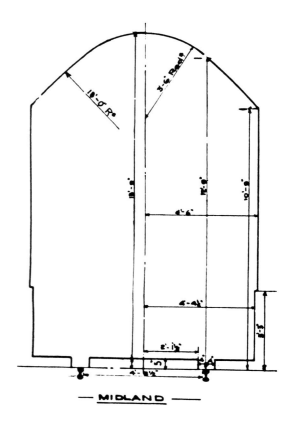

— MIDLAND —

Loading Gauge. The clearance, loading or structure gauge, all these terms were used, varied between the different British railway companies and with the increasing size of locomotives this became an important factor when locomotives from company A were required to run over the lines of Company B. In this work we refer to the Midland gauge and the Composite gauge and the need to alter the profile of the locomotives' cabs to enable LNWR locomotives to run over lines of the former Midland Railway. This need becomes very clear when we examine both companies' gauges. Whilst the Midland gauge was higher in the centre, 13ft 9in, the L&NWR was 13ft 6in; the L&NWR gauge at the side of the cab was 11ft whilst the Midland was 10ft 9in, and the three inches were the reason why L&NWR locomotives that were to run over Midland lines required to be modified. The structure gauges shown here were taken from a Midland Carriage & Wagon Department drawing dated January 1916 entitled 'Maximum Load Gauge for Various Railways'. During the Great War, operating conditions meant there was a need for locomotives and rolling stock to run over other companies' lines, rather more so than pre-1914, and it is possible this drawing was also used after the grouping had taken place to identify which engines could run over other lines. The following companies that became part of the LMS were shown and they are reproduced here: Midland and LT&SR which had recently become part of the Midland, London North Western, Furness, Lancashire & Yorkshire, Glasgow & South Western and Caledonian. My copy of the drawing was not complete which is why we have not been able to show all the companies that became part of the LMS.

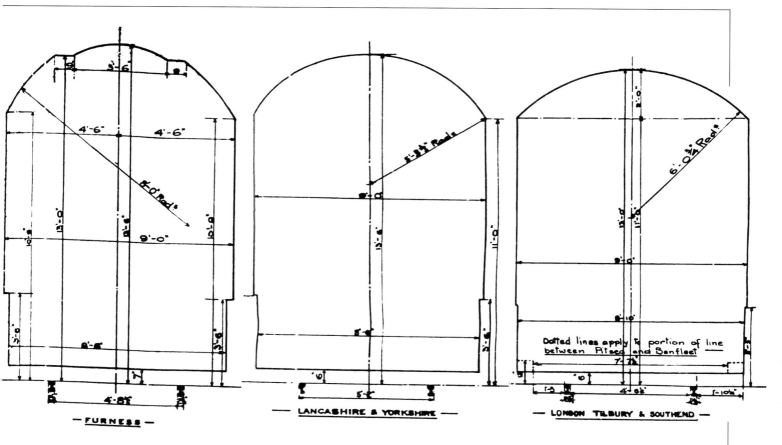

These seven loading gauge drawings were taken from a 1916 Midland Railway document as described on page 22.

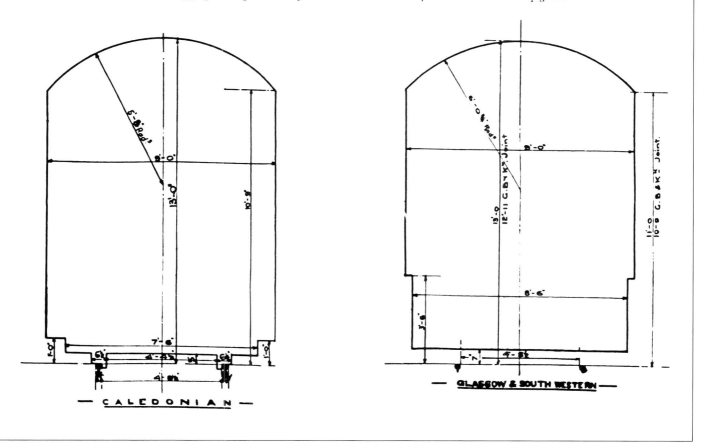

Taken at Upperby c.1923, this photograph shows LNWR No. 1452 Bonaventure which was built in October 1922 and became LMS No. 5602 in May 1926, being converted to oil burning in the same year. In 1935 it became No. 25602 and was withdrawn in June 1937. Note the bogie shields attached to the front buffer beam to protect the leading axleboxes from overspill when a pilot engine took water on the troughs. Though popular on the Midland Railway – even well into LMS days – these were only ever fitted to a handful of LNWR engines in the years after World War One. They were experimental and removed after only a few years.

COLLECTION R. J. ESSERY

began with the Red Wharf Bay branch on Anglesea in North Wales, and reference to the locomotives converted for this service together with other tank engines used on these services appears in Volume 2. Thereafter the number of Motor Train services on the LNWR increased. The position at the grouping is explained in the LMS Traffic Committee minute 1145 dated 24th November 1926, which states,

Proposed Automatic System of Regulator Control for "Push and Pull" Trains

The Chief General Superintendent reported that certain branch lines on the LMS Railway are operated by trains composed of two or more coaches, the control being so arranged as to admit of the regulator and brake being operated from a coach should that be the leading vehicle on a train.

It was explained that of the three different methods of control in use on the LMS, namely:–
(1) By rodding underneath the coaches
(2) By compressed air
(3) By vacuum control
the latter is the most economical and efficient, and, as a number of vehicles fitted with rodding arrangements are falling due for breaking up, it was recommended that 40 coaches and 20 tank engines be fitted with vacuum control at an estimated cost of £4,200, the allocation to be reported at the next meeting of the Committee. Approved, and ordered that, subject to the approval of the Locomotive & Electrical and Carriage & Wagon Committees, the matter be referred to the Board.

ALLOCATIONS

We felt that it would be helpful to provide some information about where the locomotives were allocated during the period they were LMS stock and to show the allocation of those engines still in service at the time the 'Big Four' were nationalised. Sadly the information no longer exists to allow us to present a comprehensive story for every locomotive from 1923, so what we have done under each class is to give the proposed allocation of locomotives in 1926 together with details taken from the November 1935 and 8th April 1944 lists as published by the Chief Operating Manager's Department, and finally the 31st December 1947 allocation, taken from *London Midland Scottish Railway Locomotive Allocations, The Last Day 1947*, by John Hooper.

The story of the 1926 allocation is interesting and we begin by reproducing the circular letter from F.W. Dingley.

London Midland and Scottish Railway Company
Office of Supt. of Motive Power,
(Western A Division).
Crewe
8th February 1926

EP/73/26
Circular to District Loco.
Supts and Running Shed Foremen.
Allocation and Loading of Passenger Engines.
Western 'A' Division.

For the workings commencing February 15th, the principle of allocation of passenger engines to Sheds will be that the number of engines allocated will be sufficient to cover all regular booked turns, normal requirements for specials, all Shed maintenance, examinations, washouts etc., and repairs in the C.M.E's Shops; that is, each District Loco. Superintendent or Running Shed Foreman will be responsible for arranging all the examinations, shed repairs, shopping, etc and for providing engines of the booked classification as indicated on the engine workings. A generous allocation has been given in view of the summer requirements.

The individual numbers of the engines allocated to commence this scheme will not be the engine numbers intended for the ultimate allo-

cation, which will be so arranged that as far as possible, the numbers of each Class at a Depot will run consecutively.

The types and classification of the engines as shewn in the re-numbering books, which you have had at your depot for some time, i.e.

Claughton type and Old L&Y 4–6–0 engines	} Classification 5.
Prince of Wales and Standard Compounds George the Fifth	} Classification 4.
Precursor Experiment	} Classification 3.
Renown Alfred the Great Straight Links	Classification 2. Classification 2. Classification 1.

And ultimately the Chief Mechanical Engineer will have the classification numbers fixed on the cabside panels of the engines.

The first essential is that the District Loco. Supt. or Running Shed Foreman must provide the type of engine for each train so shown on the working arrangements. Personal attention must be given to ensure that the engines are in proper mechanical order and sufficiently equipped.

If at any time, you are not able to provide an engine of the proper classification, I wish you to advise the Control Office in your District (except in the case of Camden, Willesden and Crewe) as soon as you have arrived at this decision and state what Classes of engines you can substitute. Crewe must advise the Divisional Passenger Control, Crewe Station and Camden and Willesden the Trains Office, Euston.

Only in extraordinary cases will engines be loaned from one district to another, and this, only by arrangements with this office or my representative who will be in close touch with the Control Section at Crewe.

At certain times there are events such as Race Meetings, Football Cup Ties, etc which will necessitate a number of additional specials, and from your knowledge, these events should be anticipated, and you should prepare in advance to be able to meet the traffic requirements, and, in all cases you must cooperate with the District Controllers and Station Masters in order, as far as possible, to anticipate the engine requirements.

Copies of amended engine workings to commence February 15th have already been sent out, so that you have ample opportunity of carefully making the necessary engine arrangements for the successful introduction of the scheme, from the same date as new loading instructions for passenger trains on Main Lines will be introduced. These tables shew the loading classification under the headings of 'full load', 'limited load' and 'special limited load', also instructions as regards assisting engines: and copies will be issued to all concerned.

In order to successfully carry out the new allocations scheme throughout the line, engines must be returned to their 'owning' depots as quickly as possible, by arrangements with Control. The present arrangements of advising me at the Divisional Control Office, Crewe Station, of engines away from their home stations and foreign engines on hand must be continued.

Engines allotted to you must have the Shed number plates fitted so as to assist the Control in returning engines to their home Depots.

At present it is the practice when nearing shopping time for big passenger engines to be frequently used on freight workings. This is an undesirable practice, and is one that, by degrees, is to be eliminated. This policy is to be adopted straight away as far as Claughtons, Class 8 (ex LYR 4–6–0s) and Standard Compounds are concerned.

It will be necessary for you to keep up the conditions of these large passenger engines so that they are available for passenger workings right up to the time they are called into the Shops, and you should have as few as possible of these engines in the Shops during the busy periods of the Summer Season.

This system of allocation will eventually be adopted for all classes of engines, and these instructions will similarly apply.

If there are any points not clear, please correspond with me under the title of 'Allocation of Engines' as soon as possible.

F.W. Dingley.

This picture was taken at Aston, one of two LNWR engine sheds in Birmingham, on 12th June 1935, and apart from the unidentified Standard Class 4F seen in the middle of the picture, the other three locomotives were built pre-1923, two by the LNWR and one by the Midland. To the right we can identify a 4–6–2T No. 6978 and on the left the 'Cauliflower' was probably No. 8553. The other engine was an ex-Midland Class 2F whose stock number cannot be identified. The purpose of including this picture, taken almost at the midway point of the LMS company's existence as a separate company, is to draw attention to the variety of pre-1923 stock that could be seen.

M. F. YARWOOD

What is particularly interesting about this first circular advising what was planned is that it was dated 8th February 1926 and a circular about passenger tender engines followed this on 17th March. Almost six months went by before the tank engines, both passenger and freight, were dealt with, and the final document providing details of the freight tender locomotives was dated 13th December 1926.

This suggests the ultimate allocation plan was implemented, but how long it lasted before the tidy number blocks began to be broken up by changed operating requirements is not clear. However, what it does provide is a very clear picture of where and how many of each ex-LNWR class was allocated at this time.

It is worth noting that F.W. Dingley started on the LNWR in 1875, and in 1923 he was Superintendent of Motive Power 'A' Division.

NOTE ON ALLOCATIONS

When presenting the story of the allocations, we encounter the problem of how the various depots were described; for example, to the modern-day enthusiast, Crewe was either 5A Crewe North or 5B Crewe South, but in Dingley's 1926 lists only the name Crewe was used, whilst the depot that became 4A Shrewsbury is shown as Salop. Therefore some changes have been made to simplify matters for the reader. The second problem was that after the 1926 allocation list was published, many of the 0–8–0s were converted or rebuilt, but generally they retained their first LMS numbers. Therefore to assist readers who wish to follow the 'allocation story', I have added some information about dates of rebuilding and reclassification of the various classes of 0–8–0 locomotives that will be found in Volume 3. It is interesting to note that in the allocation lists produced by the LMS, this is overcome by showing each locomotive's power classification together with its allocation, which on some lists appears as a shed code number but on others as a name.

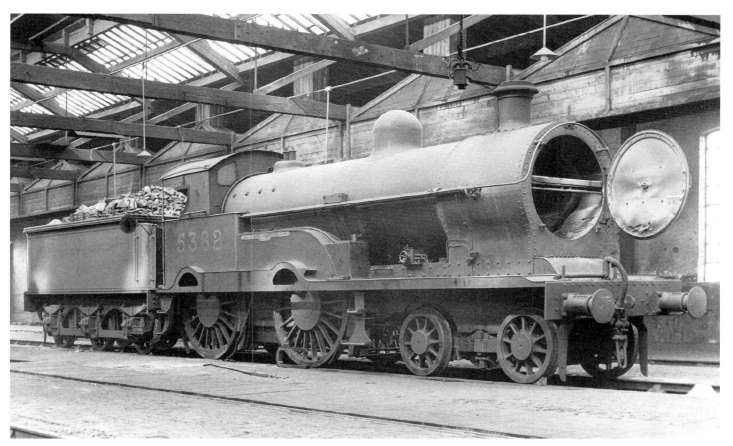

Taken at Crewe North shed on 16th August 1936, this picture shows 'George the Fifth' class No. 5362 on shed. The sign that can be seen at the front of the tender was probably a 'Not To Be Moved' sign which, although they cannot be seen, suggests the fitters were working on it. The open smokebox door allows the fastening dart and the two bars across the entrance, between which it passed, to be seen. When the door was closed, the dart handle was raised to the horizontal position to clear the bars. Once clear, the handle was allowed to fall to the vertical position, the screw handle (or wheel) could then be tightened. Note the burning of the inner lining of the door caused by red-hot ashes (char). Built in July 1911 as LNWR No. 12360 Fire Queen, the LMS stock number was applied in August 1927 and in April 1937 it became 25362 and continued in service until March 1939 when it was withdrawn.
C. F. OLDHAM/KIDDERMINSTER RAILWAY MUSEUM

During their final years the 'Straight Links' were often used as pilots double-heading mainline express passenger trains. This picture of No. 5011 was taken at the north end of Rugby c. 1930–31 when it was assisting a 'Claughton' which cannot be identified other than it was not a named engine. No. 5011 was built in November 1888 as LNWR No. 696 Director and was renumbered in September 1927, remaining in service until 1933 when it was scrapped. As we can see, it was painted black (livery code C18). However, the buffer beam still carried LNWR lining. Although we are a few years into the LMS period, apart from the LMS insignia numbers lamp holders and smokebox door mounted shedplate on 5011 the scene is pure LNWR.

COLLECTION R. J. ESSERY

CHAPTER ONE

THE INHERITED STOCK
PASSENGER TENDER ENGINES

LNWR 'Straight Link' 2–4–0 No. 1745 Glowworm *after being renumbered by the LMS as No. 5034 assisting a 'Claughton' 4–6–0 No. 5957 on a Glasgow to Manchester passenger train approaching Oxenholme. With a train of this moderate weight, the pilot is probably AENR (Assisting Engine Not Required) working back to its home shed (Oxenholme) having assisted a heavy Northbound train to Carlisle.*
T. S. STEEL COLLECTION

In this series we will follow the same sequence as adopted by the LMS in 1923 when the constituent and subsidiary companies stock was renumbered. As shown on page 4, the LMS divided the locomotive stock into passenger and freight, beginning with the passenger tender engines, followed by the tank engines. The tank engines were divided into passenger and freight classes, with the freight tender engines in the final number series. With each series the lowest numbers were given to the least powerful class. However, it must also be pointed out that a number of LNWR locomotives were withdrawn before the renumbering list was agreed and many were withdrawn still displaying their L&NWR stock numbers. The 1923 engine renumbering does not give any motive power classification numbers and I am not sure when it began to be applied to locomotives other than those from the Midland Railway, but in the absence of an official list I have included the classification given in the 5th October 1929 list reproduced on page 5, although it should be noted that F. W. Dingley's circular letters written in 1926 used power classification numbers, and this information appears in the class sections.

The LMS inherited three different wheel arrangements of LNWR passenger tender locomotives; the smallest were the 2–4–0s, but although these locomotives were similar, there were two different driving wheel diameters. They were renumbered in the series 5000–5109. In addition to the 2–4–0s there was a variety of designs of both saturated and superheated 4–4–0s, which carried numbers between 5110–5409. Finally, there were three classes of 4–6–0s, the earliest design of which was not superheated. The LMS allocated the number series 5450–6029 to these locomotives. The

total number of 2–4–0s taken into stock was 110, there were 299 4–4–0s and 650 4–6–0s. In percentage terms, this amounted to 30.585% of the L&NWR locomotive stock on 31st December 1922. We begin our survey with the 2–4–0s, but having set out the principles for allocating locomotives, we must first reproduce F. W. Dingley's letter about passenger engines. This was headed 'Allocation of Passenger engines' and was dated 17th March 1926.

> With reference to my Circular dated 8th February reference EP/73/26 headed "Allocation and Loading of Passenger engines 'A' Division."
>
> Attached is a list shewing the ultimate allocation of passenger tender engines.
>
> When rendering the Engine Stock Summary, in future, the number to be shewn as required in the special Link, will be the number left of your total allocation after you have taken into consideration the number required for your booked turns, so that the two figures will make together the total allocation.
>
> The engines apportioned to your Station, which are not already on your stock, will be sent after repairs in the Chief Mechanical Engineer's shops, and if you already have sufficient engines of any particular class, those which have been allocated to other stations, will be withdrawn and transferred to the proper station.
>
> In making the allocation, the additional summer working has been taken into account, and during the winter months it may be necessary to withdraw engines which are not required and loan them to stations at which suitable work can be found for them, but as far as possible, arrangements will be made to take the surplus passenger engines to the C.M.E.'s shops during the winter period.
>
> Enc.

Unfortunately, when these documents came into my possession, the various enclosures were missing and only circular letters and list of ultimate allocations were available.

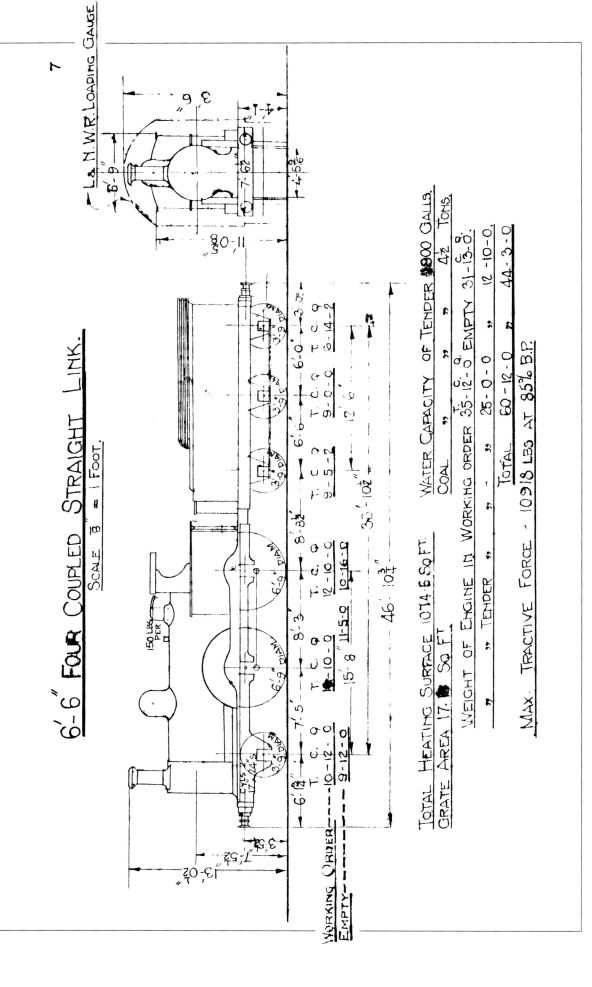

Prior to 1923 the LNWR considered the 2–4–0s as two separate series and they were shown on pages 7 and 12 of the LNWR Engine Diagram Book with the variation in wheel diameter clearly given, but following the grouping the LMS combined both the 6ft 9inch and 6ft 3inch 2–4–0s into a single class. The reason was simply the power classification, which determined the load the locomotive could pull; this was the deciding factor not the wheel diameter. At the heading of the diagram the wheel diameter appears as 6ft 6inch, which was included in the LNWR name for the class, but the wheel diameter on the diagram, which is a document that gives all the dimensions, appears as 6ft 9inches. As previously mentioned, this is due to the L&NWR practice of not including the nominal tyre dimension as part of the wheel diameter in class descriptions and this applies to all diagrams. These locomotives, also referred to as 'Precedent' class, were allocated LMS stock numbers between 5000–5079. Note that both series of 'Straight Links' were coupled to 1,800 gallon tenders that had a 4½ ton coal capacity. Comparison of the two diagrams will show that the smaller wheel locomotives had a higher tractive effort at 85% boiler pressure whilst understandably the larger wheel engines were slightly heavier.

6'-6" Four Coupled Straight Link.

Scale ⅛" = 1 Foot.

L & N.W.R. Loading Gauge.

Total Heating Surface 1014·6 Sq Ft.
Grate Area 17·1 Sq Ft.

Water Capacity of Tender 1800 Galls.
Coal   "   "   "   4½ Tons.

Weight of Engine in Working Order 35-12-0 Empty 31-13-0.

		T. C. Q.	T. C. Q.
" Tender "	"	25 - 0 - 0	12 -10 - 0
		Total 60 -12 - 0	44 - 3 - 0

Max. Tractive Force - 10,918 Lbs at 85% B.P.

Working Order - - - 10-12-0
Empty - - - - - - 9-12-0

2–4–0 Passenger Tender; LNW Straight Link

Motive Power Classification 1, post-1928 1P.
Allocated LMS locomotive number series 5000–5109.

LARGE 'JUMBO'

This 'Large Jumbo', built January 1888 as LNWR No 1522 Pitt, *became LMS No. 5005 in June 1927 and remained in service until July 1932 when it was scrapped. It is seen here at Chester in September 1929.*   H.C. CASSERLEY

Enthusiasts and historians usually divide the LNWR 2–4–0s into two classes, the first being known as the 'Renewed Precedent' class or 'Large Jumbos'. Officially they were regarded as rebuilds of the Ramsbottom 1866 and Webb 1874 designs, but in effect they were new engines built between 1887–1897, with the final pair entering service in 1898 and 1901. Withdrawals began in 1905 and by 1st January 1923 there were eighty of the 6ft 6 inch driving wheel engines still in stock; they were allocated LMS numbers between 5000–5079.

The second series were known as the 'Waterloo' or 'Whitworth' class and, whilst similar to the 'Precedents', they had smaller driving wheels 6ft 0 inch in diameter and were also known as 'Small Jumbos'. Officially they were regarded as rebuilds of the Ramsbottom/Webb 'Samson' class of 1863–79, but they were also new engines. Ninety were built between 1889–1896, but by the formation of the LMS the number in service had been reduced to thirty-six. Two were withdrawn before LMS stock numbers were allocated and four were transferred to Departmental stock and are considered later. The remainder were allocated numbers between 5080 and 5109. Both types were classified as Power Class 1, later IP, and they were the only ex-LNWR passenger tender locomotives to be given this classification. Their story in LNWR ownership is complex, but in 1923 the LMS ignored the difference in driving wheels and they were all classified as 'Straight Link'

regardless of driving wheel diameter. Therefore in this book we will consider them as one class.

They were usually coupled to 1,800 gallon Webb tenders with wood framing and buffer beams, and the wheelbase was 6ft 6in × 6ft. From about 1895 three coal rails were fitted. By the time they became LMS stock, almost all had received replacement taper body buffers, and from 1925 lamp irons, also known as lamp holders, replaced the original LNWR lamp sockets. They were fitted with Ramsbottom safety valves but at least Nos. 25001 and 5018 are recorded as being fitted with Ross safety valves.

In their prime they were splendid locomotives hauling the Company's principal express passenger trains; they were probably the finest passenger engines that Webb produced during his term of office. They were very free-running and able to generate plenty of steam, which enabled them to be driven hard, characteristics that earned them the nickname 'Jumbos', but the increasing weight of trains saw them replaced by more powerful classes of 4–4–0s. By 1923 they were generally employed as mainline pilots or on passenger trains, usually working over branch lines, but, as mentioned, some were withdrawn from capital stock and employed as departmental engines. The LNW had allocated several to departmental stock and these engines are described in Vol. 3. As new locomotives entered service, the older engines were withdrawn, and in the case of the Straight Links, withdrawals continued in 1923. Of the 110 locomotives allocated LMS numbers, at least 49 never carried them. To the best of my knowledge, the following did not receive their allocated LMS numbers or livery.

5004	5025	5047	5061	5073	5086	5100
5006	5028	5049	5063	5074	5089	5101
5008	5033	5052	5065	5076	5093	5103
5010	5037	5055	5066	5077	5094	5105
5015	5038	5056	5067	5079	5096	5106
5017	5043	5059	5071	5081	5098	5107
5024	5044	5060	5072	5082	5099	5109

Five of the engines which did not receive their allocated numbers or livery were transferred to Departmental stock: Nos. 5086 to *Engineer Northampton* in May 1923, 5094 *Engineer Walsall* in June 1923, 5099 *Engineer* in May 1923, 5100 *Engineer Lancaster* in February 1924, and 5101 *Engineer Watford* in May 1923.

LIVERY

Under LMS ownership they should have been painted red, but only four appear to have been so treated, Nos. 5012 *John Ramsbottom*, 5036 *Novelty*, 5050 *Merrie Carlisle* and 5069

This picture was taken at Northampton Engine Shed on 26th June 1920 and shows the driver and fireman in the cab of LNWR No. 231 Firefly at their home shed; note the code 5 for Northampton on the rear of the cab roof. This locomotive was built in June 1890 and did not receive an LMS stock number; it was scrapped in August 1922. However, it is the best picture we have found that shows the footplate of an LNWR locomotive as at the grouping.   R.S. CARPENTER

This picture of LNWR No. 1748 Britannia *at the head of an ordinary passenger train was taken c.1926 and shows a 'Large Jumbo' in LMS ownership but still carrying LNWR insignia and stock number. Built in 1889, the LMS number 5016 was not applied until September 1927, and nine months later in June 1928 it was scrapped. There does not appear to have been any change from its 1923 condition, and it still retained its LNWR lamp holders.*   COLLECTION R.S. CARPENTER

Penrith Beacon. The rest of the class remained black, and pre-1928 the most common arrangement for those repainted was plain black, no lining, LMS coat of arms on the cabside, and a smokebox numberplate. The tender usually retained LNWR lining but no number was carried. The renumbering of the survivors began again in 1926/7, but many did not receive their allocated LMS number until the 1928 livery style had been introduced. From this point in time they were painted plain black and usually the stock number was executed in hand-painted characters on the side of the cab.

By 1934, with the exception of No. 5001 *Snowdon*, all locomotives in capital stock had been withdrawn, but No. 5001 was renumbered under the 1934 renumbering scheme when it became No. 25001, a number it carried for a short period before it was withdrawn in October 1934. During its final months, it was stationed at Penrith where it was employed on local work, both passenger and freight, rather different from its early years. According to the January 1935 edition of *The Journal of the Stephenson Locomotive Society*, this locomotive was the only survivor of eight original members of the class, four of which were inherited by the LMS, that retained their original frames throughout their lifetime. The difference between the original and replacement frames were: thickness increased from $\frac{7}{8}$ inch to 1 inch, the bottom edge of the frame between the leading axle and driving axle was deepened by 1 inch, and the top edge of the frames above all driving wheels heightened by 2 inches. The trailing hornblocks were

strengthened and stronger bolts were fitted to all hornblocks. Fortunately, an example of this class is preserved as part of the National Collection at the NRM, where No. 790 *Hardwicke*, which ran as LMS No. 5031 before it was withdrawn in January 1932, can be seen. However, certain LNWR features were not included when it was restored.

Ultimate Allocations 1926
6ft 0in & 6ft 6in Straight Links

Springs Branch	5000–5003
Warrington	5004–5005
Llandudno Junc	5007 & 5009
Rugby	5010–5016
Peterborough	5017–5021
Northampton	5022
Bletchley	5023–5024, 5026–5027, 5029–5033
Preston	5034–5038
Edge Hill	5039–5040
Stafford	5041–5042
Patricroft	5043, 5045–5046, 5097–5098
Carlisle	5048–5056, 5092–5093, 5095–5096
Longsight	5057–5058
Nuneaton	5060–5063
Colwick	5064–5065, 5067
Tebay	5068–5069
Chester	5070–5072
Bangor	5073–5075
Birkenhead	5076–5078
Crewe	5081–5085, 5087–5091
Workington	5102–5105, 5107–5108

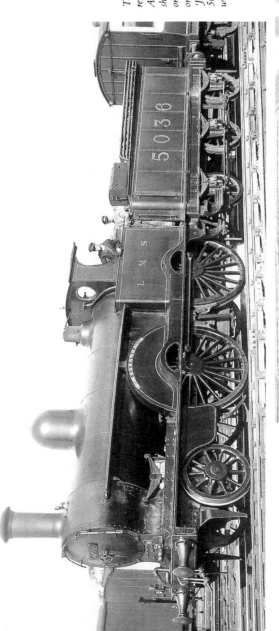

This picture of LNWR No. 1682 Novelty, after being renumbered and painted in the correct LMS red livery (Code A4) in 1923, has been included to show what the 'Jumbos' should have looked like when the LMS number was displayed on the tender and by means of a smokebox door numberplate, on the locomotive. Built in June 1892, it was one of four 'Jumbos' to receive this livery; the others were Nos. 5012, 5050 and 5069. No. 5036 remained in service until it was withdrawn in July 1928.

COLLECTION R.J. ESSERY

Here we see LNWR No. 1674 Delhi after it had been renumbered by the LMS in June 1927 when it became No. 5020. The picture was taken at Keswick shortly before withdrawal in November 1930.

COLLECTION T. S. STEEL

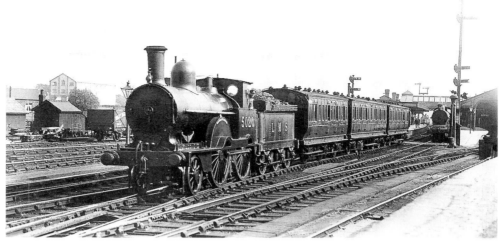

LNWR No. 1674 Delhi *after being renumbered LMS 5020; although it had acquired LMS lamp brackets, it retained Webb buffers. It is seen at Whitchurch at the head of an ordinary passenger train for Chester via Malpas (probably the 10.30am) comprising three LNWR carriages, two 6-wheel and one bogie vehicle, sometime between when it was renumbered in June 1927 and 1929–30 when it was transferred to Penrith. A Shrewsbury to Crewe passenger train can be seen standing in the down platform (probably the 10.00am from Shrewsbury due to depart 10.29am but running late).*
COLLECTION R.J. ESSERY

This picture of No. 5002 General, *one of four original (not renewed) 'Precedents' inherited by the LMS, at Crewe Works was taken after the introduction of the 1928 livery and, judging by the external condition, the locomotive was ex-works. A three-link coupling had been left on the front hook after the engine was shunted from the paint shop – soon a screw-coupling would have been fitted. The lamp irons were now LMS type. The change from red to black for this class had taken place and there is no sign of any lining on either the engine or tender. No 5002 remained in traffic until 1931 when it was withdrawn and scrapped.*   COLLECTION R.J. ESSERY

Built in November 1894 as LNWR No. 860 Merrie Carlisle, it became LMS No. 5050 in October 1923 and remained in service until withdrawn in June 1933. This undated picture was taken at Penrith after it had been repainted in the post-1927-style livery, code C18. No smokebox door numberplate but it had been fitted with LMS-type lamp holders. COLLECTION
T. S. STEEL

This undated picture was taken at Carlisle c.1924 and shows LMS No. 5012 John Ramsbottom coupled to ex-L&Y 4-6-0 No. 1670 waiting to take over an Up express. Built in 1888 as LNWR No. 1211, it was renumbered by the LMS in December 1923 when the small letters LMS were applied to the cabside, but later the correct post-1928 style was used. This picture shows livery code A4 and the locomotive was withdrawn in December 1930.
W.H. WHITWORTH/
REAL PHOTOGRAPHS

I have included this picture taken at Lichfield Trent Valley to show an example of a locomotive in black, carrying the LMS coat of arms on the side of the cab and, just visible on the original print, power class 1 on the cab sidesheet. The only evidence of renumbering is the smokebox door numberplate. In this condition some locomotives were coupled to tenders that retained LNWR lining, but this does not apply to this locomotive, a 'Large Jumbo' built in 1896 as LNWR No. 2185 Alma. It became LMS No. 5058 in February 1927 and was withdrawn in November 1928.
COLLECTION
R.J. ESSERY

During their final years the 2–4–0s were to be seen at Chester and along the North Wales line. Here we see 'Large Jumbo' No. 5048 Henry Pease, which entered traffic as LNWR No. 364 in October 1894, being coaled at Chester on 6th September 1929. The locomotive which had been renumbered is seen in plain black livery code C16, and remained in traffic until withdrawn in September 1930.   L. W. PERKINS

'Large Jumbo' No. 5029 Speke entered traffic in 1891 as LNWR No. 1684 and was renumbered by the LMS in December 1926, but later it was repainted in black without lining, displaying livery code C18. This picture was taken at Crewe North c.1929 and shows the locomotive in its final condition prior to being withdrawn in September 1931.   COLLECTION R. S. CARPENTER

This picture of LNWR No 2190 Princess Beatrice, which had been renumbered LMS 5000 in July 1928, was taken at Birmingham New Street in 1930 where, judging by the headlamp code, it was on station pilot duty. This engine was built in April 1875 and re-boilered and the frames strengthened in 1890 three years before the renewal of the class as 'Improved Precedents' began. Thus it was the oldest survivor of the eight members of the class never renewed, four of which became LMS stock. It remained in service until July 1932 when it was scrapped. However, I am sure the crew would have to have explained why the engine was blowing off while standing at the side of the platform!

This is a copy of page 12 of the LNWR Engine Diagram Book and refers to the 'Small Jumbos'. A copy of page 7, 'Large Jumbos', will be found on page 30 together with a brief summary of the difference between the two types.

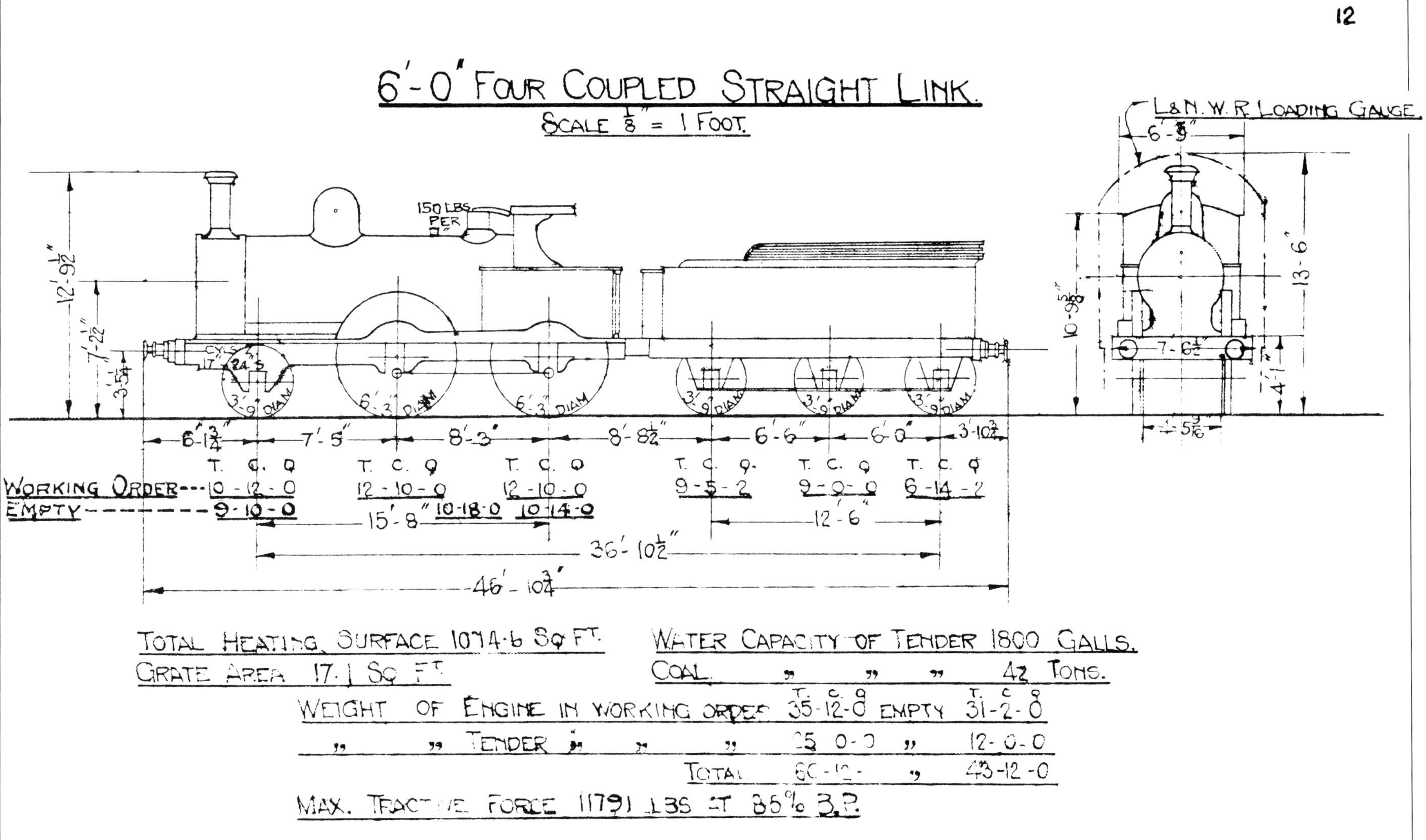

L&N.W.R. LOADING GAUGE

13'-6"

6'-0" FOUR COUPLED STRAIGHT LINK
SCALE 1/8" = 1 FOOT.

WORKING ORDER --- 10'-2'-0 9'-10-0
EMPTY --------- 9'-10-0

TOTAL HEATING SURFACE 1074.6 SQ.FT.
GRATE AREA 17.1 SQ.FT.

WATER CAPACITY OF TENDER 1800 GALLS.
COAL " " " " 42 TONS.

	T.C.Q	T.C.Q
WEIGHT OF ENGINE IN WORKING ORDER	35-12-8	EMPTY 31-2-8
" " TENDER "	25-0-0	12-0-0
	TOTAL 60-12- "	43-12-0

MAX. TRACTIVE FORCE 11791 LBS. AT 85% B.P.

SMALL 'JUMBO'

LNWR No. 604 Narcissus *was built November 1890 and was an example of a 'Small Jumbo'. Although it is not possible to date this picture, it is representative of the condition of the 2–4–0s when they became LMS stock. The locomotive was allocated to Crewe North when renumbered 5087 in October 1926, the livery style was as* Alma *seen at page 36, but before it was withdrawn in September 1930 it was repainted in black livery code C18.*   REAL PHOTOGRAPHS.

No. 5088 Charon *was built in 1892 as LNWR No. 735 and received its LMS stock number in October 1926; withdrawal came in December 1928. Clearly this picture was taken before the locomotive was taken out of traffic but since it was carrying post-1927 freight livery code C16, it could not have been in this condition for more than a year.*
COLLECTION R.J. ESSERY

Prior to 1923 the LNWR exercised running powers over the Furness Railway and following the grouping ex-LNWR engines continued to work over these lines. This picture of No. 5104 Woodlark, a 'Small Jumbo', originally LNWR No. 764 built in January 1895, was taken at Barrow station in 1930 at the head of an ordinary passenger train. Painted in black, the locomotive displays livery code C18 but soon it was to be withdrawn and this took place in January 1931. The LMS stock number was applied in September 1927 and the original LNWR lamp sockets had been replaced by LMS lamp holders.

J. A. G. H. COLTAS

Photographed at Penrith, this shows LNWR No. 642 Bee that was built in August 1890 running as LMS No. 5084 taking water while working an ordinary passenger train. The LMS stock number was applied in March 1928 and the locomotive was withdrawn in January 1932.

T. S. STEELE COLLECTION

As explained in the text, the LNWR had separate engine diagrams for compounds in their original or rebuilt form, but in 1929 the LMS combined the survivors into one series. However, we have included the three diagrams that were in use when the LNWR became part of the LMS. Page 2 of the LNWR Diagram Book shows the 7ft 0in Four Coupled Compound 'Jubilee' Class, the 7ft 0in Four Coupled Compound 'Alfred The Great' Class', and Page 1 the 7ft 0in Four Coupled Simple 'Renown' Class'. The major difference between the three diagrams is the tender size, 2500 gallons for the 'Jubilees', 3000 gallons for the 'Alfred The Great', but only 2000 gallons for the 'Renowns', although coal capacity for each size of tender was 5 tons. In practice there were few 2000 gallon tenders left in service in LMS days and all three classes usually ran with Webb 2500 gallon tenders, although exceptions are No. 5117 Polyphemus, which ran (as a 'Renown') with a 2000 gallon tender until withdrawn in December 1930 (see page 43) and No. 5185 King Edward VII, also a 'Renown', photographed with a Whale 3000 gallon tender at Crewe in 1929. According to the diagrams, in terms of starting tractive effort, the most powerful were the Jubilees (because they alone retained 200psi boiler pressure), with the 'Alfred the Great' least powerful, but under the LMS Power classification system they were all Power class 2, which for the survivors from 1928 became 2P Diagram Page 2 the 'Alfred the Greats' will be found on page 46 and diagram page 1 the 'Renown' on page 50.

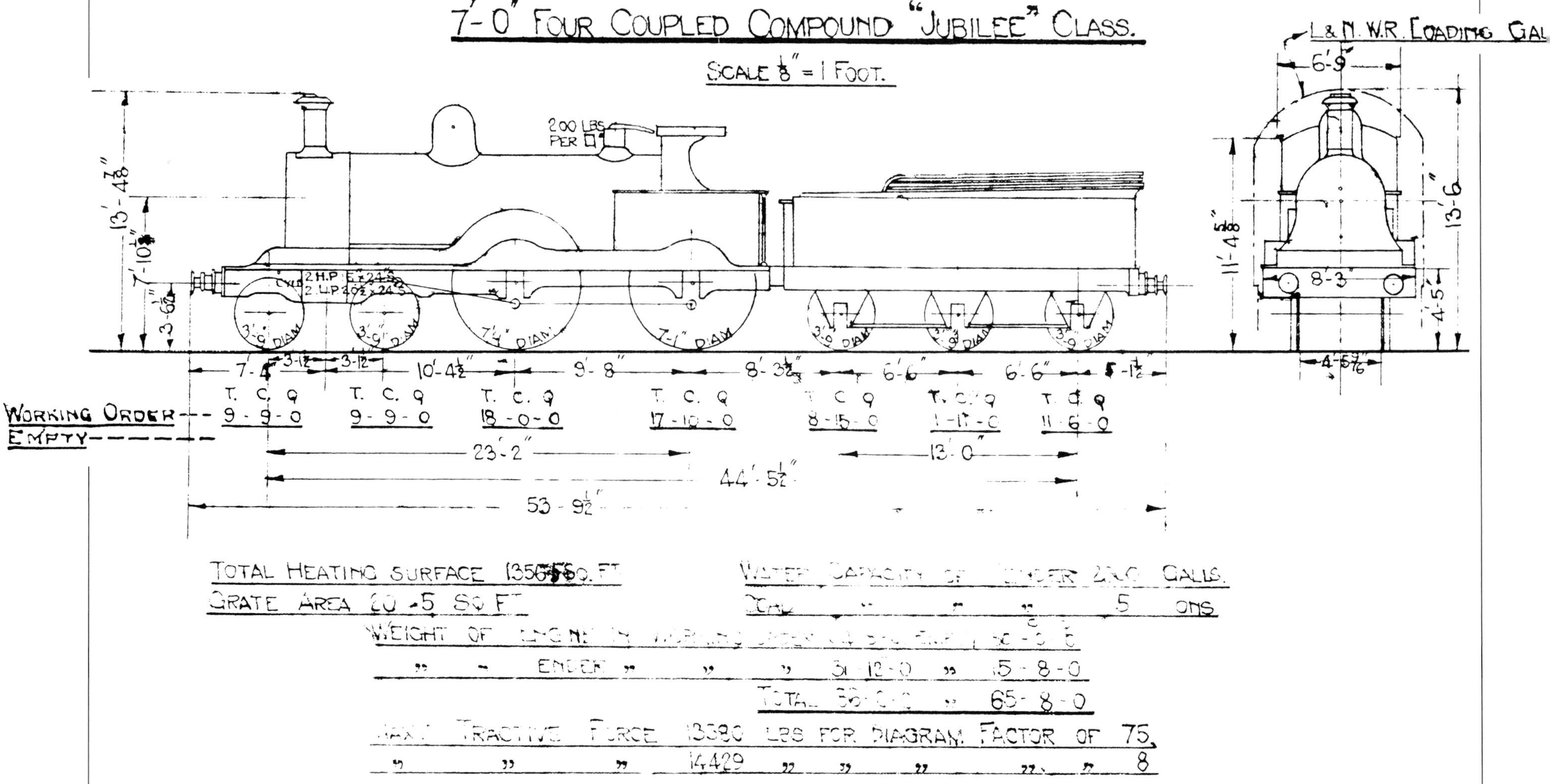

L&N.W.R. LOADING GA

7'-0" FOUR COUPLED COMPOUND "JUBILEE" CLASS.

SCALE 8" = 1 FOOT.

200 LBS PER □"

TOTAL HEATING SURFACE 1356 SQ. FT.

GRATE AREA 60.5 SQ. FT.

WEIGHT OF ENGINE

WATER CAPACITY OF TENDER 2500 GALS.

COAL — 5 TONS

MAX. TRACTIVE FORCE 18390 LBS FOR DIAGRAM FACTOR OF 75

WORKING ORDER

EMPTY

4–4–0 Passenger Tender, LNW 'Renown'

Motive Power Classification 2, post-1928 2P
Allocated LMS locomotive number series 5110–5186.

Although the LMS allocated three separate but consecutive number series to the Webb Compounds, some were still in their original form and others had been rebuilt as two-cylinder simple expansion locomotives. Collectively this group of engines did not form a significant contribution to the LMS locomotive stock. In 1923 the new company classified them in this number series, subdividing them under three headings, 'Jubilees', 'Alfred the Great' and 'Renown', but the 1929 locomotive stock summary simplified matters and the sur-

viving locomotives originally allocated numbers between 5110–5186 were all considered to be a single class that was described as 'LNW Renown'. Although the number of engines involved was small and their importance and life expectancy limited, they are interesting insofar as they represent what could be considered today as unusual LMS stock during the early years of the Company. In this work they are described using the original 1923 LMS classifications.

'Jubilee' Class Allocated LMS locomotive series 5110–5117.

We begin our pictorial survey of this series with a picture of a 'Jubilee' compound LNWR No. 1923 Agamemnon *built in March 1900 and allotted LMS stock number 5115. However, it was scrapped in March 1925 before the number was applied. The train was the return working of the 'Eastern Counties Express' photographed on the first day it ran – 9th July 1923 – near Tutbury on the North Staffordshire Railway. This service ran daily in the summer months connecting Liverpool Lime Street and Manchester London Road with Yarmouth and Lowestoft, with a through portion to Cromer. The Liverpool and Manchester portions joined and divided at Stoke. With the exception of the leading coach, in LMS livery, the others were in LNWR livery, the second coach being the twelve-wheeled restaurant car which ran between Liverpool Lime Street and Lowestoft. A Midland & Great Northern Joint engine would have worked the train to Nottingham Midland where the 'Jubilee' took over, avoiding Derby by using the Sheet Store Junction to Willington Junction line.* COLLECTION R. J. ESSERY

The two four-cylinder 4–4–0s built at Crewe in 1897 marked the beginning of the 'Jubilee' class. One was a four-cylinder simple engine, which was built for comparative purposes with the other, a four-cylinder compound. The simple expansion locomotive was originally number 1501 and carried the name *Iron Duke*, but within six months it had been renamed *Jubilee*. Webb quickly decided in favour of the compound locomotives and in 1898 the simple expansion engine was rebuilt and the following year it was renumbered, becoming No.1901. The second locomotive, the compound, entered traffic as No.1502 *Black Prince*, but it was renumbered in 1899, becoming No.

1902. As compounds they were to form the basis of the 'Jubilee' class and a further thirty-eight locomotives were constructed between 1899–1900.

In 1908 No. 1918 *Renown* was rebuilt as a 2-inside-cylinder simple expansion locomotive, and the later rebuilds were referred to as 'Simple Renown'. In due course all but three of the 'Jubilee' class were rebuilt as simple expansion engines, although several compounds were not rebuilt until after they became LMS locomotive stock. In 1923 the surviving compounds, nine in total, came to the LMS, but one locomotive, old LNW No. 1908 *Royal George*, was scrapped in January

1923 before the new LMS locomotive stock numbers were allocated, and the surviving eight were allocated stock numbers 5110–5117, all except Nos. 5111/15 receiving them. Two locomotives, Nos. 1912 and 1929, came to the LMS with Belpaire boilers, together with modified spectacle plates, but both were rebuilt as 'Renowns', in May and February 1924 respectively. None of the locomotives were renumbered while they were compounds. The class was noteworthy for

introducing coupled wheels with the distinctive large circular boss, a feature that was continued by later LNWR CMEs.

As 'Jubilees' they retained the socket lamp holders, and when replacement buffers were fitted, the taper-bodied type was used. In their rebuilt form they were to remain in service for a few years and as such are dealt with later at page 51 ('Renown' Class).

This picture shows another 'Jubilee', LNWR No. 1929 Polyphemus (built April 1900) as rebuilt with a Belpaire boiler in 1904 and as it was when it became LMS stock in 1923, but before being rebuilt as a 'Renown'. Note the tall capuchon fitted to the chimney. These were fitted to several different Webb classes in the 1903–4 period.
G. W. SHOTT

Polyphemus *again, this time after it had been rebuilt as a 'Renown' in February 1924 and renumbered by the LMS, as No. 5117, in March 1928, at which time the cab roof was altered to the MR profile. It was photographed at Rugby shortly before its withdrawal from service in December 1930.*   COLLECTION R. J. ESSERY

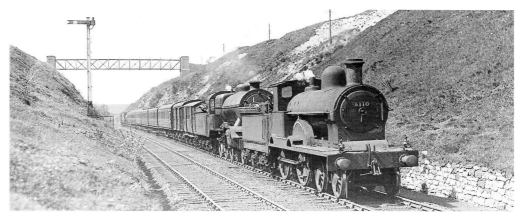

Taken at Shap, this undated picture shows a Glasgow to Birmingham train headed by 'Renown' Class 4–4–0 No. 5110 Jubilee *as pilot engine with LYR 4–6–0 No. 10436 as train engine. No. 5110 was built as a compound in June 1897 named* Iron Duke, *being renamed* Jubilee *in December 1897. It was rebuilt as a 2-cylinder simple in April 1919. The LMS stock number was applied in June 1926 and it was withdrawn in November 1931.*
T. S. STEEL COLLECTION

Built as LNWR No. 1927 Goliath *in March 1900, this locomotive became LMS stock prior to being rebuilt as a 'Renown' in January 1924. The LMS No. 5116 was applied in November 1926 and it remained in traffic until withdrawn in December 1931. As an ordinary passenger train the spare headlamp, in the LNWR tradition, had been turned sideways – a practice which ceased when standard LMS lamp holders replaced the sockets.* W.T. STUBBS

This picture of LNWR No. 1911 Centurion, *built in June 1899, now running as LMS No. 5112, was taken at Crewe in 1931. Rebuilt as a 'Renown' in December 1924, the LMS stock number was applied in February 1928 when the LNWR lamp sockets were replaced by LMS lamp holders and the cab roof altered to the MR profile. The locomotive was withdrawn in December 1931.*
H. J. STRETTON-WARD

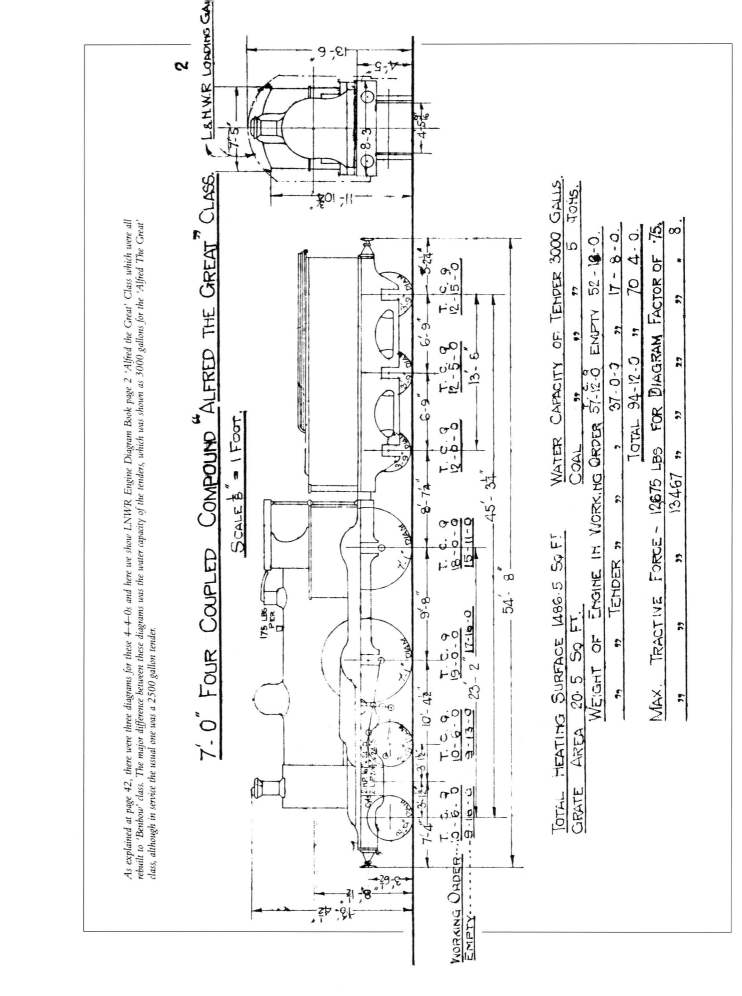

As explained at page 42, there were three diagrams for these 4-4-0s and here we show LNWR Engine Diagram Book page 2 'Alfred the Great' Class which were all rebuilt to 'Benbow' class. The major difference between these diagrams was the water capacity of the tenders, which was shown as 3000 gallons for the 'Alfred The Great' class, although in service the usual one was a 2500 gallon tender.

7'-0" FOUR COUPLED COMPOUND "ALFRED THE GREAT" CLASS.

SCALE ⅛" = 1 FOOT.

L&N.W.R LOADING GAUGE

2

TOTAL HEATING SURFACE 1486·5 SQ.FT.

GRATE AREA 20·5 SQ.FT.

WATER CAPACITY OF TENDER 3000 GALLS.

COAL   ″   5 TONS.

WEIGHT OF ENGINE IN WORKING ORDER 57-12-0 EMPTY 52-18-0

     ″   ″ TENDER   ″   37-0-3   ″   17- 8-0

                    TOTAL 94-12-0 ″   70 4 0

MAX. TRACTIVE FORCE — 12675 LBS FOR DIAGRAM FACTOR OF ·75

          ″   ″   13467 ″   ″   ″   ″   ″   ·8

'Alfred the Great' Class

Allocated LMS locomotive series 5118–5130.

This name was allocated to a second class of forty 4–4–0 compounds that were built at Crewe between 1901–1903. They were generally similar to the 'Jubilees', but with a 4 inch larger diameter boiler. They were modified between 1903/7 but remained as compounds. The work entailed modifications to the valve gear and running plate and a rearward extension to the cab. The first locomotive to be altered was No. 1952 *Benbow* and some sources refer to the rebuilds as 'Benbows', but since the LMS document reproduced at page 4 refers to them as 'Alfred the Great', that is how they will be described in this work. The alterations were in connection with the valve gear and the need to be able to adjust the inside and outside valve gear independently; all the compound 'Alfreds' were modified but none of the compound 'Jubilees'. Later a

total of thirty-three 'Alfred the Greats' were rebuilt as 'Renowns' (see below) but those that were still compounds in 1923 were allocated numbers in the series 5110–5130. Of the surviving compound 'Alfreds' in 1923, six, Nos. 5120, 5121, 5123, 5126, 5127 and 5129, had LMS numbers applied after they had been rebuilt as 'Renowns'. Two, Nos. 5119, 5125, were withdrawn, as 'Renowns', before their LMS numbers were applied and the remaining five were all withdrawn as compounds without receiving their new LMS numbers, including the unique No. 5128 (ex No. 1974) *Howe*, the only Webb compound ever to be superheated (in May 1921). When scrapped in March 1928, it was the last surviving Webb passenger compound.

We have mentioned that a number of LNWR locomotives became LMS stock but were withdrawn before their LMS stock number could be applied. This picture of LNWR No. 1944 Victoria and Albert *has been included to show such an example. Built June 1901, this locomotive was allotted LMS stock number 5118 but it was never applied, the engine being withdrawn as a compound in February 1927.*
G.W. SHOTT

LNWR No. 1969 Dominion, running under Ordinary passenger train headlamp code, was built in March 1903 and rebuilt as a 'Renown' in April 1924 before being renumbered LMS 5126 in March 1927. This picture, taken following renumbering but before it was withdrawn in April 1930, shows LNWR lamp sockets still in place, the LMS number displayed on the tender and smokebox numberplate, and the LMS coat of arms on the side of the cab.
COLLECTION R.J. ESSERY.

Again running under ordinary passenger train headlamp code, here we see LNWR No. 1969 Dominion, *this time at Tamworth shortly after the engine was renumbered in March 1927. The LNWR lamp sockets were still in place and the locomotive displayed the number on the tender (still in LNWR lined black livery), and had the LMS coat of arms on the side of the cab whilst the previous picture of this locomotive shows it carrying a smokebox door numberplate.*   COLLECTION R. J. ESSERY

This picture, taken at Crewe Works, shows compound No. 1974 Howe *that was built in July 1903 and rebuilt as a superheated compound in May 1921. Although it was allotted LMS stock number 5128, this was not applied before the engine was scrapped in January 1928. The absence of a tender suggests that it had been withdrawn and was waiting to be scrapped, and this assumption is reinforced by the presence of NSR tank engine No. 1560, seen on the left, which was withdrawn in April 1928.*
W. POTTER

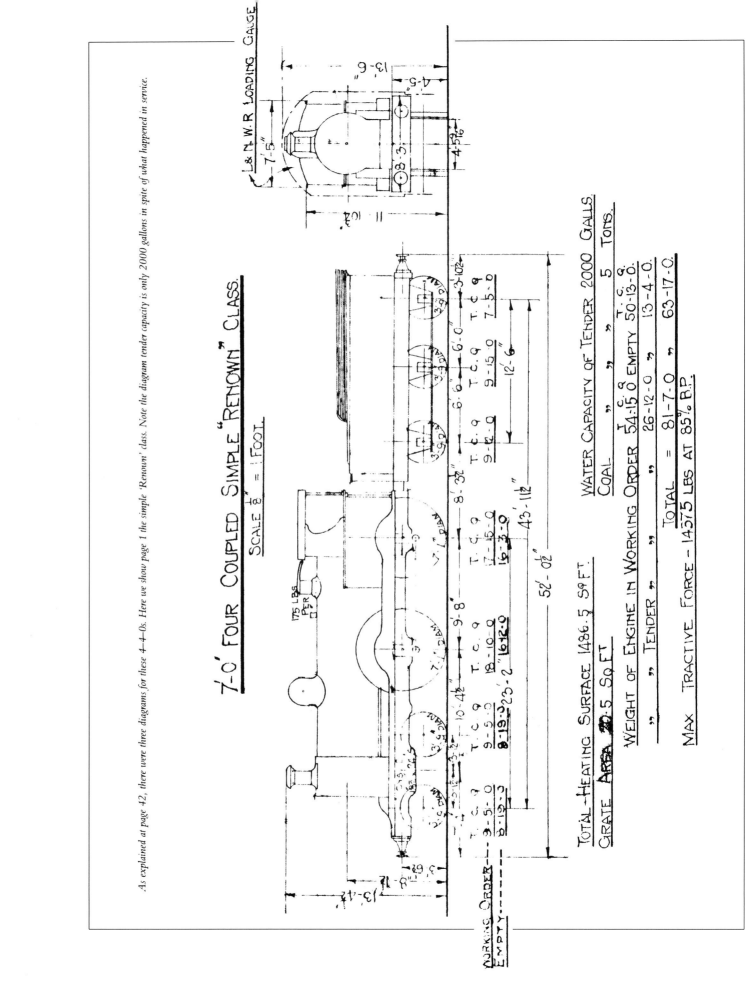

As explained at page 42, there were three diagrams for these 4–4–0s. Here we show page 1 the simple 'Renown' class. Note the diagram tender capacity is only 2000 gallons in spite of what happened in service.

7'-0' Four Coupled Simple "Renown" Class.

Scale ⅛" = 1 Foot

Total Heating Surface 1486.5 Sq Ft.

Grate Area 20.5 Sq Ft

Weight of Engine in Working Order	I.c.q.	Empty	T.c.q.
	54·15·0		50·13·0.
,, Tender ,, ,,	26·12·0	,,	13·4·0.
,, Total =	81·7·0	,,	63·17·0.

Max Tractive Force – 14575 Lbs at 85% B.P.

Water Capacity of Tender 2000 Galls

Coal ,, ,, ,, 5 Tons.

L & N.W.R Loading Gauge

'Renown' Class
Allocated LMS locomotive number series 5131–5186.

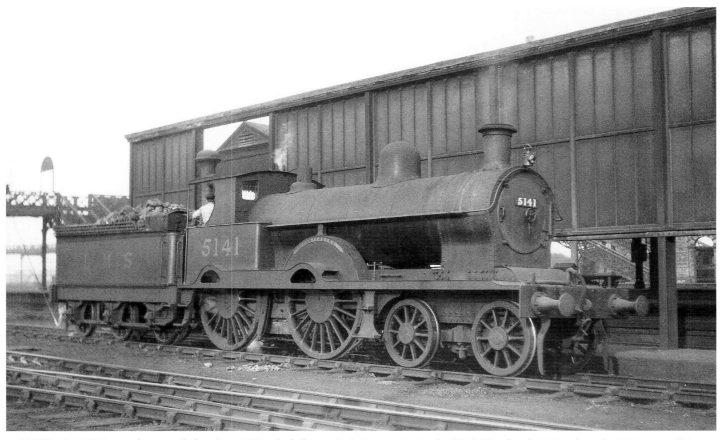

LNWR No.1948 Camperdown *was built in June 1901 and rebuilt as a simple 'Renown' in October 1915. The allotted LMS stock number 5141 was applied in October 1926, but since this picture shows the 1928 livery, the original renumbering was probably a smokebox door numberplate for the locomotive with a number on the side of the tender. This engine was to remain in traffic until August 1930 when it was scrapped.* COLLECTION R.J. ESSERY

Following the modification of the 'Alfred the Great' class, attention was turned to the 'Jubilees', and in 1908 No.1918 *Renown* was rebuilt as a two-cylinder simple expansion locomotive, hence the description used by some sources, 'Simple Renown'. The rebuilding entailed the removal of the two outside cylinders, the inside cylinders were retained and altered to 18½ inches, and an 'Alfred the Great' boiler was fitted. Although the first locomotive to be rebuilt as a simple was a 'Jubilee', a number of 'Alfreds' were also rebuilt before 1923 in a similar way by the LNWR. When the work of rebuilding ceased, thirty-seven 'Jubilees' and thirty-three 'Alfreds' had been rebuilt as simples. Generally they retained their original Webb tenders, but although rebuilding continued after 1923, the class did not survive many years and was extinct by the end of 1931. As a result of the slow renumbering of LNWR locomotives, many were withdrawn still carrying their old LNWR numbers and did not display their allocated LMS numbers, namely, 5132, 5134, 5136, 5146, 5147, 5150, 5151, 5159, 5162, 5168, 5169, 5171, 5174, 5175, 5178.

The first locomotives from this series to be renumbered in April 1926 were Nos. 5127, 5131, and at this time the usual approach was to apply a smokebox door numberplate to a plain black engine, with or without a coat of arms being on the cabside. Some locomotives had the LNWR numberplate removed, and the LMS stock number was shown by using small numbers whilst other locomotives had the number painted onto the side of the tender. The retention of LNWR lining on either the locomotive and/or tender was not uncommon.

During the LNWR period they began by being employed on the principal express passenger trains, but within a few years they had been largely replaced by the more powerful 'Precursors' and 'George the Fifth' Classes, and their work was now confined to ordinary passenger and parcels trains and some express freight trains, together with assisting as pilot engine when the train was too heavy for the allocated locomotive. In 1925 the LMS began to withdraw these locomotives from service but the largest single group to be withdrawn came in December 1931 when 5112, 5116, 5138, 5149, 5156, 5165, 5173, 5180, 5182, 5183, 5184 and 5186 were taken out of service and the class became extinct.

Built September 1900 as LNWR No. 1931 Agincourt, this engine was rebuilt as a 'Simple Renown' in December 1921 and is seen here on the turntable at Oxford shed attached to a 2000 gallon tender still fitted with the first (1890) pattern of oil axleboxes. The LMS stock number 5176 was applied in April 1926 and it was scrapped in June 1930. A picture of this locomotive as LMS No. 5176 will be found at page 54. R. GRIEFFENHAGEN.

This picture illustrates an example of renumbering when the LNWR cast numberplate had been removed and the new LMS stock number painted onto the cabside in its place. The LNWR lining on the engine and tender remained and would not be removed until the locomotive was repainted. Built in September 1900 as LNWR No 1931 Agincourt, it was rebuilt as a 'Renown' in December 1921 and remained in service until June 1930 when it was scrapped. It was seen here attached to a 2000 gallon tender.
COLLECTION R.J. ESSERY

No. 1910 Cavalier at Oxford on 30th April 1925. This was another 4-cylinder compound that was built in 1899 and rebuilt as a 'Simple Renown' in August 1921. The LMS stock number 5172 was applied in October 1926 and the locomotive was withdrawn in April 1931. In this picture we see the locomotive taking water in the shed yard.
R. GRIEFFENHAGEN

LIVERY

The early demise of these locomotive, together with the slow renumbering, meant that relatively few 'Renowns' received proper LMS livery styles before they were withdrawn. To the best of my knowledge, none received the correct pre-1928 livery and the most common treatment was to fit a new smokebox door numberplate to a locomotive finished in plain black. Some carried a cabside coat of arms but not all carried the LMS stock number on the side of the tender. Using the livery codes reproduced at page 16, Code C18 was carried by some locomotives during their final years in traffic.

Ultimate Allocations 1926

Bushbury	5110, 5112–5114, 5116.
Patricroft	5117–5119
Northampton	5120–5121
Carlisle	5123–5125
Nuneaton	5126–5127
Sutton Oak	5128–5129
Carnforth	5131–5132

Preston	5133–5135, 5137
Chester	5138–5141
Camden	5142–5144
Holyhead	5145–5147
Edge Hill	5148–5149
Bangor	5152–5153
Crewe North	5154–5159
Stafford	5160
Warrington	5161, 5163–5165
Birkenhead	5166–5167, 5169–5171
Bletchley	5172–5173, 5175–5176
Llandudno Junction and Rhyl	5177–5186

During 1931 the allocation of these locomotives still in service was:

Crewe	5116, 5149, 5184, 5186
Holyhead	5138
Warrington	5165
Edge Hill	5173
Llandudno	5182, 5183

*This picture of a 'Renown' Class loco-
motive running as LMS No. 5143 was
taken between October 1926 when the
LMS stock number was applied and
January 1928 when it was withdrawn.
Built as LNWR No. 1959* Revenge
*in March 1902, it was originally an
'Alfred the Great' compound but was
rebuilt as a 'Renown' in April 1916.*
T.S. STEEL COLLECTION

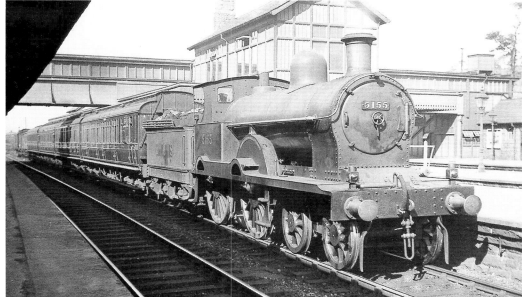

*Taken at Chinley on 12th July 1928,
this picture shows LNWR No. 1916*
Irresistible *working the 8.10am Liverpool Central to Chinley and running
under express passenger headlamp code.
A note on the reverse of the print states
this train conveyed a through coach to St
Pancras. Built in July 1899, the engine
was rebuilt as a 'Renown' in February
1919 and the LMS stock number 5155
was applied in January 1928; it was
withdrawn in September 1930. This
picture clearly shows the 1928 livery,
number on cabside and 'LMS' on the
side of the tender with the retention of
the smokebox numberplate. Note the
LNWR lamp holders had not yet been
replaced.* COLLECTION
R.J. ESSERY

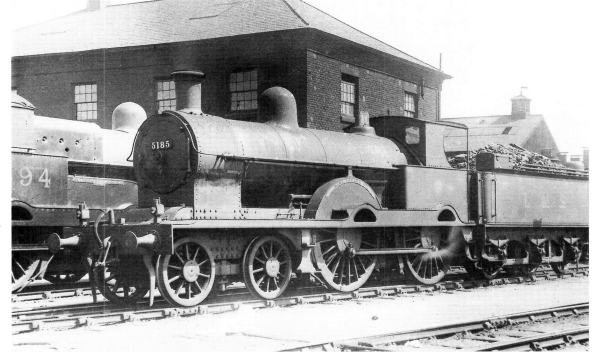

*This undated picture shows
No. 5185 at Coleham shed,
Shrewsbury. Built in May
1901 as LNWR No. 1942
King Edward VII, it was
rebuilt as a 2-cylinder simple
in September 1922. The
LMS stock number was
applied in September 1926
and it was withdrawn in February 1930. The livery carried
is interesting: the LMS coat of
arms was on the side of the
cab, 'LMS' on the tender and
the stock number on the smokebox door. LNWR lamp
sockets had been retained.*
T. S. STEEL
COLLECTION

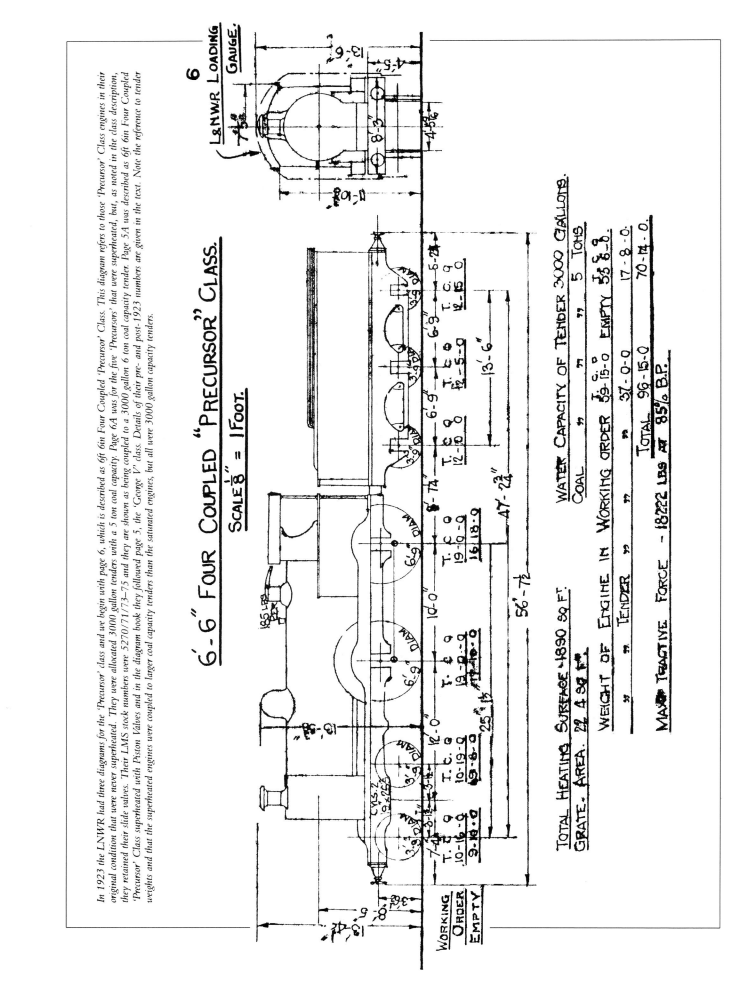

In 1923 the LNWR had three diagrams for the 'Precursor' class and we begin with page 6, which is described as the 'Precursor' Class. This diagram refers to those 'Precursor' Class engines in their original condition that were never superheated. They were allocated 3000 gallon tenders with a 5 ton coal capacity. Page 6A was for the five 'Precursors' that were superheated, but, as noted in the class description, they retained their slide valves. Their LMS stock numbers were 5270/71/73–75 and they are shown as being coupled to a 3000 gallon 6 ton coal capacity tender. Page 5A was described as 6ft 6in Four Coupled 'Precursor' Class superheated with Piston Valves and in the diagram book they followed page 5, the 'George V' class. Details of their pre- and post-1923 numbers are given in the text. Note the reference to tender weights and that the superheated engines were coupled to larger coal capacity tenders than the saturated engines, but all were 3000 gallon capacity tenders.

6'-6" Four Coupled "Precursor" Class.

Scale ⅛" = 1 Foot.

Total Heating Surface 1890 sq ft.
Grate. Area. 22.4 sq ft.

Water Capacity of Tender 3000 Gallons.
Coal ,, ,, ,, 5 Tons

Weight of Engine in Working Order 59-15-0 Empty 53-8-0

,, ,, Tender ,, ,, 37-0-0   17-8-0
                              _____
                    Total 96-15-0   70-14-0.

Max. Tractive Force – 18222 lbs at 85% B.P.

4–4–0 Passenger Tender, LNW 'Precursor'

Motive Power Classification 3, post-1928 2P
Allocated LMS number series 5187–5266

by PETER DAVIS

A saturated 'Precursor' seen at Crewe in 1929 – this was No. 5220 photographed in September. As LNWR No. 1784 Python *it was built in October 1905 and renumbered by the LMS in October 1927, being withdrawn from service in November 1931. At the time it retained the original type of boiler with two washout plugs on either side of the firebox as well as LNWR lamp sockets and had been fitted with an oil reservoir above the boiler handrail.* H. C. CASSERLEY

The introduction of George Whale's 'Precursor' class 4–4–0 in 1904 gave the LNWR an excellent, large by contemporary standards, two-cylinder simple expansion express passenger locomotive. Between March 1904 and August 1907 Crewe turned out 130 of them. The design was in essence an enlarged 6ft 6in wheeled Webb '18in Goods' 0–6–0 with the Double Radial Truck (bogie) from the 'Jubilee/Alfred the Great' coupled to a new design of steel-framed tender (with two coal rails). As its name suggests, *Precursor* was the progenitor of a family of related designs using Joy valve gear and covering 4 and 6-coupled tender and tank engines and later developed, in superheated versions, by Whale's successor Charles Cooke – better known among enthusiasts as C. J. Bowen Cooke on account of his early fame as an author of books and articles on the subject of locomotive engines. The whole 'family', comprising six classes of engines, became LMS stock in 1923.

Following the successful introduction, in 1910, of the superheated piston-valved version of the 'Precursor' – the 'George the Fifth' (referred to henceforth as 'George V') – the LNWR rebuilt 43 of its 'Precursors' as 'George V' class engines between January 1913 and January 1923. In addition there were eleven 'Precursors' equipped with superheated boilers, while retaining their original slide valve cylinders, between February 1913 and September 1919 (LMS Nos. 5270, 5271, 5273, 5274, 5275, 5278, 5302, 5303, 5304, 5305 and 5306) of which four (Nos. 5278, 5302, 5303 and 5304) had been converted to 'George Vs' by January 1923. All 50 superheated engines are dealt with later including the 21

converted to 'George V' by the LMS between January 1923 and June 1928, a total which itself included three of the seven inherited superheated slide-valve engines. It is hardly surprising that this somewhat confusing situation led to the compilers of the LMS renumbering scheme making several mistakes within this class. These errors have added to the confusion faced by the locomotive historian.

The eighty unsuperheated members of the 'Precursor' class at the LMS takeover largely remained unaltered and in LNWR livery, apart that is from the eighteen that were gradually converted to 'George V' class, until renumbering began in earnest in February 1926. By this time many had acquired LMS lamp holders in place of the original sockets and would go on to receive Ross safety valves in place of the Ramsbottom type. They all had Beames oil reservoirs fitted above the boiler handrails and Cooke lft 7½in buffers in place of the original Whale lft 4½in type. Their boilers, interchangeable with those of the 'Precursor Tanks', were all gradually modified with four washout plugs in each side of the firebox wrapper in place of the original two.

From 1920 Crewe Works began to fit horizontal handrails on the cab side, above the rectangular panel plates, to all the Whale and Cooke passenger tender engines. This process was continued in LMS days until all the engines of these classes were so equipped. It is thought that there had been a serious accident to an engineman while walking forward on the foot-framing as was a traditional practice. It had been relatively easy on the smaller engines with a narrower cab and shorter

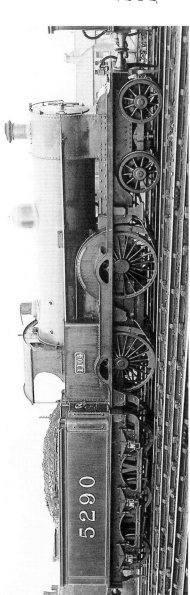

Here we show two examples of engines coupled to tenders that did not carry the same numbers as the engines to which they were attached. Unfortunately, this happened from time to time during the early LMS years.

The Midland practice of displaying the engine number on the tender side could, in the case of LNWR or L&Y tenders, lead to confusion. It was the practice at Crewe, and Horwich, to attach to an engine when outshopped the next available tender of the right type, tenders requiring less time for overhaul than engines. Thus both those railways built fewer tenders than tender engines and numbered them in a separate series. The following seems to be the most likely scenario depicted in these photographs, both of which date from 1926. Saturated 'Precursor' No. 1104 Cedric, built in February 1905, left Crewe Works attached to a Cooke third type tender which happened to be that relinquished by 'Superheated Precursor' No. 5290 Achilles when it entered Crewe Works a while after Cedric. When Achilles was ready to leave the works the next available tender was that separated from 'G1' 0-8-0 No. 9229, renumbered in October 1925, which entered works, probably for a Light Intermediate overhaul shortly after Achilles did. Thus we see a black engine with a red tender (No. 5290 Achilles had been renumbered and repainted in LMS code A2 livery in September 1923) and a red engine with a black tender. Achilles was built as No. 310 in December 1904 and superheated with piston valves in June 1914, was later given a Belpaire boiler and in March 1932 had its cab altered to the Midland loading gauge and was withdrawn in October 1936. Meanwhile Cedric was eventually renumbered as 5199 in August 1928 and withdrawn in December 1933.

Both COLLECTION R.J. ESSERY

Seen at Crewe on 13th March 1926, Precursor' No. 1117 Vandal was among the first three engines of the saturated class to acquire its LMS number, 5194, stencilled in the space left by the LNWR plate, during the previous month. Apart from losing the Roscoe displacement lubricator from the smokebox side, and gaining cabside handrail, the only alterations it had received since it was new in November 1904 were Cooke 1ft 7½in buffers, a set of coupled wheels with large bosses and a boiler with two extra washout plugs per side. It was even attached to a Whale tender still in LNWR lined black. It would have received Beames oil reservoirs above the boiler handrails and LMS lamp holders, probably Ross safety valves and possibly a smokebox door numberplate before it was withdrawn in October 1931.   COLLECTION R. J. ESSERY

panel plate to negotiate the bit between the cutaway and the boiler handrail but was hazardous on the bigger engines. This is another detail to 'spot' on photographs.

According to Baxter, only one of this class, LNWR No. 117 *Alaska*, received a Belpaire boiler fitted at an unspecified date but replaced by a round-topped one in 1927, probably at the time it was renumbered as LMS No. 5222 in October of that year. Tenders and coupled wheelsets were fitted on a first come first served basis to all 'Precursor' and 'George V' class engines upon leaving works so that the saturated 'Precursors' could be seen with any of the Whale or Cooke 3,000-gallon tenders, except the 1916 type, or wheels with large or small bosses.

In LMS days these engines were employed exclusively on the A Division (Western Lines) both as pilots to heavy expresses and in working secondary passenger services as well as parcels and fitted freight services. For this reason no saturated 'Precursor' ever had its cab roof modified to suit the Midland loading gauge. Seven of the saturated engines were withdrawn between October 1927 and February 1928 before

Crewe had got round to applying their LMS numbers which would have been 5195, 5209, 5224, 5227, 5247, 5251 and 5256. The last of the class to be scrapped was No. 5235 *Moonstone*, withdrawn in April 1935 from Crewe South shed.

Saturated 'Precursor' Allocations 17th March 1926

Longsight	5189–5193
Chester	5194–5199
Springs Branch	5200–5202
Carlisle	5203–5206
Camden	5208–5210, 5213–5215
Northampton	5217, 5219–5222
Stafford	5224, 5226–5230
Crewe	5232–5233
Warrington	5234–5236
Edge Hill	5237–5238
Bletchley	5240, 5242, 5244, 5246–5247, 5249
Patricroft	5251–5259
Preston	5260–5261
Carnforth	5262–5263
Warwick	5264–5265
Aston	5266

Precursor Class in original condition on 1st January 1923 with subsequent changes

LNW No.	Name	Built	Rebuilt as GV	LMS No.	Applied	2XXXX Dup. No.	Withdrawn
2023	Helvellyn	4/04	3/24	5187	6/26	11/34	3/36
412	Marquis	6/04	3/23	5188	4/26	10/34	4/40
510	Albatross	6/04	–	5189	7/28	–	8/33
639	Ajax	10/04	–	5190	11/26	–	9/28
648	Archimedes	10/04	–	5191	2/27	–	1/28
685	Cossack	10/04	–	5192	11/26	–	4/32
1102	Thunderbolt	11/04	–	5193	11/26	–	9/31
1117	Vandal	11/04	–	5194	2/26	–	10/31
622	Euphrates	12/04	–	(5195)	–	–	11/27
638	Huskisson	12/04	–	5196	7/27	–	4/33
645	Mammoth	1/05	–	5197	5/27	–	11/30
40	Niagara	3/05	–	5198	1/28	–	11/30
1104	Cedric	2/05	–	5199	8/28	–	12/33
1111	Cerberus	3/05	–	5200	2/26	–	9/34
1431	Egeria	3/05	–	5201	11/26	–	11/30
520	Panopea	3/05	–	5202	8/27	–	1/34
2031	Waverley	3/05	–	5203	4/27	–	11/31
184	Havelock	5/05	–	5204	6/27	–	9/31
1115	Apollo	4/05	–	5205	6/26	–	2/28
1545	Cyclops	4/05	–	5206	10/27	–	5/32
2061	Eglinton	4/05	3/25	5207	8/27	11/34	8/36
519	Messenger	5/05	–	5208	10/27	–	11/31
2120	Trentham	5/05	–	(5209)	–	–	10/27
1430	Victor	5/05	–	5210	9/27	–	10/31
113	Aurania	7/05	12/24	5211	11/27	11/34	9/36
315	Harrowby	7/05	4/23	5212	2/27	11/34	12/36
311	Emperor	9/05	–	5213	9/27	–	5/33
1509	America	7/05	–	5214	5/26	–	3/28
2257	Vulture	8/05	–	5215	2/27	–	12/33
911	Herald	9/05	3/23	5216	9/27	11/34	2/36
1114	Knowsley	9/05	–	5217	11/26	–	2/33
1116	Pandora	9/05	4/23	5218	2/26	11/34	4/36
1510	Psyche	9/05	–	5219	10/27	–	12/30
1784	Python	10/05	–	5220	10/27	–	11/31
2202	Vizier	10/05	–	5221	6/27	–	12/30
117	Alaska	10/05	–	5222	10/27	–	9/33
127	Snake	11/05	3/23	5223	4/28	11/34	11/36
229	Stork	11/05	–	(5224)	–	–	11/27
1301	Candidate	10/05	5/25	5225	12/26	5/36	11/36
1396	Harpy	11/05	–	5226	12/27	–	11/30
2007	Oregon	11/05	–	(5227)	–	–	10/27
2012	Penguin	11/05	–	5228	5/28	–	10/31
2115	Servia	11/05	–	5229	5/27	–	4/32
2576	Arab	12/05	–	5230	10/26	–	9/33
2579	Ganymede	12/05	2/25	5231	6/27	–	2/36
2580	Problem	12/05	–	5232	5/28	–	11/31
2581	Peel	12/05	–	5233	11/26	–	8/34
2582	Rowland Hill	12/05	–	5234	12/26	–	11/28
2583	Moonstone	12/05	–	5235	4/28	–	4/35
2585	Watt	1/06	–	5236	9/27	–	12/33
234	Pearl	3/06	–	5237	12/27	–	2/32
526	Ilion	3/06	–	5238	12/26	–	12/28
723	Coptic	2/06	7/23	5239	1/28	–	1/36
837	Friar	2/06	–	5240	12/27	–	10/33
1311	Napolean	3/06	4/23	5241	8/28	–	1/36
1312	Ionic	2/06	–	5242	3/27	–	11/30
1642	Lapwing	3/06	5/24	5243	1/28	–	11/35
2017	Tubal	3/06	11/26	5244	11/26	–	11/35
561	Antaeus	4/06	12/24	5245	1/27	4/36	3/41
675	Adjutant	4/06	6/26	5246	6/26	–	2/36
772	Admiral	4/06	–	(5247)	–	–	10/27
804	Amphion	4/06	3/23	5248	6/27	–	10/35
988	Bellerophon	4/06	–	5249	9/27	–	6/33
1433	Faerie Queen	4/06	3/25	5250	6/27	–	11/35
1650	Richard Trevithick	5/07	–	(5251)	–	–	2/28
1787	Hyperion	5/07	–	5252	2/27	–	12/30
1	Clive	6/07	–	5253	8/28	–	11/30
218	Daphne	6/07	–	5254	11/26	–	8/33
469	Monarch	6/07	–	5255	5/28	–	12/30
665	Mersey	6/07	–	(5256)	–	–	10/27
1011	Locke	7/07	–	5257	11/27	–	1/33
1364	Clyde	7/07	–	5258	10/26	–	12/30
2053	Edith	7/07	–	5259	11/27	–	3/34
2181	Eleanor	7/07	–	5260	1/28	–	12/33
276	Doric	7/07	–	5261	12/26	–	11/27
754	Celtic	7/07	–	5262	8/27	–	12/30
807	Oceanic	8/07	–	5263	11/26	–	12/33
976	Pacific	8/07	–	5264	11/26	–	11/28
1297	Phalaris	8/07	–	5265	5/27	–	10/31
1516	Alecto	8/07	–	5266	5/28	–	10/31

LMS numbers in brackets were allotted but never applied. LMS numbers 5267-5269 were never used.

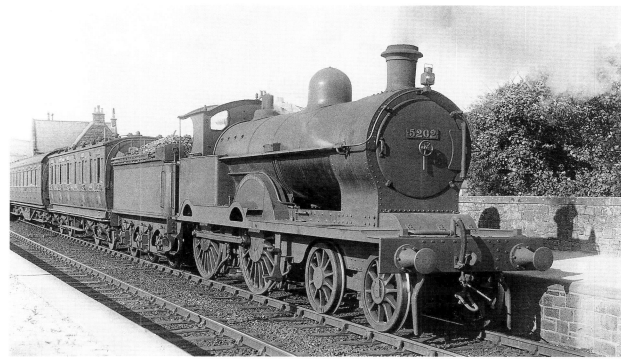

During the LMS period ex-LNWR locomotives were to be found away from their home territory, as shown by this picture taken at St Bees, which is on the old Furness Railway between Sellafield and Whitehaven. Here LNWR No. 520 was running under ordinary passenger train headlamp code. Built in March 1905 and named Panopea, *it was one of the class that was never superheated. In August 1927 the LMS stock number 5202 was applied and it remained in service until January 1934 when it was withdrawn.*
W. POTTER

Seen at Crewe in June 1929, No. 5262 was built in July 1907 as LNWR No. 754 Celtic *and renumbered by the LMS in August 1927. When the picture was taken there were still eighteen months to go before the engine was withdrawn in December 1930.*
COLLECTION R. J. ESSERY

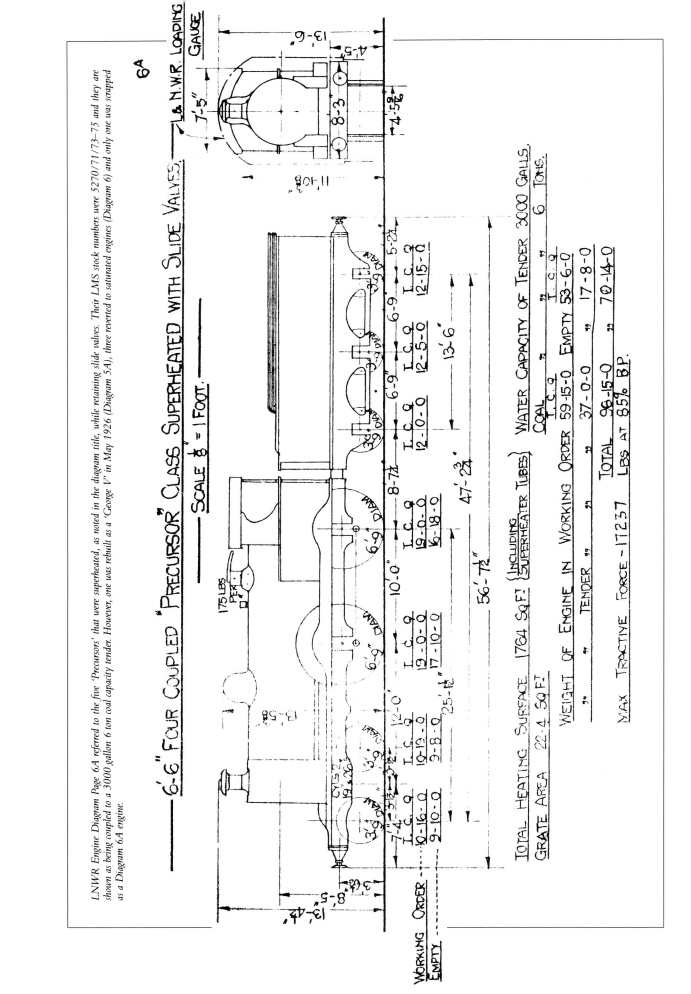

LNWR Engine Diagram Page 6A referred to the five 'Precursors' that were superheated, as noted in the diagram title, while retaining slide valves. Their LMS stock numbers were 5270/71/73–75 and they are shown as being coupled to a 3000 gallon 6 ton coal capacity tender. However, one was rebuilt as a 'George V' in May 1926 (Diagram 5A), three reverted to saturated engines (Diagram 6) and only one was scrapped as a Diagram 6A engine.

6A

L & N.W.R. LOADING GAUGE

— 6′-6″ FOUR COUPLED "PRECURSOR" CLASS SUPERHEATED WITH SLIDE VALVES —

SCALE ⅛″ = 1 FOOT.

TOTAL HEATING SURFACE 1764 SQ.FT {INCLUDING SUPERHEATER TUBES}

GRATE AREA 22.4 SQ.FT

WATER CAPACITY OF TENDER 3000 GALLS.

COAL 6 TONS.

	I.C.G	I.C.G	
WEIGHT OF ENGINE IN WORKING ORDER	59-15-0	EMPTY	53-6-0
" TENDER "	37-0-0	"	17-8-0
" "	TOTAL 96-15-0	"	70-14-0

MAX TRACTIVE FORCE - 17257 LBS AT 85% B.P.

WORKING ORDER -------

EMPTY - - - - - - - -

4–4–0 Passenger Tender, LNW 'Rebuilt Precursor'

Motive Power Classification 4, post-1928 3P
Allocated LMS number series 5270–5319

by PETER DAVIS

Photographed at Edge Hill on 25th April 1925 this shows LNWR No.1439 Tiger, *which was built in November 1905, superheated in June 1918 and became LMS No. 5275 in 1924. It acquired a new Belpaire boiler, probably when renumbered and repainted in red livery code A2 and the cab altered to MR load gauge. It reverted to a saturated boiler in April 1930, being withdrawn in February 1933.*

W. POTTER

For some unexplained reason the LMS left the Nos. 5267 to 5269 blank, beginning the superheated series of 'Precursors' with No. 5270. Not surprisingly this series began with what the compilers believed were the six engines running with superheated boilers and the original 19in cylinders with slide valves. In fact only five of these, allotted Nos. 5270, 5271, 5273, 5274 and 5275, were in this category – No. 5272 had been converted to 'George V' in May 1918. Two further slide valve superheated engines, LNWR Nos. 303 *Himalaya* and 1287 *Lang Meg*, were allotted Nos. 5305 and 5306 respectively in the piston valve series by mistake. These seven engines looked almost identical to the saturated engines, retaining 3ft 9in bogie wheels and 3ft 7in long smokebox. The only telltale difference was the Wakefield mechanical lubricator fitted on top of the right-hand frame plate in front of the leading splasher. Three of the seven, Nos. 5274, 5305 and 5306, joined the 'George V' class and of the remaining four, three reverted to saturated boilers in 1929–30; only No. 5270 remained as a superheated slide valve engine until withdrawal in May 1936.

To the 43 'George V' conversions it inherited from the LNWR, between March 1923 and June 1928 the LMS added a further 21 (including the three slide-valve superheaters), as and when 'good' saturated engines came into works in need of replacement cylinders. Including the four slide valve engines, the eventual total of superheated 'Precursors' was 68.

The 'George V' rebuilding, apart from the superheated boiler which differed from the saturated boiler only in internal arrangements, entailed fitting new 20½in diameter cylinders with 8in piston valves in place of the original 19in with slide valve, an extended smokebox 5ft long, a rocker shaft to reverse the Joy valve gear events to suit inside admission valves, and 3ft 3in bogie wheels to lower the truck frame to clear the deeper cylinders. The smokebox extension was not necessary to accommodate the superheater (as is evidenced by the slide valve conversions) but was desirable as the larger volume equalised the draught through the tubes, reducing the tendency to tear holes in the fire when working hard. All the superstructure remained unaltered including the retention of a separate splasher for the driving wheels. This is the only feature that marks out a superheated 'Precursor' from a 'George V' in photographs. Many acquired Belpaire boilers: -

Superheated 'Precursors' with Belpaire boilers.

No.	Date	Date reverted to R.T.	Notes
5187	prob. 6/1926	when reno.	also as 25187
5188	–	–	also as 25188
5207	1933	–	also as 25207
5211	1934	–	also as 25211
5216	9/1926	–	also as 25216
5218	1932	–	also as 25218
5225	–	–	photo 10/1934
LNW 2579	4/1925	–	also as 5231 (applied 6/1927)

continued

This picture was taken near Kenton in or around 1926 and shows the up 'Royal Scot' express. The train engine was a 'Claughton' No. 5985 and the pilot 'Precursor' No. 5273 Jason. The only difference in the engine as seen here, compared with the views below, are a boiler with Ross safety valves and the application of code A1 livery.

T. S. STEEL

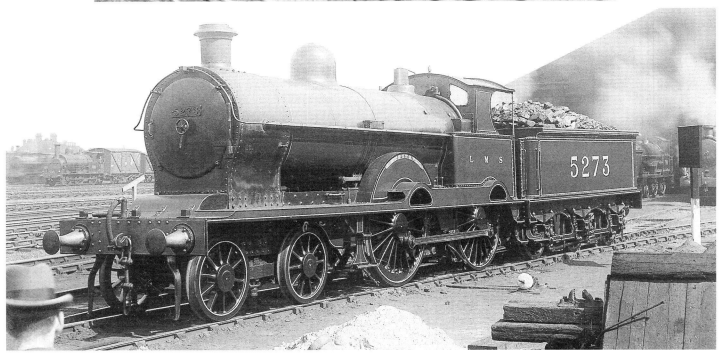

The date of these pictures of No. 5273 Jason is late 1923 illustrating a locomotive in the first LMS red livery style for passenger locomotives; the stock number was on the tender and the initials 'LMS' on the side of the cab. Later, when the LMS coat of arms was agreed, this was placed on the side of the cab and the small initials were no longer used. When this livery style was applied, the locomotive stock number was also displayed on a smokebox door numberplate, as seen here. Built in March 1905 as LNWR No. 2064, it was superheated in May 1918 but a boiler change in July 1929 saw No. 5273 receive a saturated boiler, which was retained until it was withdrawn in August 1931. The centre view shows the engine heading an up express near Kenton. Note the interesting mix of carriages, both LNWR and Midland, in Crimson Lake with the Dining Car still in LNWR 'plum and spilt milk' livery. The lower view was taken at Camden shed. BOTH COLLECTION R.J. ESSERY

No.	Date	Date reverted to R.T.	Notes
5239	–	–	photo of 5/1930
5242	10/1927	–	–
5243	–	–	photo 1935
5245	prob. 12/1924 when reb. to GV		also as 25245
LNW 675	prob. 6/1926 when reb. to GV and re. no 5246		photo 1928
5248	–	–	
5250	–	–	photo 1930
5270	?	–	Baxter gives 'BG' not 'BF'
5274	–	–	photo 1924
5275	prob. 1923–4 when reno.	4/1930	Wdn 2/1933 with RT saturated
5276	–	–	photo 1935
5277	–	–	photo post 1928, also as 25277
5278	–	–	photo 1934
5279	–	–	also as 25279, 1937
5281	9/1927	–	–
5282	1932		also as 25282
5284	–		also as 25284
5286	1933		also as 25286
5287	12/1927	–	also as 25287
5288	–		photo 1935
5289	–		photo 1930
5290	–		also as 25290
5292	Prob. 7/1926	–	also as 25292
5293	–		also as 25293
5294	1/1928	–	–
5295	–		photo post 1928
5296	–		photo 1934
5297	11/1927	–	also as 25297
5300	1/1928	–	also as 25300
LNW 300	4/1925	–	also as 5301
5302	–	–	–
5304	1931		also as 5304
5306	–		–
5307	1935		also as 25307
5310	11/1927	–	also as 25310
LNW 811	4/1925	c.1930–31?	BF again by 1937 as 25311
5313	–	–	–
5315	1934		–
5317	4/1925	1927	BF again later
5319	1931		also as 25319

Without exception the above engines had their cab roofs modified to suit the Midland loading gauge, presumably indicating that the Midland Division preferred Belpaire boilered examples. It is rare to encounter a photograph of a round-top boilered superheated 'Precursor' with a Midland profile cab before around 1930, but by the mid 1930s many of the surviving round-top members of the superheated class had them.

Three 'Precursors' had their nameplates removed while still in service in order to end duplication after the names had been bestowed upon two 'Jubilees' and one 'Royal Scot' 4–6–0s. 'Jubilee' No. 5703 was given the name *Thunderer* on 6th May 1936 and 'Jubilee' No. 5706 became *Express* on 26th of the same month. The 'Precursors', Nos. 5310 and 5311, lost their respective names four months later in September 1936. Inexplicably, having named 'Royal Scot' No. 6148 *Velocipede* sometime before April 1928, it took the LMS until July 1933 to realise that it already had an engine of that name in stock. It removed the name from 'Precursor' No. 5312 in

that month. Ironically, almost two years later, the 'Royal Scot' in question was renamed so that the name *Velocipede* could have been restored to No. 5312 for the last six months of its life – it was withdrawn at the end of December 1935 – had the original plates not been, supposedly, destroyed. Certainly they are not recorded among the 30 ex 'Precursor' nameplates surviving into preservation. There were two other examples of duplication of names, but in each case the 'Precursors' retained their names until withdrawal. The name *Ajax* appeared on 'Royal Scot' No. 6139 in March 1928 but saturated 'Precursor' No. 5190 retained its *Ajax* nameplates until withdrawal in the following September, and 'Superheated Precursor' No. 5310 *Achilles* retained its name until withdrawn in October 1936, although 'Jubilee' No. 5697 had been given the same name in the previous April.

Whereas the saturated 'Precursors', and other older and less powerful LNWR passenger tender engines, worked out their lives exclusively on the ex-LNWR routes, the fact that the LMS went to the trouble and expense of altering the cabs of almost all the later and more powerful LNWR passenger classes to the MR (LMS Composite) loading gauge indicates that those engines were intended to have much wider use on the system. There is no evidence, however, that any of these classes, other than the 'Claughtons', did any more than visit Midland Lines in the course of through workings. Certainly there is no record of the allocation of any member of these classes to a Midland shed. As far as the superheated 'Precursors' are concered, they were employed on main line express trains in the early LMS days, but as more modern engines began to displace them, they found employment on cross-country passenger, parcels and fitted freight trains. By 1935 the majority were stationed at Rugby (14), Crewe (11), Stafford and Bletchley (7 each), but in their final years the survivors had moved westwards, being concentrated in Chester. They were to be seen on the North Wales main line as well as the Mold, Denbigh and Corwen branches. With the withdrawal of No. 25297 *Sirocco* from Chester shed in June 1949, the LNWR 4–4–0s became extinct.

LIVERY
Following the decision of December 1923 (see p.11) to adopt Midland livery, as passenger engines the 'Precursors' were entitled to receive the lined crimson lake livery and a number of the superheated engines did receive this livery, with small letters 'L M S' on the cab side and the number on the side of the tender, in the 1923–4 period. When the reorganisation of Crewe Works began, renumbering and repainting of locomotives virtually ceased until early 1926. The most common, and easiest option with regard to renumbering was to remove the cast LNWR plate and replace it with a stencilled LMS number in the vacant space, sometimes with a smokebox numberplate as well. In 1927 the LMS livery changes were introduced under which lesser passenger classes were to receive black with red lining and yellow numbers on the cab side. Although a number of styles are identified in *Liveries of the LMS, Vol. 1*, from this time onwards the most common for 'Precursors' was livery code C18.

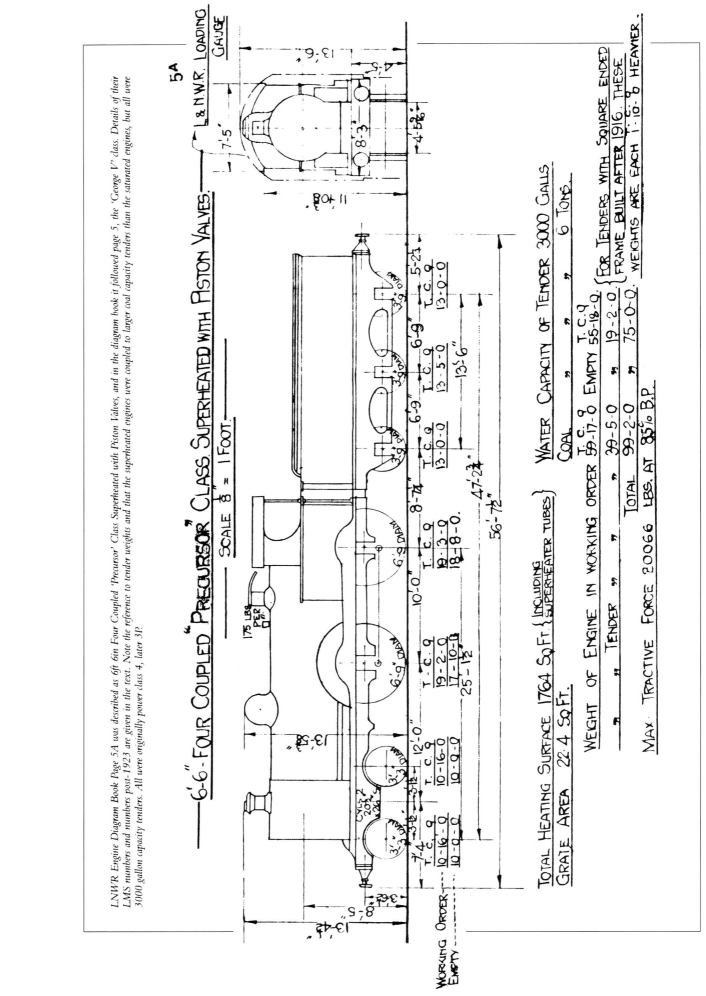

LNWR Engine Diagram Book Page 5A was described as 6ft 6in Four Coupled 'Precursor' Class Superheated with Piston Valves, and in the diagram book it followed page 5, the 'George V' class. Details of their LMS numbers and numbers post-1923 are given in the text. Note the reference to tender weights and that the superheated engines were coupled to larger coal capacity tenders than the saturated engines, but all were 3000 gallon capacity tenders. All were originally power class 4, later 3P.

— 6·6 - FOUR COUPLED "PRECURSOR" CLASS SUPERHEATED WITH PISTON VALVES.

— SCALE ⅛ = I FOOT.

5A

L & N.W.R. LOADING GAUGE

13'-6"

TOTAL HEATING SURFACE 1764 SQ.FT. { INCLUDING SUPERHEATER TUBES}

GRATE AREA 22·4 SQ.FT.

WATER CAPACITY OF TENDER 3000 GALLS.

COAL " " " 6 TONS.

WEIGHT OF ENGINE IN WORKING ORDER

		T.C.Q		T.C.Q
" "	" "	59-17-0	EMPTY	55-18-0
" TENDER "	"	39-5-0	"	19-2-0
" "	"	TOTAL 99-2-0	"	75-0-0

{ FOR TENDERS WITH SQUARE ENDED FRAME BUILT AFTER 1916. THESE WEIGHTS ARE EACH 1·10·6 HEAVIER.

MAX· TRACTIVE FORCE 20066 LBS. AT 85% B.P.

Superheated Precursor Class with slide valves, 1917–19, and piston valves, 1913–28.

LNW No.	Name	Built	Super-heated	Piston valves	LMS No.	Applied	2XXXX Dup. No.	Withdrawn
469	Marmion	6/07	5/18	–	5270	8/26	4/34	5/36
802	Gaelic	7/07	5/18	–	5271	7/27	–	11/31
1363	Brindley	10/05	5/18	5/18	5272	8/27	10/36	12/39
2064	Jason	3/05	5/18	–	5273	3/24	–	8/31
688	Hecate	7/05	6/18	3/23	5274	6/27	–	10/35
1439	Tiger	11/05	6/18	–	5275	3/24	–	1/33
7	Titan	6/04	1/13	1/13	5276	4/28	–	10/35
2184	Oberon	4/04	1/13	1/13	5277	11/27	9/36	8/46
513	Precursor	3/04	2/13	2/13	5278	5/27	–	7/36
2062	Sunbeam	8/05	2/13	2/13	5279	10/27	6/36	8/39
2166	Shooting Star	10/05	2/13	2/13	5280	5/27	–	11/35
564	Erebus	6/07	9/13	9/13	5281	9/27	–	9/36
515	Champion	12/04	9/13	9/13	5282	11/27	6/36	12/39
2011	Brougham	8/07	9/13	9/13	5283	8/27	–	3/36
333	Ambassador	12/04	11/13	11/13	5284	2/24	8/36	8/36
1419	Tamberlane	3/04	11/13	11/13	5285	8/26	–	3/36
1573	Dunrobin	4/05	4/14	4/14	5286	4/26	5/36	9/37
365	Alchymist	4/05	5/14	5/14	5287	12/27	5/36	6/37
1469	Tantalus	3/05	5/14	5/14	5288	2/27	11/36	3/37
301	Leviathan	11/04	6/14	6/14	5289	9/27	–	5/36
310	Achilles	12/04	6/14	6/14	5290	9/23	–	10/36
1395	Harbinger	3/04	9/14	9/14	5291	3/27	12/36	6/37
366	Medusa	5/05	11/14	11/14	5292	7/26	12/36	4/45
2513	Levens	3/06	11/14	11/14	5293	7/27	12/36	6/39
106	Druid	10/04	12/14	12/14	5294	1/28	12/36	5/37
1723	Scorpion	8/05	12/14	12/14	5295	5/27	–	11/36
659	Dreadnought	6/04	1/15	1/15	5296	3/24	–	5/36
643★	Sirocco	11/04	3/15	3/15	5297	11/27	12/36	6/49
60	Dragon	10/04	4/15	4/15	5298	4/27	9/36	11/38
1137	Vesuvius	2/05	4/15	4/15	5299	4/27	5/36	8/36
1617	Hydra	8/05	5/15	5/15	5300	1/28	12/36	6/40
300	Emerald	7/05	1/17	1/17	5301	2/28	–	10/35
1309	Shamrock	8/07	1/17	11/22	5302	4/28	9/36	6/37
323	Argus	2/05	6/17	1/23	5303	2/27	–	10/36
302	Greyhound	7/05	7/17	7/22	5304	1/27	8/36	1/47
303	Himalaya	1/05	1/19	6/28	5305	6/28	–	1/36
1287	Lang Meg	3/06	9/19	5/26	5306	4/28	–	2/36
305	Senator	11/04	6/20	6/20	5307	4/28	1/37	2/37
2	Simoom	6/04	8/20	8/20	5308	10/27	–	10/36
2578	Fame	12/05	8/20	8/20	5309	10/23	–	8/36
1120	Thunderer	1/05	10/21	10/21	5310	6/26	7/36	8/39
811	Express	9/05	11/21	11/21	5311	11/27	12/36	3/41
2584	Velocipede	1/06	1/22	1/22	5312	5/27	–	12/35
2577	Etna	12/05	2/22	2/22	5313	8/27	–	2/36
282	Alaric	4/06	4/22	4/22	5314	2/28	–	11/35
2051	Delamere	8/07	6/22	6/22	5315	4/26	–	9/36
1737	Viscount	3/05	10/22	10/22	5316	3/27	–	7/36
374	Empress	9/05	12/22	12/22	5317	9/27	–	6/36
806	Swiftsure	1/05	1/23	1/23	5318	5/26	–	10/35
990	Bucephalus	4/06	1/23	1/23	5319	7/27	5.36	12/40

Superheater removed from 5271 (6/30), 5273 (7/23) and 5275 (4/30).
★Allotted BR No. 58010 March 1948 but never applied.

Superheated 'Precursor' Allocation

	17th March 1926	28th September 1935	8th April 1944	31st December 1947
Longsight	5187–5188	5310		
Chester	–	5282, 5294, 5316, 5318	25204, 25292, 25297	25297
Camden	5207, 5211–5212, 5216, 5313–5315			
Northampton	5218, 5316–5319	5292, 5306, 5308, 5311, 5315		
Stafford	5223, 5225, 5231	5272, 5274, 5276–5279, 5281		
Crewe	5270–5300	5231, 5284, 5285, 5288, 5290, 5293, 5295, 5296, 5297, 5298, 5299		
Bletchley	5239, 5241, 5243, 5245, 5248, 5250	25187, 25188, 5239, 5241, 5245, 5313, 5319		
Patricroft	–	25207, 25211, 25212, 25216, 25223		
Aston	–	5225		
Warrington	–	5317		
Rhyl	–	25218		
Stoke	–	5280		
Rugby	5301–5312	5243, 5244, 5246, 5248, 5286, 5300–5305, 5307, 5312, 5314		
Llandudno Junction	–	5250, 25270, 5283, 5287, 5289, 5291, 5309	25277	

The footbridge just to the North of Whitchurch station made a
fine vantage point from which to photograph this 'Precursor'
hauled Crewe to Shrewsbury stopping passenger train. The engine
was LNW No. 515 Champion built in December 1904 and
converted to a 'George V' in September 1913. At this date,
sometime around 1924-25, it was still in LNW condition and
had yet to acquire Beames oil reservoirs on the boiler handrail; it
was renumbered as LMS 5282 in November 1927, was fitted
with a Belpaire boiler and had its cab altered to the Midland
loading gauge by 1932. It was renumbered as No. 25282 in
June 1936 and withdrawn in December 1939. The leading
carriage in the train, a GWR corridor composite, would have
been a through coach from Manchester to the West of England to
be attached to a Liverpool North to West express at Shrewsbury.
The rest of the train was one of the LNWR Manchester London
Road District sets of six 50ft 0in arc-roofed carriages and an arc-
roofed bogie full brake, probably for parcels, at the rear.

COLLECTION R. J. ESSERY

LNWR No. 2579 Ganymede was built in December 1905 and rebuilt as a 'George the Fifth' in February 1925 and in April 1926 had its cab altered to the Midland loading gauge, was fitted with a Belpaire
boiler and, incredibly, turned out in LNWR lined livery complete with company crest on the splasher. Shortly after this photograph was taken it was renumbered LMS No. 5231 in June 1927 when it was, presumably,
repainted in LMS lined black livery and given LMS lamp holders.

COLLECTION R.J. ESSERY

Built in December 1904 as LNWR No. 333 Ambassador, this engine was superheated and fitted with piston valves in November 1913. In February 1924 it was renumbered into LMS stock as No. 5284 and repainted in crimson lake livery, code A2, having had its boiler modified to the future standard of four washout plugs on each side of the firebox instead of the LNWR two. Otherwise the engine is seen in LNWR condition.

T. S. STEEL COLLECTION

Photographed at Camden in September 1927, LNWR No. 323 Argus was built in February 1905 and superheated in June 1917, being fitted with piston valves at the same time. The LMS stock number 5303 was applied in February 1927 and it was withdrawn in October 1936. The cab profile had not been altered but LMS-type lamp holders had been fitted. Note the 'S' on the side of the cab; this was used for a while on locomotives that were in 'good nick', to use a railway expression that may have also been used to describe LNWR locomotives that were in first class condition.
H. C. CASSERLEY

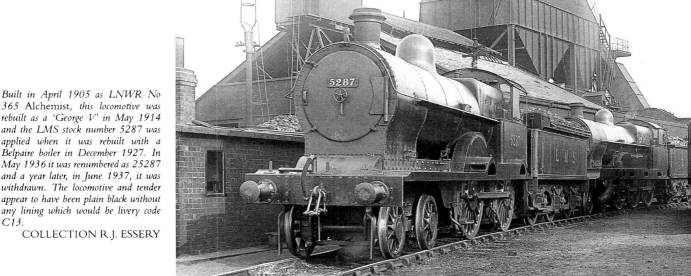

Built in April 1905 as LNWR No 365 Alchemist, this locomotive was rebuilt as a 'George V' in May 1914 and the LMS stock number 5287 was applied when it was rebuilt with a Belpaire boiler in December 1927. In May 1936 it was renumbered as 25287 and a year later, in June 1937, it was withdrawn. The locomotive and tender appear to have been plain black without any lining which would be livery code C13.

COLLECTION R.J. ESSERY

Photographed at Cambridge, note the LNER tender on the left of the picture, this shows a superheated 'Precursor' departing with an ordinary passenger train for Bletchley. Built in December 1905 as LNWR No. 2577 Etna, it was superheated in February 1922 and the LMS stock number 5313 applied during August 1927. When this picture was taken, LMS lamp holders had replaced the LNWR lamp sockets and an oil reservoir was fitted above the boiler handrail. This locomotive was not renumbered in the 2xxxx series being withdrawn in February 1936.
                                                                                                             G. H. SOOLE

This picture of No. 5298 was taken at Crewe during June 1929. Built in October 1904 as LNWR No. 60 Dragon, it was rebuilt as a 'George V' class in April 1915 and received its allotted LMS stock number in April 1927. As we would expect, LMS lamp holders had been fitted together with an oil reservoir above the boiler handrail. During September 1936 it became No. 25298 and withdrawn in November 1938.
                                                                                                             H. C. CASSERLEY

This picture shows the cab layout of a round-top boiler 'Precursor' Class locomotive. The driver was on the left-hand side of the engine, the fireman on the right, and the footplate could not be described as 'roomy'. Note the heavy cast steel drag box, the top of which formed the upward sloping cab floor, with its chequer-pattern square holes into which renewable hardwood blocks were pressed. In the centre of the floor can be seen the hole through which the intermediate drawbar pin was inserted.
COLLECTION
R.J. ESSERY

Taken near Basford Hall, which is clo[se to]
Crewe, this picture shows No. 5288 Tan[hauser]
hauling six coaches under Express passenger[]
headlamp code. Built in March 1905 as LN[WR]
No. 1469, the engine was rebuilt as a 'C[eorge]
V' in May 1915. Its allotted LMS stock n[umber]
was applied in February 1927. In Nov[ember]
1936 it was renumbered as 25288 and [con-]
tinued in service until withdrawal in [May]
1937.   E.R. MOR[TEN]

Photographed in 1930, a Down express
at Tring hauled by No. 5310 Thunderer. Built in January 1905 as
LNWR No. 1120, it was rebuilt as a
'George V' Class in October 1921 and
received its LMS number in June 1926.
The name was removed in September
1936 to avoid duplication with 4–6–0
'Jubilee' Class No. 5703. In December
1936 it was renumbered and became
25310 and was withdrawn in August
1939.   COLLECTION
R.S. CARPENTER

Photographed at Chester, this picture shows LNWR No. 213 Aurania built in July 1905 and superheated in December 1924. The LMS stock number 5211 was applied
during November 1927 and, as seen here, during 1934 it acquired a Belpaire boiler. During November of that year it was renumbered 25211 before being withdrawn in
September 1936.
                                                                                                      H. C. CASSERLEY

This front view of No. 5277, which was built in April 1904 as LNWR No. 2164 Oberon, was taken on 10th September 1933 and shows the smokebox door with the LMS numberplate and shedplate 14, which was the code for Stafford. This locomotive was rebuilt as a 'George V' in January 1913 and received the allotted LMS stock number in November 1927. Later, in September 1936, it was renumbered as 25277. While still carrying a smokebox number plate, as expected at this date, LMS lamp holders had replaced the LNWR sockets and the cab had been cut back to the Midland loading gauge. No. 25277 was withdrawn from Llandudno Junction shed in August 1946. COLLECTION R.J. ESSERY

Built in December 1904 as LNWR No. 333 Ambassador, this locomotive was superheated and piston valves fitted in November 1913. The LMS stock number 5284 was applied in February 1924 and on 11th August 1936 the figure '2' was added in front of the number at Rugby Works, shortly before being withdrawn during the week ending 22nd August 1936. As with all Belpaire-boilered 'Precursors', the cab profile had been altered to the composite gauge and oil reservoirs had been fitted above the boiler handrail. Ross safety valves had replaced the Ramsbottom type and LMS lamp holders had replaced the LNWR lamp sockets. Although the engine retained the original type of driving wheels, the fact that the side rods had been removed suggests that it perhaps suffered a serious mechanical failure and that led to its somewhat premature withdrawal from Crewe North shed.
W. L GOOD

In this photograph taken in the Western side of Birmingham New Street station during July 1935, we see LMS No. 25188 displaying ordinary passenger train headlamp code which suggests it was waiting to take over a passenger train. Built in June 1904 as LNWR No. 412 Alfred Paget, it was renamed Marquis in November 1904 and the LMS stock number was applied in April 1926. However, when this took place, the engine had been superheated in March 1923 and received a Belpaire boiler. It was renumbered in October 1934, becoming 25188, and withdrawn in April 1940.
H. C. CASSERLEY

This picture of No. 25298 Dragon was taken between September 1936 when it was renumbered and November 1938 when it was withdrawn. It was built in October 1904 as 'Precursor' class LNWR No. 60 and rebuilt as a 'George V' in April 1915. It received its allotted LMS stock number in April 1927. Although retaining a round-top boiler, as one would expect, Ross safety valves and LMS lamp holders had been fitted.

L. HANSON

It is not clear if this picture shows a locomotive that had been withdrawn, set aside awaiting repairs or had been stored; the last option seems the most likely. It was normal practice at Rugby to store locomotives out of use by the coal stack and this is where it was photographed sometime during July 1935 several months before it was withdrawn in February 1936 as LMS 5306. Built in March 1906 as LNWR No. 1287 Lang Meg, it was superheated in September 1919, retaining slide valves. Rebuilding with piston-valve cylinders came in May 1926...

H. C. CASSERLEY

Above: Seen here at Bletchley shed in September 1937, No. 25304's tender had been fully coaled which suggests that the engine would soon have left the shed on its next turn of duty. Built in July 1905 as No. 302, this engine was superheated in July 1917 while retaining its original cylinders and slide valves. Rebuilt with new piston valve cylinders as a 'George V' in July 1922, it was renumbered as LMS No. 5304 in January 1927. A Belpaire boiler was fitted in 1931 and in December 1936 it was renumbered as 25304. Greyhound was the last but one member of the class to be withdrawn, lasting until January 1947.

H. C. CASSERLEY

Right: A view of the nameplate of No. 25304 probably taken shortly after the engine had been renumbered in December 1936. The lined black livery shows up well and the lids can be seen above both sandboxes together with the operating rodding for the same.

L. HANSON

During their later years the 'Precursors' were to be seen running over the North Wales line with a reasonable number allocated to Llandudno Junction. This picture of LNWR No. 2164 Oberon, built in April 1904, was taken at Llanfairfechan in July 1941 when it was working an Ordinary passenger train. This locomotive was rebuilt as a 'George V' in January 1913 and the LMS stock number 5277 was applied during November 1927. The duplicate number 25277 was applied in September 1936 and it was withdrawn in August 1946.

H. C. CASSERLEY

The headlamp code for this train was for Express Freight or Cattle train with the continuous brake in use on not less than four vehicles and as such indicated by a Maltese Cross in the working time table. However, the same headlamp code was also used for trains where none of the wagons had the continuous brake, or, if they did, less than four were connected to the engine. When a signalman offered the train to the signal box in advance, he used a bell code that applied to the braking power of the train; the more braking power, the less time would be spent running point to point, which was essential information for signalmen. Built in April 1906 as LNWR No. 561 Antaeus, this engine was rebuilt as a 'George the Fifth' class in December 1924 and the LMS stock number 5245 was probably applied when it was rebuilt. Conversion to the Midland Loading Gauge took place in November 1931, and in May 1936 it was renumbered again as 25245 and withdrawn in March 1941.

W. H. WHITWORTH

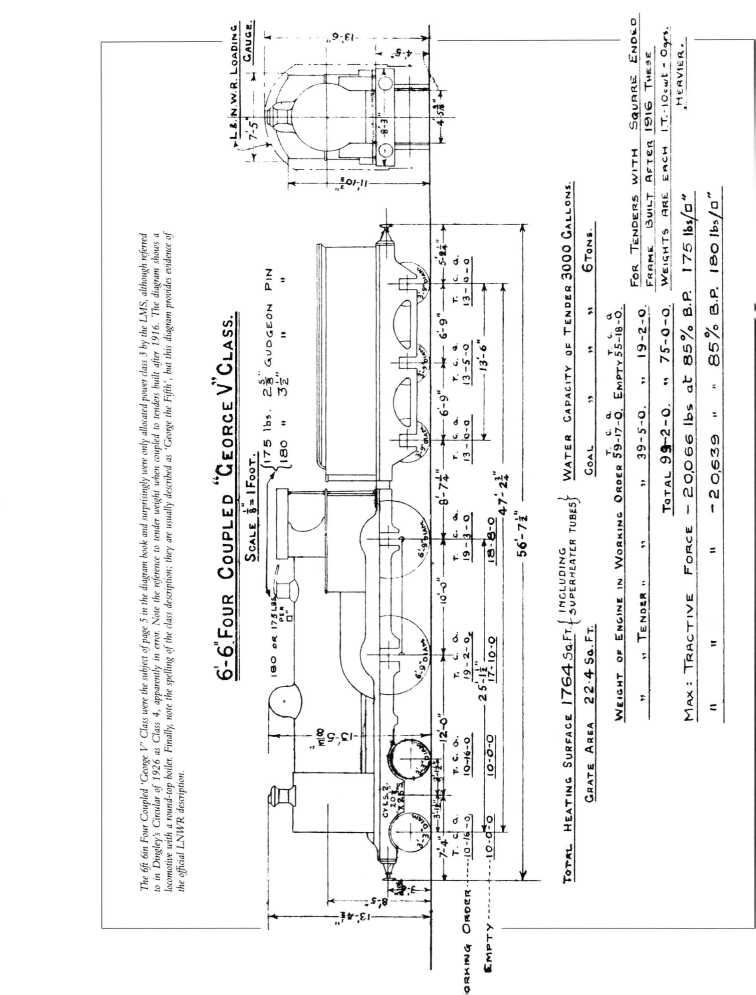

The 6ft 6in Four Coupled 'George V' Class were the subject of page 5 in the diagram book and surprisingly were only allocated power class 3 by the LMS, although referred to in Dingley's Circular of 1926 as Class 4, apparently in error. Note the reference to tender weight when coupled to tenders built after 1916. The diagram shows a locomotive with a round-top boiler. Finally, note the spelling of the class description; they are usually described as 'George the Fifth', but this diagram provides evidence of the official LNWR description.

4–4–0 Passenger Tender, LNW 'George the Fifth'

Motive Power Classification 3, post-1928 3P
Allocated LMS locomotive number series 5320–5409.

LNWR No.215 Newcomen *was built in October 1910, one of ten 'Queen Mary' class that were built as saturated steam locomotives for comparison with the superheated steam 'George the Fifth' class. All the 'Queen Mary' class were rebuilt in 1913/4 and became part of the 'George the Fifth' Class. The allotted LMS stock number 5334 was applied in September 1926 and during 1937 it was renumbered 25334 and ran as such for a few months before being withdrawn in November 1937. The lamp holders were now LMS type and Ross safety valves had replaced the Ramsbottom type.*
COLLECTION R.J. ESSERY

The 'George the Fifth' (henceforth 'George V') was an outstanding design of inside-cylinder 4–4–0. In effect they were a superheated version of the earlier 'Precursors' and eventually there were ninety superheated engines constructed between 1910 and 1915. The story begins in June 1910 when two locomotives were built at Crewe for comparison purposes, No. 2663 *George the Fifth*, was superheated and No. 2664 *Queen Mary* was saturated. It would appear that in order to evaluate the benefit of superheating, a decision was made to construct a further nine 'Queen Mary' class, which were built, during October/November 1910, and nine superheated 'George V' class during November to January 1911. The results soon became obvious and a further seventy superheated engines were built whilst all the 'Queen Mary' class received superheaters, this work being completed by October 1914.

The saturated engines were built with piston valves and their bogie wheels were the same diameter as the superheated engines, but by the time they became LMS locomotive stock, they were part of the 'George V' class and the new company ignored their origin. The modifications and alterations to the 'George V' class followed a similar pattern to the 'Precursors'; cabs were modified to suit the Composite loading gauge, and boiler changes during the LMS period saw some of the class fitted with Belpaire boilers.

List of Belpaire boilered 'George the Fifths'
Prepared by Peter Davis

	No.	Date	Date reverted to round-top boilers	Notes
	5320	–	–	–
	5321	8/1927	–	also 25321
	5322	–	–	also 25322
	25323	–	–	–
	5324	9/1924	–	also 25324
	5325	12/1927	–	also 25325
	5326	–	–	–
	5327	–	–	photo 1934
	5329	–	–	–
	5331	–	–	also 25331
	5333	–	–	–
	5335	–	–	photo 1934
	5336	–	–	photo 1934
	5337	–	–	–
	5338	10/1927	–	–
	5339	–	–	also 25339
	5340	12/1927	–	–
	5342	2/1928	–	–
LNW	5343	1928	–	–
	5345	–	–	also 25345
	5346	3/1928	–	–
	5347	1934	–	also 25347
	25348	1937	–	–
	5350	8/1927	–	also 25350

continued

This delightful early LMS period picture of No. 5365 Race-horse was taken just south of the bridge carrying the Met./GC Line near Kenton and shows an up express in the early LMS period with eight of the twelve carriages in LNWR livery and the locomotive in the first LMS livery style. applied in 1924. The engine number was carried on the tender and on a smokebox door numberplate, with the small letters 'L M S' on the side of the cab. Built in August 1911 as LNWR No. 1631, the engine received its LMS stock number in 1924, and later, in 1930, the cab was altered to conform to the Midland loading gauge. Rebuilding with a Belpaire boiler came in 1935 and in July 1936 the locomotive was renumbered 25365, but less than a year later, in June 1937, it was withdrawn.

Renumbering, by removing the LNWR cast numberplate and painting the new LMS stock number in small letters where the numberplate had been, was a simple way for a locomotive to display its new number without the need for a complete repaint. In this picture LNWR No. 681 St George, taken after becoming LMS No. 5390 in April 1926 and before the cab was altered to MR loading gauge in January 1930, is seen in LNWR unlined black and overall condition, apart from Ross safety valves and LMS washout plugs. Attached to a fully-coaled Whale tender and displaying express passenger headlamp code suggests that it would soon have been at the head of an express passenger train.   COLLECTION R.J. ESSERY

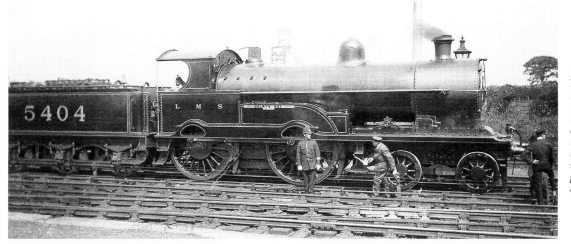

This picture of No. 5404 Colwyn Bay illustrates a locomotive in early LMS red lined livery Code A2. Built in June 1915 as LNWR No. 226, it was renumbered as seen here early in 1924 and was withdrawn in March 1936. This picture was taken at Trentham Junction in 1925 with a policeman in the centre of the picture, the driver with an oil can and other railwaymen present.

L&GRP

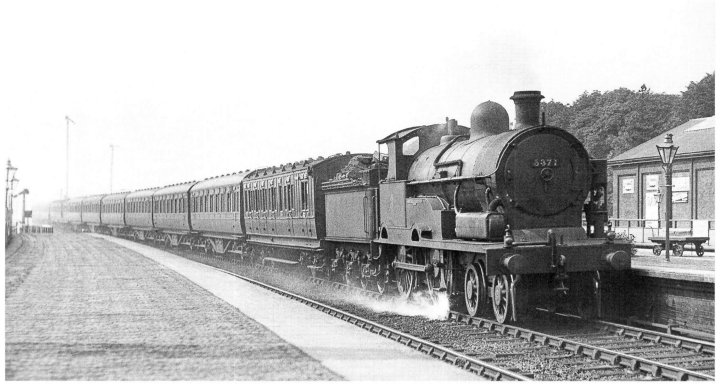

Photographed at Berkhamsted at the head of an up Manchester express, LNWR No. 1472 Moorhen *had been fitted with Weir feed-water heater by 1917. Seen here after it had been renumbered 5371 in July 1927 and before the Weir apparatus was removed in 1928, it became No. 25371 in August 1936. The following year it was observed with a Belpaire boiler and withdrawn from traffic in October 1939.*   COLLECTION R.J. ESSERY

No.	Date	Date reverted to round-top boilers	Notes
LNW 882	–	–	also 5351
5353	–	–	–
5354	–	–	–
LNW 2212	–	1927	(prob. RT when renumbered 5355 9/'27)
LNW 2291	6/1925	–	also 5356 and 25356
LNW 2495	9/1925	–	also 5357 and 25357
5358	–	–	–
5359	1934	–	–
5360	–	–	–
5361	1933	–	–
5364	1934	–	–
5365	1935	–	–
5368	9/1927	–	–
5369	–	–	–
25371	1937	–	–
5372	6/1925	–	–
5375	11/1927	–	–
5376	–	1937	also 25376
5377	–	–	photo 1934
5378	10/1927	–	also 25378?
5379	–	–	–
5381	1931	–	–
5382	–	–	also 25382
5385	8/1927	–	–
5386	–	–	–
5387	–	–	also 25387
5388	–	–	–
5389	9/1927	–	also 25389
5391	–	–	photo 1935
5392	–	–	also 25392
5393	1932	–	also 25393
5394	–	–	–

No.	Date	Date reverted to round-top boilers	Notes
5395	–	–	also 25395
5397	–	–	–
5399	1931	–	–
5400	–	–	–
LNW 789	4/1925	–	also 5401
5403	1929	–	–
5405	3/1928	–	–
5406	–	–	–
5407	–	–	–
5408	1933	–	–
5409	3/1928	–	also 25409

NB. The entries under 'date' with month specified are from official sources. Those with just the year are from observation and therefore signify 'running with' only. This applies to 'Precursors' too.

The coupled wheel bosses on the first twenty engines were normal LNWR size, but in April 1911 the wheel with a large diameter boss became standard. However, because the wheel centre had a long life and wheels could be used with other members of the class, it was not unknown for a locomotive to run with wheels that were different to those fitted when it was built. From about 1933, replacement buffers were of the Stanier type with a parallel buffer socket or body (an alternative name) and square base. They were originally coupled to tenders that were similar to those attached to the 'Precursor' class, with a single coal rail. Later they were coupled to a variety of Whale and Bowen Cooke tenders and a few also ran with ROD type tenders. Photographic evidence confirms the following were at one time coupled to the ROD class of

This picture shows LNWR No. 2155 W.C. Brocklehurst displaying its LMS stock number 5326, which was applied in June 1927 and hauling an express freight train with a 'fitted head' (automatic brake in use on at least the first four, but less than half the vehicles in total). This class of freight train was also known as a 'Maltese' because it was indicated by a Maltese Cross in the working timetable. The picture shows a 'George the Fifth' with a Belpaire boiler, LMS lamp holders and a smokebox door numberplate. Allotted No. 25326 in the duplicate list, the engine was withdrawn in December 1936 before the new number was applied.
COLLECTION R.J. ESSERY

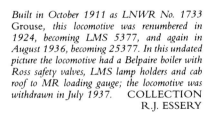

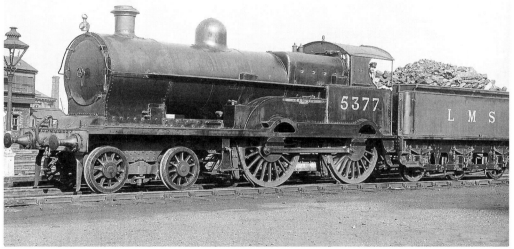

Built in October 1911 as LNWR No. 1733 Grouse, this locomotive was renumbered in 1924, becoming LMS 5377, and again in August 1936, becoming 25377. In this undated picture the locomotive had a Belpaire boiler with Ross safety valves, LMS lamp holders and cab roof to MR loading gauge; the locomotive was withdrawn in July 1937.   COLLECTION R.J. ESSERY

This picture of LMS No. 5393 was taken at Bletchley during March 1932 when it was working a passenger train. Note the headlamp on the top of the smokebox in front of the chimney. The driver is seen looking back, waiting for the 'right away' signal from the guard or one of the station staff. The guard was responsible for giving this signal, but depending upon circumstances, long train, platform on a curve, or view obstructed by buildings on the platform, the 'right away' signal could be relayed from the guard to one or more station staff, and the signal to the driver would come from a foreman, inspector or station master as was appropriate. Built in April 1913 as LNWR No. 1680 Loyalty, the LMS stock number was applied in February 1924, and in March 1936 it was renumbered, becoming 25393. Five years later, in December 1941, it was withdrawn.   H. C. CASSERLEY

tender: Nos. 5336, 5349, 5350, 5366, 5375, 5376, 5382, 5402 and 5406. The arrival of the 5XP 'Jubilee' class saw some locomotives lose their nameplates, as recorded by the *Railway Observer*, Nos. 5350 *India*, 5356 *Gibraltar*, 5358 *Malta*, 5359 *Cyprus* in September 1933 and 5398 *Meteor* in July 1933.

When they became LMS stock, they were still employed on mainline express passenger work as either train engine or pilot, and as we can see from the 1926 allocations, there were thirty-one at Crewe North and sixteen at Chester, but the influx of new standard locomotives, beginning with the Standard Compounds, saw the rate of withdrawal increase and only thirty-three received 2xxxx numbers during the mid-1930s. These were Nos. 5321–5326, 5331, 5334, 5339, 5345, 5347, 5348, 5350, 5356, 5357, 5360, 5362, 5365, 5368, 5369, 5371–5374, 5376–78, 5382, 5387, 5389, 5392, 5393 and 5409. By 1935 the survivors were concentrated at Crewe North, Rugby, Chester and Llandudno Junction, although there were a number stationed at Aston and Patricroft. In their

A number of 'ROD' tenders were coupled to 'George the Fifth' class locomotives and in this picture we can see they were somewhat larger than the LNWR tenders and visually not a good match. Built in February 1913 as LNWR No. 2124 John Rennie, the allotted LMS stock number 5382 was applied in July 1927, and in September 1936 the number altered to 25382, which was carried for a few months prior to withdrawal in June 1937. In this undated picture we can see the engine had been rebuilt with a Belpaire boiler.   W.L. GOOD

LMS 5406 photographed at its home shed Rugby in 1932, Note the '8' shedplate on the smokebox. Built in June 1915 as LNWR No. 2153 Llandrindod, this engine was renumbered in June 1926, and later withdrawn in April 1937. The date when it was rebuilt with a Belpaire boiler, Ross safety valves and the cab altered to conform with the Midland loading gauge, is not known to the author. The work was probably done at the same time and we must not overlook that it now has LMS-type lamp holders. This picture has been included to show another 'George the Fifth' class coupled to an ROD tender.   J.A.G.H. COLTAS

This picture of No. 25322 F.S.P. Wolferstan at Chester on 8th August 1936 enables readers to see the cab roof profile after it had been modified to suit the Midland loading gauge. Built in November 1910 as LNWR No. 1294, the engine received its LMS stock number 5322 in November 1927 and was renumbered again in July 1936, becoming No. 25322. It was withdrawn in December 1938. L. HANSON

'George V' No. 5396 acquired its LMS number in June 1928 and when captured on film at Euston, sometime after that date, the engine still carried one of the original LNWR boilers with only two washout plugs, albeit modified to take Ross safety valves on the original Ramsbottom mounting. LMS lamp holders were fitted but the cab remained unaltered at this date and a Cooke tender of the fourth type was attached. Built as LNWR No. 1481 Typhoon in April 1913, the engine was withdrawn in October 1936.   V. R. WEBSTER/ KIDDERMINSTER RAILWAY MUSEUM

When this locomotive was completed in June 1911 it was hailed as the 5000th locomotive to be built at Crewe and for a short time 1800 was its first (and official as far as the accountants were concerned) stock number, but, doubtless at the behest of the Publicity Department, it was soon renumbered, becoming LNWR No. 5000, which was carried until June 1927 when the LMS stock number was applied. In fact it was probably the 498th engine to be built at Crewe because Crewe motion numbers 3784 and 3785 were allotted but never used. In August 1936 it was renumbered again and, at about the same time, was fitted with a Belpaire boiler. It carried the number 25348 until it was withdrawn in June 1940. The upper picture was taken at Crewe in March 1936 whilst the lower picture has been included to provide a close-up view of the rather special nameplate which bore the words '5000th engine built at the locomotive works Crewe June 1911'. After withdrawal there was a proposal to preserve the engine but, sadly, it was finally scrapped in April 1942. However, one of these plates was sold for £21,000 at auction in 1992.   A. C. ROBERTS and G. H. PLATT

In this undated picture we see LNWR No. 1059 Lord Loch, *at the head of a three-coach train running under express passenger train headlamp code. It became LMS No. 5321 in July 1927 and was also rebuilt with a Belpaire boiler that year. A note on the reverse of the print states 'Warrington to Wigan stopping train at Winwick, but the headlamp code is for an express!' Renumbered as 25321 in 1936, this engine was the last but two of the class to remain in service and was withdrawn in February 1948.*
COLLECTION
DAVID JENKINSON

Ultimate Allocations	*17th March 1926*	*28th September 1935* *	*8th April 1944*	*31st December 1947*
Crewe North		5362, 25365, 5369, 5373, 5382, 5389, 5391		
Rugby		5409, 5327, 5329, 5339, 5377, 25392–93		
Camden				
Northampton		5337, 5359, 5376		
Stafford	5320–5324	5277		
Willesden	5325–5328	5320		
Bushbury	5329–5332	5331		
Aston	5333–5337	5321, 5334, 5352, 5357, 5378		
Monument Lane	5338–5343	5338, 5344		
Hereford	5344–5346			
Longsight	5347–5354			
Chester	5355–5370	25326, 5333, 25345, 5348, 5356, 5358, 5360–61, 5363–65, 5368, 5370, 5375, 5394–95, 5406	25321, 25350, 25376	25321, 25350, 25373
Bangor	5371–5374	25374		
Holyhead	5375–5377			
Edge Hill	5378–5390	5366, 5381, 5390		
Salop/Shrewsbury	5391–5395			
Llandudno Junction	5404 5409	5341–43, 5350, 5353–54, 25371–72, 5379–80, 5385, 5397, 5402–5, 5407–08	25373	
Warrington		5323–24, 5388		
Carnforth		5327, 5384		
Bletchley		5330, 5335, 5340		
Speke Junc		5332, 5386		
Rhyl		5336		
Workington		5346		
Patricroft		5347, 5355, 5383, 5396, 5398–5401		
Buxton		5351		
Preston		5367		
Stoke		25373, 5387		

At the foot of the 1926 table there was a note 'Total 140, included in Precursor Nos. 16, Grand Total 156'.

* Note the locomotive numbers are as stated in the LMS list, but it is clear that in some instances the renumbering into the 25xxx series had not been recorded. The numbers given above are as recorded by the LMS.

final years they were employed upon a variety of turns ranging from mainline pilots, stopping passenger trains, station pilots and freight train working. Three members of the class, Nos. 25321, 25350 and 25373, became British Railways stock; No. 25321 was withdrawn in February 1948 and the other two in May, leaving a 'Precursor' No. 25297 *Sirocco* as the sole survivor of the LNWR 4–4–0s.

LIVERY

As previously mentioned, in 1923, the LMS decided to paint the company's passenger locomotives red and generally the sequence of change was similar to that described for the 'Precursors'. It was not until 1928 that they began to display a uniform appearance, running in either lined black livery or plain black with various types of transfers or hand-painted numbers on the cabside. As with the 'Precursors', Livery Code C18 was the most common.

Photographed at Chester on 24th April 1947 when it was displaying a 6A Chester shed plate, this locomotive was built in October 1911 as LNWR No. 1730 Snipe *and received its LMS stock number 5376 in July 1927. A further renumbering took place in October 1936 when it became No. 25376 which it retained until December 1947 when it was withdrawn.* H. C. CASSERLEY

The subject of this picture, taken at Crewe Works on 31st May 1947, No. 25373 was the other final survivor of the 'George V' class. Built in September 1911 as LNWR No. 1681 Ptarmigan, *the allotted LMS stock number 5373 was applied in May 1926 and in May 1936 it became No. 25373. Following nationalisation in 1948 the British Railways stock number 58012 was allocated to this engine, but it was withdrawn in May 1948 before it could be applied. When photographed, the engine was sandwiched between 'Coal Engine' No. 28100 and an ex-MR 3-plank dropside wagon in internal use. Both engines were overhauled, the 'Coal Engine' giving another five years service.*
H. C. CASSERLEY

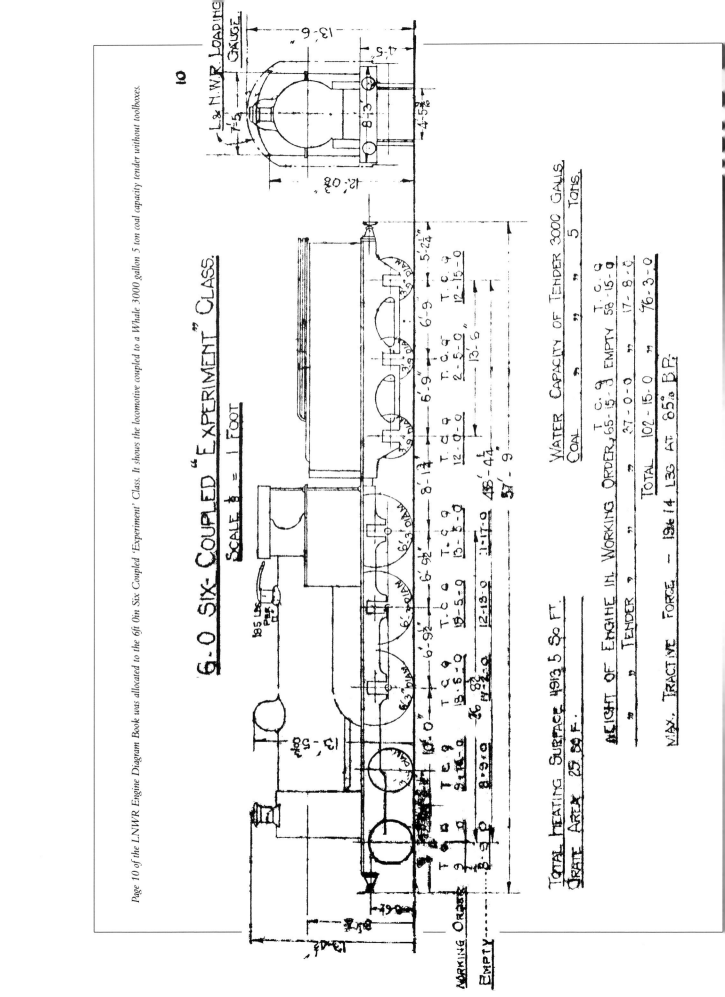

Page 10 of the LNWR Engine Diagram Book was allocated to the 6ft 0in Six Coupled 'Experiment' Class. It shows the locomotive coupled to a Whale 3000 gallon 5 ton coal capacity tender without toolboxes.

"6.0 SIX-COUPLED "EXPERIMENT" CLASS.

SCALE ⅛ = 1 FOOT

WATER CAPACITY OF TENDER 3000 GALLS.
COAL " " " 5 TONS

TOTAL HEATING SURFACE 1913.5 SQ FT.
GRATE AREA 25 SQ F.

WEIGHT OF ENGINE IN WORKING ORDER 65-15-3 EMPTY 58-15-9 T.C.Q
" " TENDER " " 37-0-0 " 17-8-0 "
TOTAL 102-15-0 " 76-3-0 "

MAX. TRACTIVE FORCE — 13414 Lbs AT 85% B.P.

4–6–0 Passenger Tender, LNW 'Experiment'

Motive Power Classification 3, post-1928 3P
Allocated LMS locomotive number series 5450–5554.

No. 5469 was among the first four 'Experiments' to be renumbered in April 1926. Seen here in May 1927 'on shed' at Water End, Peterborough, the LMS numbers had been stencilled in the space left by the LNWR plate and, apart from the boiler with four washout plugs each side, the engine was unaltered from LNWR condition. The first batch of 'Experiments' to be renumbered did not receive cast smokebox numberplates, but most of the later ones did. This engine, built in October 1906 as LNWR No. 1990 North Western, *had yet to receive horizontal cabside grab rails. Presumably the fireman had put the lamp in the socket 'up top' ready for working an Ordinary passenger train from Peterborough East station to either Rugby or Northampton.*
H. C. CASSERLEY

The 4–6–0 'Experiment' class were introduced in 1905 and in many respects they were an enlarged 'Precursor' with 6ft 3in rather than 6ft 9in driving wheels. They were largely intended for work north of Crewe over the more difficult line to Carlisle and 105 were built, the last entering service at the beginning of 1910. All except one were saturated engines when they became LMS stock, but later two more were superheated. The first was LNW No. 1361 *Prospero*, which had been rebuilt as a 4-cylinder superheated engine with Dendy Marshall valve gear in March 1915, becoming LMS No. 5554 in February 1927. It was withdrawn in June 1933. The second engine to be superheated was LNW No. 2624 *Saracen*, which, although allotted LMS stock number 5507, was never renumbered. This locomotive was fitted with a Belpaire boiler and superheated in February 1926, but two years later it was withdrawn in February 1928. The third locomotive was LNW No. 1993 *Richard Moon*, which became LMS No. 5472. This locomotive was superheated in December 1926 and it ran in this condition until it was withdrawn in December 1933, both locomotives retaining their original smokebox.

Ninety-two locomotives carried the allotted LMS numbers; those that failed to receive them were Nos. 5455, 5465, 5481, 5486, 5493, 5503, 5507, 5515, 5517, 5527, 5530, 5538 and 5544. A number of locomotives were renumbered under the 1934 programme and had 20000 added to their LMS number; these locomotives became Nos. 25456, 25473, 25502, 25504, 25508, 25509, 25511, 25514, 25525, 25528, 25531, 25532 and 25552.

During the time they became LMS stock, a number of locomotives received Belpaire boilers and others had their cabs modified to suit the composite loading gauge whilst some locomotives received both. Those recorded as running with Belpaire boilers were:

List of Belpaire boilered 'Experiments'
Prepared by Peter Davis

No.	Date	Date reverted to round-top boilers	Notes
5450	–	–	–
5451	1927	–	–
5456	2/1928	–	–
5457	2/1928	–	–
5458	8/1927	–	–
5461	9/1927	–	–
5462	4/1926	–	–

Continued

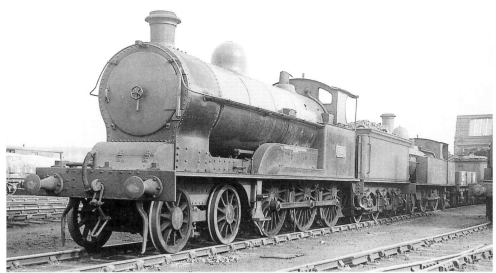

Scenes like this were commonplace during the 1920s, some locomotives displaying their original LNWR and others their new LMS number. The object of the photographer's attention was the 'Experiment' Class 4–6–0 No. 2628 Banshee, built in February 1909 and receiving its allocated LMS stock number 5511 in August 1927. It became No. 25511 early in 1935 for a short time before it was withdrawn in July 1935. Standing behind the 4–6–0 we can see a 2–4–2T displaying its LMS No. 6748, applied in September 1926, dating this picture between September 1926 and August 1927.

A. C. ROBERTS

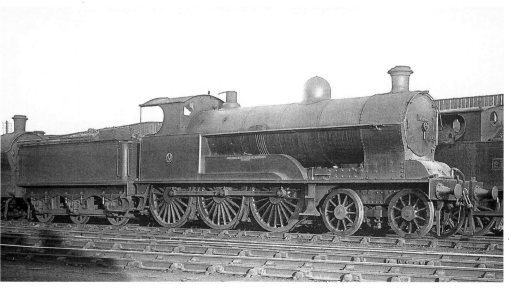

Both of these pictures show the same early LMS livery on two different locomotives. To the left we see LNWR No. 2629 Terrier at Huddersfield engine shed. Built March 1909 and renumbered as LMS No. 5512 in July 1926, it was the thirteenth 'Experiment' to be withdrawn, in February 1928. It is seen here in black without any lining and displaying the LMS coat of arms on the side of the cab and with the LMS stock number displayed on the smokebox numberplate. The picture above illustrates LNWR No. 5466 Glendower after it had been rebuilt with a Belpaire boiler and Ross safety valves in June 1926 at which time the cab was altered to conform to the Midland loading gauge. The livery was the same as No. 5512 and both engines retained their LNWR lampholders. No. 5512 was withdrawn in November 1934 before it was necessary to renumber it in order to clear the 54xx series for new Stanier Class 5MTs.

COLLECTION R.J. ESSERY

No.	Date	Date reverted to round-top boilers	Notes
5466	6/1926	–	–
5467	–	–	–
5469	–	–	–
5473	1926	1927 later refitted	also 25473
5474	11/1927	–	–
5476	9/1927	–	–
5479	9/1927	–	–
5482	1/1928	–	–
5484	–	–	–
5488	–	–	–
LNW 2624	2/1926	–	superheated
LNW 2630	1/1926	1927	RT boiler as 5513
5522	–	–	–
5523	–	–	–
5524	–	–	–
5525	9/1927	–	–
5526	–	–	–
5528	–	–	also 25528
5532	–	–	–
5534	10/27	–	–
5539	1/1928	–	–
5548	3/1928	–	–

During the LMS period, the original Ramsbottom safety valves were replaced by Ross type safety valves; this also applied to many locomotives with round-top boilers as well as those rebuilt with Belpaire boilers. There were a number of tender changes, but, based upon photographic evidence, only 5472 and 5497 are known to the author to have been coupled to 'ROD' tenders. In December 1928 the nameplates were removed from No. 5468 *Lady of the Lake* and the name was bestowed on a new 'Royal Scot' locomotive No. 6149.

LIVERY
During the 1923–1927 period, the class were entitled to be painted in the red livery, but only one of the class, No 5458 *City of Edinburgh*, appears to have been painted in this style. The others were in plain black, most running with Livery Code C18 even though black with red lining would have been correct.

They were not the most successful LNWR class to become LMS stock, and during their time on the LMS they were employed on secondary passenger train work, including excursions and freight trains, work that was undertaken by the Horwich 'Moguls' rather more effectively. As we can see from the 1926 allocations, they were distributed across the system although there were none in South Wales or at Carlisle. The arrival of the Stanier Class 5s saw the demise of the 'Experiments', although nine locomotives, Nos. 25456, 25473, 5475, 25508, 25509, 25511, 25514, 25528, and 25552, were still in service at the beginning of 1935. Before the end of the year, the class became extinct when 25473 was withdrawn in September 1935.

Ultimate Allocations	*1926*
Willesden	5450–5454, 5456–5461
Bletchley	5462–5464
Northampton	5466–5470
Walsall	5471–5473
Aston	5474–5480, 5482
Bushbury	5483–5484
Stafford	5485, 5487–5492
Birkenhead	5494–5495
Holyhead	5496–5501
Bangor	5502, 5404–5506
Huddersfield	5507–5512
Warrington	5513–5514, 5516, 5518–5520
Springs Branch	5521–5526 5528–5529
Edge Hill	5530–5534
Salop	5535–5537
Carnforth	5539–5540
Patricroft	5541–5543
Llandudno Junction	5545–5549
Rhyl	5550
Rugby	5551–5554

Taken at the LNWR station at Oxford, the terminus of the branch from Bletchley, this photograph shows an 'Experiment' at the head of an ordinary passenger train. Built in June 1905 as LNWR No. 507 Sarmation, it became LMS No. 5454 in June 1926. Seen here in the 1928 livery, the date is between that year and September 1932 when the locomotive was withdrawn. Note the retention of the smokebox numberplate, a feature that was applied to, and later removed from, many ex-LNWR locomotives. LMS-type lamp holders had been fitted. Finally, note the Ramshottom safety valves had been replaced by Ross safety valves.
COLLECTION R.J. ESSERY

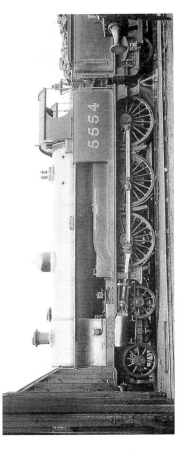

These LMS period pictures of LNWR No. 1361 Prospero illustrates the four-cylinder member of the class. Built in October 1907, it was rebuilt as a 4-cylinder superheated locomotive with Dendy Marshall valve gear in 1915, the only one to be rebuilt although, as mentioned in the text, two others were superheated. It was renumbered by the LMS in February 1927 and ran as No. 5554 until it was withdrawn in June 1933. The lower view shows the cab had not been altered but LMS lamp holders had been fitted.

H. J. STRETTON-WARD

This picture taken at Willesden on 27th July 1930 shows 5464 at the head of an empty coaching stock train. Built in January 1906 as LNWR No.1669 City of Glasgow, *it was renumbered in September 1926 and was withdrawn in December 1930, five months after the picture was taken. The locomotive had retained the LNWR cab, but LMS-type lamp holders had replaced the original lamp sockets. By this time the boiler, with four LMS washout plugs each side, had also been fitted with Ross safety valves.* COLLECTION R.J. ESSERY

During the 1920s and into the 1930s a number of LNWR locomotives were coupled to 'ROD' tenders to provide greater water capacity, but as far as I can establish, only two 'Experiments' ever ran with them; one was No. 5472 and the other was No.5497 seen in this picture, taken at Llandudno Junction in September 1932. Built in January 1909 as LNWR No. 1020 Majestic, *the LMS stock number 5497 was applied in September 1927 but it was withdrawn in November 1934 before it was necessary to renumber it to avoid clashing with the LMS Standard Class 5s that were being built.* COLLECTION R.J. ESSERY

'Experiment' Class locomotives were often used to haul freight trains and this picture shows LNWR No. 1669 City of Glasgow built in January 1906 after it had been renumbered in June 1926 as LMS No. 5464, In this picture the locomotive displays the correct 1928 livery replacing the style adopted upon renumbering, which was probably similar to that shown on No. 5466 (see page 90). It is seen here hauling a short freight train, which is usually described as a 'pick up goods' and may indicate that it was 'getting the mileage in before going to the workshop', a common practice used by shed foremen when allocating locomotives to cover various diagrams. No. 5464 was to remain in traffic until December 1930 when it was withdrawn.

COLLECTION R.J. ESSERY

This picture of No. 5487 Combermere at the head of a through up freight is typical of the trains worked by this class of locomotive during the LMS periods. A note on the back of the print suggests a date around 1933 and the location is Brock troughs; the engine has just passed under the 'Badger Bridge'. Built as LNWR No. 902 in September 1907, the LMS stock number was applied during February 1927 and the cab was altered to the Midland Loading Gauge in July 1931. It was withdrawn in October 1934.

W. S. GARTH

This locomotive, which was built in June 1909 as LNWR No. 2641 Bellona, became LMS No. 5528 in January 1928 and the cab was altered to conform to the Midland loading gauge in October 1929. It was renumbered again as No. 25528 before being withdrawn in August of that year. Therefore this picture was taken during 1935 and shows the engine waiting for the signal to be 'pulled off', allowing it to propel the horse-box somewhere. COLLECTION R.J. ESSERY

Built in February 1909 as LNWR No. 2625 Buckland, this engine was allotted LMS stock number 5508, applied in May 1927, and for a few months during 1935 it ran as No. 25508 before being withdrawn in August 1935. It is impossible to see the number on either the cabside or tender, so suggesting a date the picture was taken is not easy; however, the engine had LMS-type lamp holders and Ross safety valves. It had also been in a collision causing damage to the front buffer beam and running plate, the latter having been bent upwards, so it is possible that it was photographed at the time of withdrawal.

H. J. STRETTON-WARD

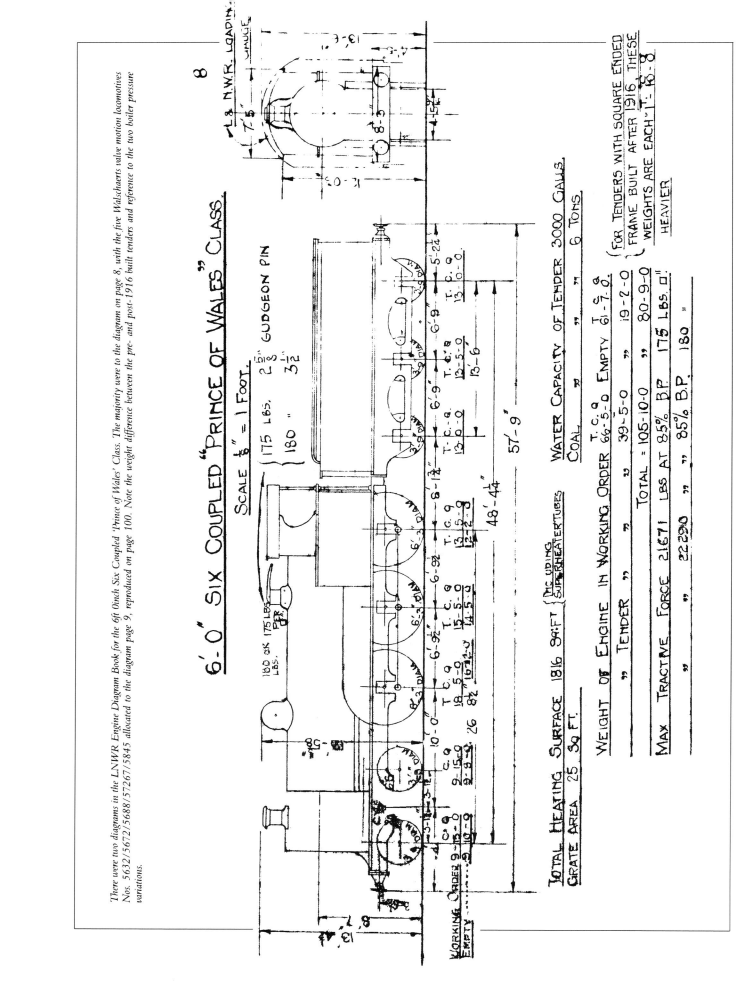

There were two diagrams in the LNWR Engine Diagram Book for the 6ft 0inch Six Coupled 'Prince of Wales' Class. The majority were to the diagram on page 8, with the five Walschaerts valve motion locomotives Nos. 5632/5672/5688/57267/5845 allocated to the diagram page 9, reproduced on page 9. Note the weight difference between the pre- and post-1916 built tenders and reference to the two boiler pressure variations.

8

L & N.W.R. LOADING GAUGE

6'-0" SIX COUPLED "PRINCE OF WALES" CLASS.

SCALE ⅛" = 1 FOOT.

175 LBS. 2⅝" GUDGEON PIN
180 " 3½"

TOTAL HEATING SURFACE 1816 SQ.FT { INCLUDING SUPERHEATER TUBES

GRATE AREA 25 SQ.FT.

WATER CAPACITY OF TENDER 3000 GALLS
COAL " " 6 TONS

	T.C.Q			
WEIGHT OF ENGINE IN WORKING ORDER	66-5-0	EMPTY	61-7-0	
" TENDER " "	39-5-0	"	19-2-0	
TOTAL =	105-10-0	"	80-9-0	

MAX TRACTIVE FORCE 21671 LBS AT 85% B.P. 175 LBS. ◻"
" " 22290 " " 85% B.P. 180 "

(FOR TENDERS WITH SQUARE ENDED
FRAME BUILT AFTER 1916 THESE
WEIGHTS ARE EACH 1'- 16 - 8
HEAVIER

4–6–0 Passenger Tender, LNW 'Prince of Wales'

Motive Power Classification 4, post 1928 4P

Allocated LMS locomotive number series 5600–5844. (5845 was built by Wm. Beardmore & Co. Ltd
in February 1924 for the Wembley Exhibition.)

Seen at Rugby in July 1935, newly renumbered 25638, Charles James Lever *had been built as LNWR No. 2443 in March 1914 and given the LMS No. 5638 in April 1926 – possibly at the same time as it was converted to oil burning. The cab was altered to the Midland loading gauge in December 1930 and the engine was withdrawn in April 1936.*
H. C. CASSERLEY

Expressed in numerical terms, this was the largest class of passenger tender locomotives owned by the LNWR. Two hundred and forty-five became LMS stock in 1923, and in 1924 another locomotive was built by Wm. Beardmore & Co. for display on their stand at the Wembley Exhibition, April to November 1924. After the close of the exhibition, it was taken into stock by the LMS. The circumstances whereby this came about are explained in this extract from the Locomotive Building Programme Winter 1923/1924, as submitted by George Hughes, Chief Mechanical Engineer. 'Messrs. Beardmore's, who had, in the past, built engines for the London & North Western Company, were anxious to complete a new engine of the same class as previously supplied, for exhibition on their stand at the Wembley Exhibition next year, and provided they would supply an engine at the same price as it could be built for in the Company's Works, permission would be granted to them to do so.' This locomotive was displayed as No. 5845 *Prince of Wales*, and the nameplates which were new, not transferred from No. 5600, were removed before the locomotive entered traffic. Thereafter it ran without a name.

For many years prior to the grouping, Crewe Works had built the locomotives required to work the line, but the 'Prince of Wales' class proved to be an exception. Ten were built at Crewe in 1911 and a further thirty in 1913–14. The next batch of fifty locomotives was built in 1915–16, twenty by the North British Locomotive Co., the remainder at Crewe.

The final one hundred and fifty-five were built between 1919–1921; ninety were built by Wm. Beardmore. None of this series was ever named although some of the final sixty-five built at Crewe were eventually named. The contractor-built locomotives became LMS stock carrying the builders' works plates, but these were removed as the locomotives were renumbered by the LMS, the Company renumbering them in the order in which they entered traffic irrespective of origin.

The 'Prince of Wales' class were essentially a six-coupled version of the 'George V' class, although some sources regard them as a superheated version of the 'Experiment' class. The coupled wheels were 6 inch less in diameter than the 'Precursor' at 6ft 3in, and the wheel boss was not the large circular type seen on the 4–4–0s. Because the LNWR was still 'feeling its way' with superheating, the first forty engines were fitted with a pyrometer on the right-hand side and a damper on the left-hand side. From about 1916 these fittings began to be removed, but a few were still in place when the locomotives became LMS stock. Shortly after the grouping, Belpaire boilers began to replace the original round-top design, but it was not unknown for locomotives to be reboilered and change from round-top to Belpaire and then back to round-top. Those locomotives that have been identified from photographic sources and contemporary observation (listed in Baxter, *British Locomotive Catalogue Vol. 2B*) with Belpaire boilers are listed on page 99.

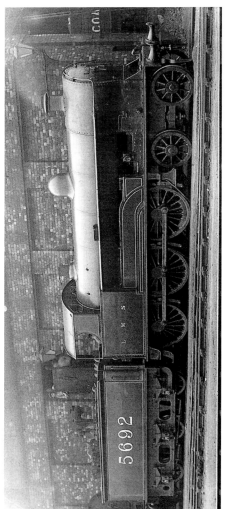

Built at Crewe as LNWR No. 295 in January 1919, this locomotive was not named. It became LMS No. 5692 in 1924 and in January 1936 it was renumbered 25692. It was withdrawn in July 1937. As we can see, it had been painted in red livery. Code A2, with the stock number displayed on the side of the tender and on the smokebox door. It retained the Ramsbottom safety valve and LNWR lamp sockets, but the cab roof had been altered to the Composite loading gauge.
COLLECTION R. J. ESSERY

As described in the text, a number of 'Prince of Wales' Class locomotives were built by the trade, and in this picture we see LNWR No. 53, that was built by William Beardmore & Co in March 1922. In keeping with the policy at that time, it was not named. The LMS stock number 5834 was applied in 1924, when a smokebox door numberplate was fitted, the letters 'LMS' were applied on the cabside where the LNWR numberplate would have been, and the locomotive number was put on the side of the tender. This engine was rebuilt with a Belpaire boiler in 1933, renumbered as 25834 in 1934 and withdrawn in January 1936.
COLLECTION R. J. ESSERY

This picture of No. 5668 provides a good example of the first LMS livery style, with the engine number on the side of the tender and a smokebox door number, with the initials 'LMS' on the side of the cab, livery code A2. This locomotive was one of a batch of twenty built during late 1915/early 1916 by the North British Locomotive Company Ltd and it entered traffic as LNWR No. 446 Pegasus during November 1915. The LMS stock number was applied in 1924 and the cab was altered to conform to the Midland loading gauge in 1931. In 1935 it was renumbered, becoming 25668, and in August 1935 it was withdrawn.

REAL PHOTOGRAPHS

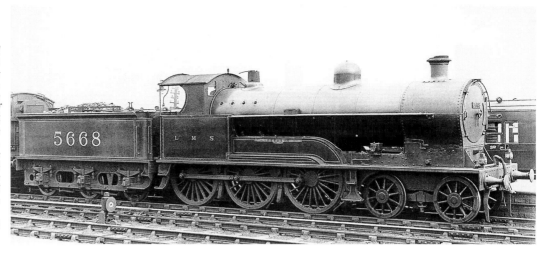

List of Belpaire boilered 'Prince of Wales' class
Prepared by Peter Davis

No.	Date	Date reverted to round-top boilers	Notes
25601	–	–	–
LNW 1704	1923	–	and 5606
5607	1926	–	–
5614	–	–	–
LNW 2040	1923	–	also 5615 (1933) and prob. 25615
5620	–	–	–
LNW 1679	–	1927	RT as 5623
25625	1935	–	–
5628	–	–	Prob. also 25628
5629	1933	–	Prob. also 25629
LNW 979	–	–	also 5630 and poss. 25630
5632	–	–	not as LNW 964
5633	1932	–	also 25633
5636	–	–	–
5638	1923	–	also 25638
LNW 27	1923	–	also 5640 and 25640 (1934)
25643	–	–	–
25645	–	–	–
5646	–	–	–
5649	11/1929	–	–
25653	–	–	–
25655	–	–	–
5656	–	–	also 25656
LNW 2417	1932	–	also 5658 and 25658
5662	1924	–	also 25662
5665	1932	–	–
5666	3/1928	–	also 25528
5670	1932	–	also 25670
5672	3/1928	–	also 25672
5673	–	–	also 25673
5674	1931	c. 1935	also 25674 (1938)
5675	–	–	–
5680	9/1932	–	–
LNW 1324	–	1927	refitted 12/1935 to 25683
25689	1933	–	–
5694	11/1927	–	also 25694
5695	–	–	–
25700	1934	–	–

No.	Date	Date reverted to round-top boilers	Notes
LNW 707	–	–	also 5701
5703	–	–	–
25704	–	–	–
5706	9/1925	–	–
5707	12/1925	–	–
5710	–	–	–
5711	11/1927	–	–
5712	1930	–	–
5715	8/1927	–	–
LNW 1732	1925	–	also 5717
5718	1932	–	–
LNW 444	4/1925	–	also 5720
LNW 497	4/1925	–	also 5721
25722	1934	–	–
5725	2/1928	–	–
5730	1933	–	also 25730
25732	12/1935	–	–
25733	1934	–	–
LNW 812	c. 1923	3/1928	also 5734
5743	1933	–	–
LNW 889	1923	–	also 5744 (1932)
5747	1933	–	also 25747
25751	1937	–	–
25752	–	–	–
5753	1/1928	–	–
LNW 123	4/1925	–	also 5756 but RT by 1933
LNW 141	6/1925	–	also 5761
LNW 142	9/1925	–	also 5762
25763	1935	–	–
5764	–	–	–
LNW 224	–	–	also 5765
25773	–	–	–
25776	–	–	–
LNW 248	–	1927	also 5777
LNW 252	10/1925	–	also 5780 and prob 25780
5781	–	–	also 25781
5782	1932	–	–
5783	1934	–	–
5784	6/1925	–	–
5787	11/1927	–	also 25787
25788	1934	–	–
5791	1932	–	fitted 1932, also 25791
5793	4/1925	–	–
25795	–	–	–
25796	–	–	–
5797	–	3/1928	re-fitted 1932 also 25797
LNW 296	–	1928?	fitted as 5798 and 25798
LNW 331	9/1925	–	also 5802 and 25802
LNW 357	9/1925	–	also 5804

Continued

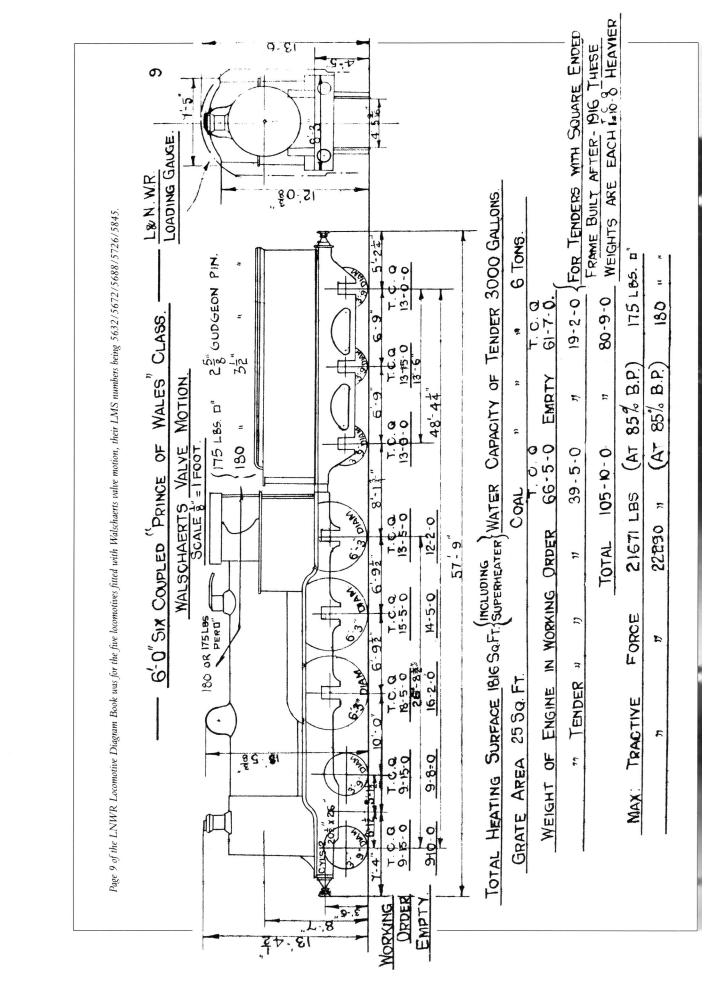

Page 9 of the LNWR Locomotive Diagram Book was for the five locomotives fitted with Walschaerts valve motion, their LMS numbers being 5632/5672/5688/5726/5845.

L&N.W.R
LOADING GAUGE.

9

— 6'-0" SIX COUPLED "PRINCE OF WALES" CLASS. —

WALSCHAERTS VALVE MOTION.
SCALE ⅛" = 1 FOOT.

TOTAL HEATING SURFACE 1816 SQ.FT. {INCLUDING SUPERHEATER} WATER CAPACITY OF TENDER 3000 GALLONS.

GRATE AREA 25 SQ.FT.

		T.C.Q	COAL		T.C.Q	6 TONS.
WEIGHT OF ENGINE IN WORKING ORDER	66·5·0	EMPTY	61·7·0
" TENDER "	39·5·0	"	19·2·0	{FOR TENDERS WITH SQUARE ENDED FRAME BUILT AFTER-1916 THESE WEIGHTS ARE EACH 1·10·8 HEAVIER
TOTAL	105·10·0	"	80·9·0

MAX. TRACTIVE FORCE   21671 LBS (AT 85% B.P.)   175 LBS. ▫"
           "   22890 " (AT 85% B.P.)   180 "   "

No.	Date	Date reverted to round-top boilers	Notes
LNW 359	6/1925	1926?	also 5805 (fitted 10/1927) and 25805
5806	1932	–	–
5811	–	–	–
5812	1933	–	–
25818	1937	–	–
LNW 198	9/1925	–	also 5819
25827	1937	–	–
25829	1932	–	–
5832	1933	–	–
25833	–	–	–
5834	1933	–	also 25834
LNW 433	12/1925	–	also 5836
5840	–	–	–
25841	–	–	–
5845	2/1924	c. 1930	also 25845 (1937)

When Belpaire boilers were fitted, the Ramsbottom type of safety valves were replaced by Ross safety valves. Other detail changes to note include the sandboxes. The first ninety locomotives to be built had the sandbox for the leading coupled wheels below the running plate behind the foot steps, but on the remainder of the class the sandbox was mounted in front of the splasher on the running plate where it was more accessible. From about 1933, any buffer replacements were of

the Stanier type as previously described in the 'George V' section. A number of locomotives had their cabs cut down to conform with the Composite loading gauge and the LNWR lamp sockets were changed to lamp holders, although this did not apply to the ninety constructed by Wm. Beardmore, which were built with lamp holders.

Over the years, a variety of tenders were coupled to locomotives of the 'Prince of Wales' class; they can be summarised as solid top with double beading in place of coal rails; two open coal rails; single open coal rail; and single beading with a solid coping, on the final style of LNW tender which had different frames from the earlier types. At least 13 locos were coupled to tenders from the 'ROD' 2–8–0s, described later in Vol 3, photographic evidence confirming the following: 5600, 5621, 5626, 5630, 5637, 5643, 5661, 5668, 5707, 5714, 5798, 5828, and 5833.

Apart from replacing the original round-top boiler with Belpaire boilers, the only other major mechanical change was the modification of four locomotives by replacing the Joy valve motion between the frames with Walschaerts valve gear outside the frames to operate the inside valves. This arrangement required the running plate to be raised. The objects were (1) accessibility of all motion parts for examination and removal in cases of running repairs. (2) The ease whereby

This picture, taken at Shrewsbury Coleham shed between August 1933 and April 1934, shows LNWR No. 867 Condor. Built by the North British Locomotive Company in January 1916, it was rebuilt with Walschaerts valve motion in March 1923 and allocated LMS stock number 5672 which was applied in October 1926. Rebuilt with a Belpaire boiler in March 1928, it later reverted to a round-top boiler. In July 1933 the name was removed, thus ending duplication with that of 'Royal Scot' No. 6145, named in February 1928. In April 1934 it was renumbered, running as No. 25672 until withdrawal in December 1936.

W. POTTER

The outside Walschaerts valve gear was fitted to five locomotives. This close-up is of LMS No. 5726 which was built in July 1919 as LNWR No. 56 and rebuilt with the outside valve gear in March 1924 and did not receive its allotted LMS stock number until February 1927. During 1926 it was converted to oil burning and in due course reverted to coal burning again. In April 1935 it was renumbered as 25726 and in July 1936 it was withdrawn.

The oil fuel conversion programme had its origins in prolonged strikes in the coal mining industry, the worst taking place during 1926, re-conversion beginning as soon as reliable coal supplies resumed. Some locomotives had one tank on the tender while others had two. This picture, taken at Stafford, shows No. 5630, with two tanks, on an Ordinary passenger train, the first coach of which, as an ex-MR vehicle, was in Midland red while the remaining four ex-LNWR carriages were still in their pre-group livery.   L&GRP

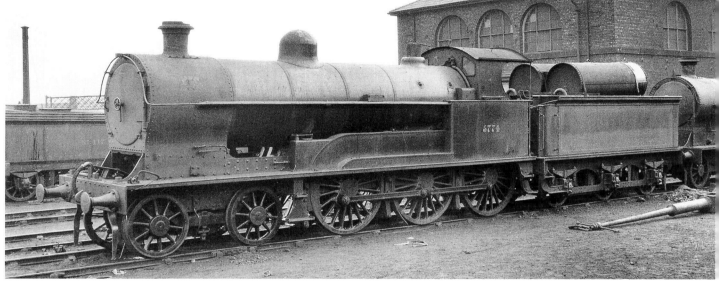

This picture of LMS No. 5774 illustrates a locomotive built by William Beardmore & Co. in September 1921 as LNWR No. 244 which was converted to burn oil in 1926, received its LMS stocknumber 5774 in February 1926 in the LNWR style on the cabside where the numberplate had been. There was no front numberplate. The locomotive was in unlined black, but the tender had LNWR lining. Allotted No. 25774 in 1934, it did not remain in traffic long enough to acquire it, being withdrawn in October 1934.   P. RANSOME-WALLIS

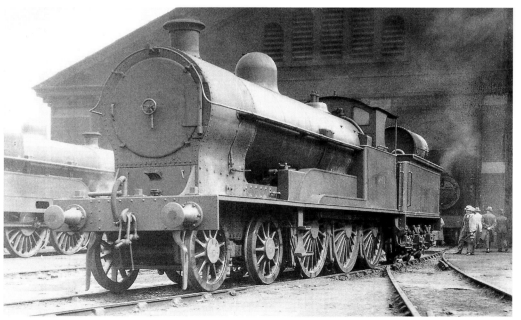

Photographed at Camden in August 1926, the year it was converted to burn oil, No. 5841 was built for the LNWR by William Beardmore & Co. in April 1922 and carried its LNWR stock number 1323 until its allotted LMS stock number was applied in April 1926. In 1934 it was renumbered 25841 and continued in service until a few months before Nationalisation, being withdrawn in September 1947.
H. C. CASSERLEY

the driver and fireman may oil and inspect parts. (3) The elimination of the hole in the connecting rod from which the drive is taken in the case of engines with Joy motion, thus causing less likelihood of bent rods when valve friction becomes excessive. (4) Decreased maintenance cost so far as the motion is concerned. (5) The advantages of an outside cylinder engine as far as accessibility is concerned and from a steady running point of view. The decision to alter these locomotives was made by the LNWR, but the work was not undertaken until after the LMS was formed in 1923. The selected locomotives were LNWR Nos. 964 (allocated LMS No. 5632, applied September 1926), 867 (allocated LMS No. 5672, applied November 1927), 56 (allocated LMS No. 5726, applied February 1927) and 2340 (allocated LMS No. 5688, applied March 1927). In this condition they acquired the nickname 'Tishy', after a famous racehorse that apparently, if the story can be believed, had a habit of crossing its legs while running. In addition to the four that were modified, a fifth, No. 5845, was built with outside Walschaerts valve gear by Wm. Beardmore. It would appear that the cost of the conversions was not justified and no further locomotives were modified. The first of these five to be withdrawn were Nos. 5632 and 5672 in September 1933, and the last was No. 5845 in December 1947.

OILBURNERS

It was reported that during the 1926 miners strike forty-six 'Prince of Wales' class were converted to burn oil, some tenders being fitted with two cylindrical tanks, others with a single rectangular tank.

Oil Fired 'Prince of Wales' class
Prepared by Peter Davis

Engine number	Name	Number of tanks
5600	Prince of Wales	–
1452 (and 5602)	Bonaventure	–
5607	Defiance	2
5608	Wolverine	–
2359	Hermione	–
362	Robert Southey	–
2075	Robert Burns	–
2198	John Ruskin	2
2213	Charles Kingsley	–
1679	Lord Byron	–
2249	Thomas Campbell	2
5628	R. B. Sheridan	–
5630	W. M. Thackeray	2
86	Mark Twain	–
146	Lewis Carroll	–
5638	Charles James Lever	–
5666	Plynlimmon	–
2175	Loadstone	–
2392	Caliban	2
88 (and 5641)	Czar of Russia	–
877 (and 5645)	Raymond Poincare	–
5651	Pluto	1
5655	Smeaton	–
5661	Gallipoli	2
849 (and 5671)	Arethusa	1
5696	–	–
5702	–	–
5703	–	–
388	–	–
1123 (and 5712)	–	–
1732	–	–

Engine number	Name	Number of tanks
56	–	–
5731	–	–
1620	–	–
5741	–	–
5750	Marathon	2
142	–	–
241	–	–
242	–	–
5774	–	2
246	–	–
252	–	–
5791	–	–
5829	–	2
433	–	–
5841	–	2

Total 46

The first conversions are believed to date from March 1926 and it took several weeks to complete all 46. Twenty of the chosen engines had already been renumbered when converted or were renumbered at the same time, while the rest retained their LNW numbers. As can be seen, five of them were actually renumbered before the oil burning equipment was removed.

LIVERY

When the LMS was formed, the 'Prince of Wales' class displayed two painting styles, plain black and lined black livery. The first ninety to be built entered traffic carrying full LNWR lining, but the final 155 were in plain black livery. Prior to October 1921 any repaints turned out of Crewe were without lining, but thereafter lining was resumed. Under LMS ownership they were at first entitled to the red livery, but, as with the other passenger classes described, the reorganisation of Crewe works meant that renumbering and repainting was not a high priority. A few were painted in red with small letters 'LMS' on the cabside, others received the LMS coat of arms on the cabside, and some were painted black without any lining.

All the 'Prince of Wales' class carried their allotted LMS stock number; the last one to be renumbered was LNWR No. 354 which became LMS No. 5820 in September 1928, over five and a half years after the grouping! The LMS 1934 renumbering scheme meant that the entire class had to be renumbered by the addition of 20000 to the 1923 stock number, but since withdrawal of the class had started in September 1933, about forty locomotives were not renumbered. Four locomotives had their nameplates removed, Nos. 5671 *Arethusa*, in September 1936, 5658 *Atlas*, 5672 *Condor*, and 5682 *Samson* in July 1933.

In their prime the 'Prince of Wales' class were to the LNWR (and indeed during the early years of the LMS Western Division) what the Stanier Class 5s became to the LMS. They were employed upon major express passenger trains, parcels and express freight turns, but with the increasing availability of the Stanier Class 5s, they were relegated to secondary work. Note that in 1926 there were twenty-six stationed in London, but by 1935 there were none and the Crewe allocation of 1926 was somewhat reduced. The two depots where they were to be found were Bletchley, and in particular Stafford, and this is confirmed by a statement in the *Railway Observer* that said, 'during the early 1940s the following locomotives, Nos. 25648, 25674, 25725, 25749,

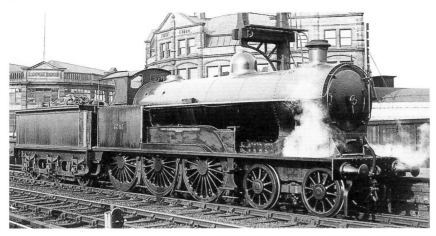

No. 5743 was built in September 1919 as LNWR No. 1178 Prince Albert. This picture was taken after the locomotive had been renumbered by the LMS in February 1926, with the number painted onto the side of the cab where the LNWR numberplate had been. In 1933 it was rebuilt with a Belpaire boiler and was withdrawn in September the following year. The locomotive is seen here in black livery without any lining.   A. C. ROBERTS

This locomotive was comparatively new when this picture was taken at Tamworth c.1925. Built in April 1922 by William Beardmore & Co., it was one of the final batch of 'Prince of Wales' class to enter service; none of them were named. The LMS stock number was applied in February 1924 and it was renumbered 25838 in October 1934 and in May 1935 it was withdrawn. We can see that the number was displayed on the side of the tender and smokebox door with a small 'LMS' on the side of the cab. Otherwise the engine was as built. Running under express passenger train headlamp code, the note on the reverse of the print states it was a down Scotch express with several of the carriages still in LNWR livery.   L&GRP

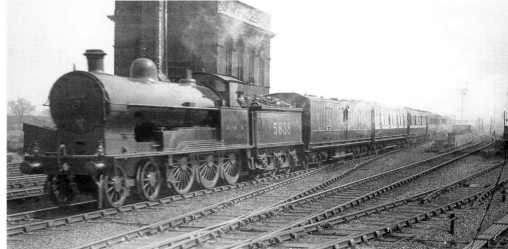

LMS No. 5607 was built at Crewe as LNWR No. 1721 Defiance in November 1911 and its allotted LMS stock number was applied in April 1926, as seen in this view. Although there was no lining on the locomotive, LNWR lining is visible on the tender. Oil-fired in 1926, it is seen here with Ross safety valves, Belpaire boiler, smokebox door numberplate, cabs to the composite loading gauge and LMS lamp holders. This locomotive was renumbered in 1904 and became 25607 in 1934 and was withdrawn during December that year.
                                                                                    REAL PHOTOGRAPHS

25752, 25775, 25787, 257981, 25818, 25841, 25845 were recorded as working in the Stafford and Crewe areas on passenger and freight trains'.

Following nationalization, the four survivors were allocated British Railway numbers 58000–58003, but Nos. 25648, 25673, 25752 and 25787 were all withdrawn before their allocated numbers were applied: the last to be withdrawn was No. 25752 in May 1949. In the final months before withdrawal, this locomotive could be seen working the 12/20pm Birmingham New Street to Stafford and the author recalls seeing this locomotive when working this service.

Built at Crewe as LNWR No. 233 in March 1916, Suvla Bay *was photographed shortly after it was renumbered by the LMS in May 1927 before the large cabside numerals were adopted as standard in 1928. It still had LNWR lamp sockets and was attached to the original type of tender (Cooke second design). The original type of boiler with two washout plugs on either side of the firebox had been modified with Ross safety valves and the 'S' on the upper side of the cab indicated an engine in 'top nick', in turn suggesting, together with the immaculate condition, that it was ex works.* COLLECTION R. J. ESSERY

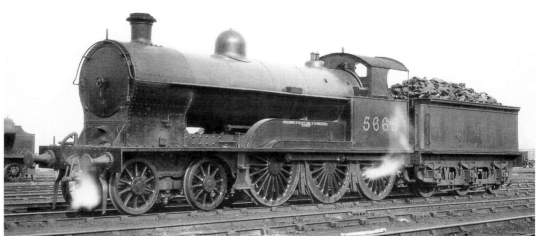

By 1930–31, when Suvla Bay *had had its cab altered to the Composite loading gauge, it had also acquired LMS lamp holders and was running with a tender of the fourth (1916) Cooke design with oval slots. Painted in the standard 1928 lined black livery, it still carried the early type of boiler for a little longer, being rebuilt with one of the Belpaire design in 1932. In June 1934 it became No. 25665 and was withdrawn from Warrington shed in April 1936.* T. S. STEEL COLLECTION

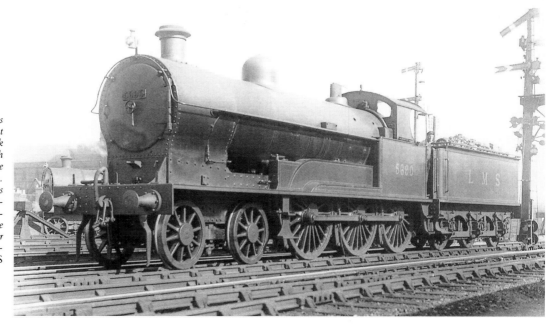

No. 5690 was built at Crewe as LNWR No. 28 in January 1919 but was never named. Its allotted LMS stock number 5690 was applied in March 1928 in small numerals where the LNWR cabside numberplate had been. In 1934 it became No. 25690 and, as we can see, it had been fitted with LMS-type lamp holders, but retained Ramsbottom safety valves. LMS lining can be seen on both the locomotive and tender and in November 1934 it was withdrawn. W. T. STUBBS

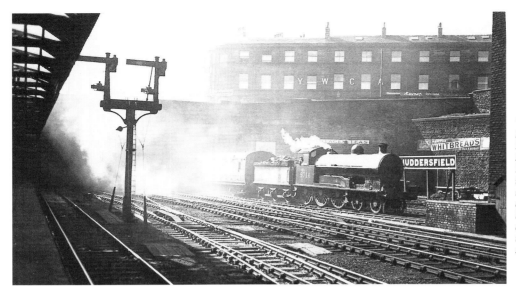

This 1932 picture of LMS No. 5716 was taken at Huddersfield when the engine was at the head of a Liverpool to Hull express passenger train. Built in May 1919 as LNWR No. 1670, it became LMS No. 5716 in February 1927, was renumbered again in January 1935 as 25716, and withdrawn a few months later in August 1935. The cab had been altered to the Composite gauge, Ross safety valve had replaced the original Ramsbottom safety valve and there was an oil reservoir above the boiler hand rail. We can also see that the original LNWR lamp sockets had been replaced by LMS type.

G.H. SOOLE

No. 5659 was built by North British in December 1915 as LNWR No. 2392 Caliban and had been converted to oil burning in 1926. The LMS number was applied in May 1928. This photograph, taken at Rugby on 2nd April 1932, shows the engine waiting to take over the 8.20 Carlisle to Euston express passenger train. Note the flat smokebox door, no centre handle, and door secured by eight bolt fixings spread around the circumference of the door. Ross safety valves and LMS lamp holders are also apparent. The following year it was fitted with a Belpaire boiler until withdrawal in September 1936.

COLLECTION R.J. ESSERY

No. 5650, seen here at Derby in June 1933, was almost certainly working the late-morning express service from Derby to Llandudno which the engine, allocated to Stoke, would have worked as far as Crewe. Built in January 1916 as LNWR No. 606 Castor, it was an early example of a red 'Prince' having been turned out of Crewe in March 1924 with LMS stock number and code A2 livery. It became No. 25650 in May 1934, ending its days in April 1936.

H. C. CASSERLEY

A number of 'Prince of Wales' class were coupled to ex-'ROD' tenders, ostensibly for working over the Midland Division where their greater water capacity was essential because of the more widely spaced water troughs However, many of these 'Princes' still worked over the Western Division where, although troughs were more plentiful, the extra ton of coal gave a longer range. Here we illustrate three 'Princes' running with this Great Central design of tender. Top No. 5798 was built by William Beardmore & Co. in November 1921 as LNWR No. 296 and was fitted with a Belpaire boiler in April 1925 before acquiring its LMS stock number in February 1927. During a visit to Crewe Works sometime between 1928 and 1930 it was fitted with a Cooke round-top boiler with only two washout plugs on either side, the cab was altered to the Midland profile and it emerged in the 1928 livery attached to the ex-'ROD' tender seen in the photograph. Becoming No. 25798 in November 1934, the engine was withdrawn in August 1939 only to be reinstated a few months later in 1940. It lasted in service until June 1945. Middle: LNWR No. 2205 Thomas Moore was a Crewe product of November 1913, becoming LMS No. 5621 in January 1927. Like No. 5798 (above) it had been fitted with LMS lamp holders and Ross safety valves but, in this case, there was no smokebox numberplate. The shed plate at the bottom of the smokebox door, Code 15 (Crewe), dates this photograph post-1930. The cab was altered to the Midland loading gauge in January 1930, and the 'ROD' tender was presumably attached at the same time. Withdrawal came in August 1934 only three months after the engine became No. 25621. Bottom: Seen here attached to a freshly coaled 'ROD' tender on 31st July 1932, No. 5833 was photographed at its home shed Carlisle Upperby (code 29). Built by Beardmore & Co. in March 1922 as LNWR No. 1339, it was renumbered by the LMS in April 1927, and again in April 1934 as No. 25833, and withdrawn in June 1937. As far as we know, this engine never had its cab altered to the Composite Loading Gauge and always worked on the Western Division.

COLLECTION R. J. ESSERY and
L. W. PERKINS/SLS COLLECTION

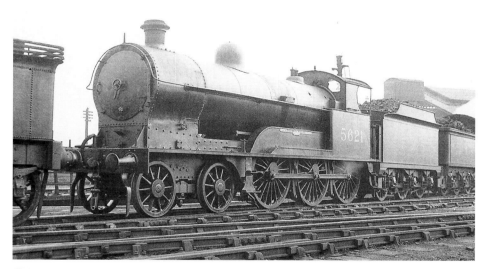

This right-hand side picture of LMS No. 25672 was taken in October 1936 at Willesden and provides a good view of the Walschaerts valve gear. LMS lamp holders had been fitted and Ross safety valves had replaced the Ramsbottom safety valves. The cab had been altered to conform to the Composite loading gauge, an oil reservoir had been fitted at the side of the boiler above the handrail, and the tender is an example of the Bowen Cooke third type.

H. C. CASSERLEY

This picture, taken at Shrewsbury on 9th May 1935, shows LNWR No. 867 Condor after it had twice been renumbered by the LMS. Full details of this engine's chequered history can be found on page 101. Here it had just backed onto the 2.25 p.m. passenger train to Hereford consisting of four GWR Dean clerestory carriages.

V. R. WEBSTER/
KIDDERMINSTER
RAILWAY MUSEUM

Here, a few minutes after the above photograph was taken, we see No. 25672 in the process of leaving Shrewsbury with the 2.25 p.m. stopping train to Hereford. The single headlamp in front of the chimney indicates the train's status as 'Ordinary Passenger'. Note the trespass notice to the right of the picture. These were found in a variety of places on the railway system and in this case was to warn passengers not to use the barrow crossing to move from one platform to another.

V. R. WEBSTER/KIDDERMINSTER RAILWAY MUSEUM

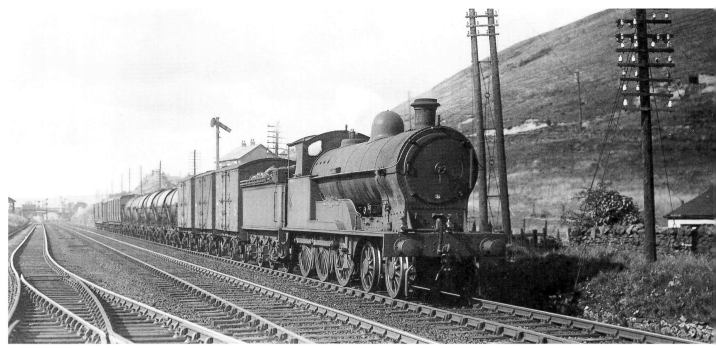

It was not uncommon to use passenger engines to work goods trains, and at first sight this south bound working seen leaving Tebay, could be described as a goods train, but the locomotive headlamp code (one lamp on the right side and one in the middle of the buffer beam) was for a parcels, newspaper, fish, milk, fruit, horse, or perishable train, composed of coaching stock, which meant stock that could run in most passenger trains. LNWR No. 88 Czar of Russia, seen in this undated picture, was built in 1915 and received its LMS stock number 5641 in July 1926 and was renumbered again in May 1934 when it became 25461. It is recorded as being rebuilt with a Belpaire boiler in 1934 which suggests this picture was taken after 1930 when shedplates were moved from cab roofs to smokebox doors and before the Belpaire boiler was fitted. This locomotive remained in service until March 1936 when it was withdrawn.

T. S. STEELE COLLECTION

We have included the two pictures of No. 25674 to show how a change of boiler from round-top to Belpaire altered the appearance of the locomotive. Built by the North British Locomotive Company Ltd as LNWR No. 1132 Scott, the changes began in August 1923 when the cab was altered to conform to the Midland loading gauge. The LMS stock number 5674 was applied in April 1926 and a Belpaire boiler replaced the round-top boiler in 1931, only to be replaced at the engine's next general overhaul, in or around 1934, with another round-top one. During 1935 the locomotive was renumbered 25674 and during a visit to Crewe Works in 1938 it acquired another Belpaire boiler. Both views were taken at Shrewsbury, the upper one on 4th August 1936 and the lower one about two years later. From the mid-1930s until it was withdrawn in February 1946 No. 25674 was allocated to Stafford shed (5C) and was probably working the Swansea portion of expresses to or from Euston when pictured.   L. HANSON

A broadside picture of a 'Prince' built in January 1914 as LNWR No. 1400 Felicia Hemens *and given the LMS stock number 5631 in February 1927. Later, in May 1934, it was renumbered 25631 and two years later, in June 1936, it was withdrawn from service. Note that Ross safety valves had replaced the Ramsbottom valves, there was an oil reservoir above the boiler handrail and the engine was coupled to the fourth type of Bowen Cooke tender. Finally, note the power class 4P displayed on the cabside.*
T. S. STEEL COLLECTION

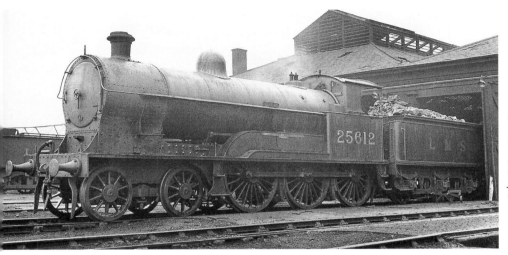

Built at Crewe in October 1913 as LNWR No. 1081 John Keats, *this engine received its LMS stock number 5612 in February 1925. Ten years later in 1935 it became No. 25612, but the second LMS number was not carried for long because the engine was withdrawn in January 1936. This picture was taken at Crewe North, the locomotive's home shed, on 13th October 1935.* L. W. PERKINS

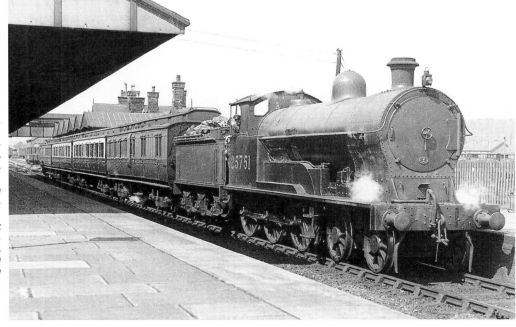

Another of Shrewsbury Coleham shed's 'Princes' was photographed at Craven Arms in the 1935–36 period heading the 2.25 p.m. Ordinary passenger train to Hereford consisting of the same set of GWR carriages shown on page 107. For the record, all four coaches were 50ft long, the first was a Diagram 24 four-compartment brake third, next came a lavatory composite, a lavatory third and finally a five-compartment brake third. Built at Crewe in November 1919 as LNWR No. 1549, this locomotive received its allotted LMS stock number 5751 in August 1925 and in January 1935 was renumbered 25751 and, two years later, acquired a Belpaire boiler. It remained in service until withdrawn from Bletchley shed in July 1944. LENS OF SUTTON

Above and right: Two 'Princes' photographed at Berkhamsted in the late 1930s. In the upper view No. 25683 was pulling away from the station with a down stopping passenger train in September 1938 while No. 25763 was leaving the station with an up stopping passenger train in April 1939. No. 25683 began life in April 1916 as LNWR No. 1324, a member of the last batch of 'Princes' to be named when built during the Great War, in this case Falaba. The allotted LMS No. 5683 was applied in May 1927 and the duplicate No. 25683 in January 1935. In December of that year the engine acquired its second Belpaire boiler, this time retaining one of that type until withdrawn from service in January 1946. No. 25763 was built by Beardmore as No. 145 in August 1921. In August 1927 the engine was turned out as LMS No. 5763 and became No. 25763 in December 1934. In 1935 it was fitted with a Belpaire boiler but had reverted to a round-top one before this photograph was taken. No. 25763 survived only a few more months until withdrawn in September 1939. These two photographs are the work of the legendary H. C. (Henry) Casserley who had moved his family to a new house in Berkhamsted overlooking the railway in that year and, hardly surprisingly (see below), there are other photos of 'Princes' at the same location at this period taken by him.   Both H. C. CASSERLEY

As described in the text, No. 25845 was built by Wm. Beardmore for display at the 1924 Wembley Exhibition and taken into LMS stock as No. 5845 in November 1924. In September 1934 it was renumbered 25845 and withdrawn in November 1947. This picture shows the outside Walschaerts valve gear and the second Belpaire boiler that in 1937 replaced the round-top boiler fitted in the early 1930s and that the engine was coupled to the final type of Bowen Cooke tender.
COLLECTION R. J. ESSERY

Here is another of Henry Casserley's photographs at Berkhamsted, this time in August 1939 and showing No. 25845 at the head of another Ordinary passenger train, probably bound for Bletchley, although with that amount of coal on the tender, the service may have been a Euston to Northampton 'out and back' with the engine being turned, but the tender would not be 'topped up' with coal, although the fireman would doubtless have cleaned the fire before the return journey.   H. C. CASSERLEY

Two more Casserley photographs both showing the same 'Prince of Wales'. The upper view dates from Friday 26th July 1940 and shows No. 25722 leaving Berkhamsted with a down Ordinary passenger train, probably the 6.5 p.m. from Euston to Bletchley, due there at 6.54 p.m. Henry would have caught an earlier train home from work in the Prudential Assurance Company and was taking advantage of the light evenings. The sidings in the foreground were host to some interesting Private Owner coal wagons in various stages of unloading. The engine was built as LNWR No. 501 in June 1919 being one of a large number of the class built after the First World War to remain unnamed. Note the sandbox mounted at the front of the splasher, a feature of all the later batches of the class. This engine was renumbered 5722 in March 1927 and its cab was altered to the Composite loading gauge in July 1931. Shortly after it became No. 25722 in 1934, a Belpaire boiler was fitted. It was withdrawn in March 1948 from Bletchley, its home shed since the late 1930s. When photographed, the engine was finished in the shortlived '1936-style' with sans serif insignia (livery code B11) with 14in letters and 10in numerals. Bottom: In May 1938 No. 25722 was captured on film while reversing onto a Bletchley train at Cambridge. As the engine had standard serif lettering and numerals at this date, it must have been one of the last to receive the '1936-style' sans serif insignia during its next works visit later in 1938 as this style was abandoned during that summer.   H. C. CASSERLEY

On this page we show two pictures of LNWR No. 2396 Queen of the Belgians, *which was built in December 1915 and received its LMS stock number 5648 in May 1927. It was renumbered as 25648 in May 1934 and withdrawn in October 1948. The top picture was taken at Rugby on 6th August 1942 and the lower picture at Stafford in April 1946. The tender was the third Bowen Cooke design and the view at Rugby suggests the engine had just come off shed and would shortly take over a train. I have fond memories of the locomotive; during the later 1940s, before I started work at Saltley, I worked in the City of Birmingham and spent my lunch hours at New Street station and frequently saw* Queen of the Belgians *which was working Birmingham to Stafford passenger trains.*

V. R. WEBSTER/KIDDERMINSTER RAILWAY MUSEUM and H. C. CASSERLEY

During their final years of service, it was common for 'Princes' to be employed on the cross-country service between Oxford and Cambridge. This picture shows the last to be built, LMS No. 25845, approaching Oxford with an Ordinary passenger train in March 1946. Readers are advised that there is a close-up of the outside Walschaerts valve gear fitted to five of the class on page 101, and the reason why No. 5845 was built is given on page 97.

H. C. CASSERLEY

No. 25673 at Crewe in May 1947. One of six to become British Railways stock in 1949, it was allocated No. 58001 as its BR stock number, but it was withdrawn in January 1949 before it was applied.

H. C. CASSERLEY

This picture of No. 25752 was taken at Crewe during May 1949 following its withdrawal that month. Built in November 1919 as LNWR No. 1557, the allotted stock number 5752 was applied in May 1927 and in June 1934 it was renumbered again, becoming 25752. The cab had been altered in January 1930 to the Composite loading gauge, and in February 1939 it was withdrawn, but following the outbreak of war in September 1939, it was not cut up and returned to traffic in 1940. It was allotted the number 58002 by British Railways, but it was not applied before it was withdrawn in May 1949. This picture provides a good view of the curve of the cab that allowed it to run over the Midland Division if required and confirms that it was coupled to the final type of Bowen Cooke tender.

H. C. CASSERLEY

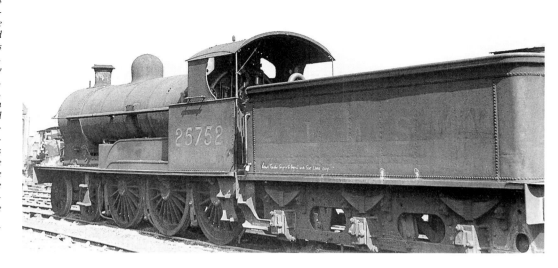

Ultimate Allocations	1926	28th September 1935	8th April 1944	31st December 1947
Camden	5670–5688			
Willesden	5664–5669			
Bletchley	5662–5663	25669, 25692, 25706, 25737, 25768, 25790, 25728, 25828	25673, 25683, 25694, 25722, 25751, 25752, 25791, 25797, 25804, 25805, 25818, 25827, 25845	25722, 25827
Rugby	5648–5661	25620, 25624, 25638, 25658, 25671, 25834, 25675, 25684, 25746, 25757, 25784, 25820		
Aston	5825–5826	25653, 25712, 25781		
Monument Lane	5827–5829	25672		
Stafford	5823–5824	25648, 25674, 25680, 25648, 25673, 25752, 25787, 25689, 25825–27, 25830	25648, 25674, 25725, 25749, 25775, 25787, 25798, 25802, 25841	25648, 25673, 25752, 25787
Crewe North	5600–5647, 5845	25612, 25627, 25631, 25637, 25640–42, 25662, 25698, 25700, 25728, 25744, 25753, 25791, 25795, 25803		
Longsight	5689–5713	25702–03, 25771, 25785, 25788, 25833		
Stockport	5783–5784			
Farnley Junction	5792–5803	25793–94, 25804		
Huddersfield	5804–5808	25792, 25796, 25800		
Holyhead	5785–5791			
Warrington	5817–5819	25625, 25644, 25665, 25697, 25779–80, 25787, 25823		
Springs Branch	5809–5816	25725, 25730, 25740, 25752, 25756, 25812–13, 25816–18		
Edge Hill	5714–5733	25717–18, 25767, 25777		
Preston	5752–5764	25670, 25776, 25822		
Carnforth	5762–5764	25708, 25764, 25821		
Oxenholme	5765–5767	25712		
Carlisle	5768–5782			
Salop/Shrewsbury	5830–5831	25645, 25672, 25726, 25751, 25775, 25845		
Patricroft	5734–5751	25693, 25732, 25739, 25741, 25747–49		
Llandudno Junction	5832–5836	25656, 25691, 25762–63, 25769, 25829, 25832		
Walsall		25626, 25660, 25721, 25723, 25835		
Chester		25657, 25683, 25685, 25704, 25720, 25750, 25772–3		
Nuneaton		25694, 25699, 25819		
Stoke		25650, 25836		
Southport		25798, 25801, 25805, 25844		
Wigan		25802, 25841		
Bury		25839, 25842–43		

'B' Division 5837–5844. No specific sheds were given, just a divisional allocation (Ex-LYR sheds)
'N.S' Division 5820–5823. They were allocated to ex-North Stafford Railway sheds but no details were given in this 1926 document.

LNWR Locomotive Diagram Book page 4, seen here, was allocated to the 6ft 6in 'Claughton' class in their original condition and this diagram shows that a 3000 gallon 6-ton capacity tender was used with this class. The diagram for those locomotives rebuilt with the larger 5ft 5in boilers will be found at page 120.

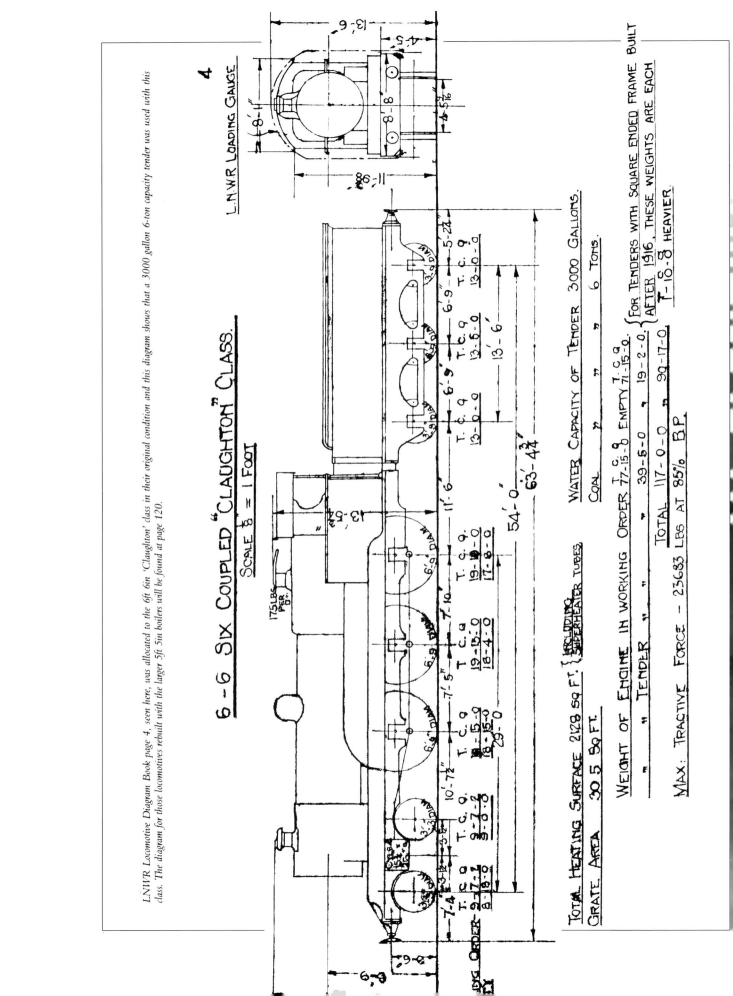

4–6–0 Passenger Tender, LNW 'Claughton'

Motive Power Classification 5 & 5X, post-1928 5P & 5XP
Allocated LMS locomotive number series 5900–6029

LMS No. 5997 was built in July 1920 as LNWR No. 11 and did not receive its allotted LMS stock number until June 1927 and later (around 1930) the cab roof was altered to conform to the Midland Railway loading gauge. When this photograph was taken, the locomotive was in red livery code A7, the most common applied to the class post 1928. No. 5997 was withdrawn in July 1933.
COLLECTION R.J. ESSERY

The 130 members of the 'Claughton' class, built between 1913–1921, represented the final and most powerful class of passenger tender locomotives built by the LNWR. Unfortunately, during the early years of the LMS, the shortcomings of these four-cylinder engines became apparent and their life, in their original condition, was rather short. Readers who may care to delve more deeply into the subject may be interested to read a detailed study of the class that has been published by Wild Swan Publications as an Historical Monograph, *The Claughton & Patriot 4–6–0s*, see Bibliography.

By July 1913 the first ten 'Claughtons' were in service and as such were a marked improvement upon the locomotives that had been available to work the principal express passenger trains for the company. There were some differences between the first locomotive, No. 2222 *Sir Gilbert Claughton* and the other nine; however, by the time they became LMS stock, the pioneer engine was similar to the other members of the class. The first thirty locomotives were fitted with a damper for the superheater and the operating gear was combined with the horizontal handrail that ran alongside the boiler. In keeping with the practice at this time, they were also fitted with a pyrometer for measuring the superheater temperature. There was a gauge in the cab connected to the smokebox by a pipe that ran along the right-hand side of the locomotive, but from about 1919 both fittings were removed. However, it is possible that some locomotives may still have been fitted with this equipment in 1923.

Sand shields were fitted close to the leading coupled wheels and later to the centre pair. The idea was to prevent the sand being blown away from the head of the rail. However, by 1922 they were being removed although some 'Claughtons' still retained them under the LMS. When they became LMS stock, all had been fitted with two oil reservoirs on each horizontal handrail alongside the boiler and had larger reversing gear covers. In 1923 it was also becoming clear that the early 'Claughtons' were showing signs of wear and tear; in particular there were problems with the trailing coupled wheel bearings, and coal consumption was rising. During 1925/6 Derby Works was engaged in trying to improve the performance of the 'Claughtons'; this work included modifications to the ashpan, firebars and arrangement of the brick arch as well as new tubeplates and tubes. Unfortunately, as described in the historical monograph mentioned above, no records of similar work undertaken at Crewe have come to light. Other changes included the replacement of the original LNWR safety valves by Ross safety valves by about 1925 and later work included replacement buffers of the Stanier type with the square base, but only a few of the 'Claughtons' in original condition received them.

In October 1921 locomotives that were repainted before returning to traffic were given full LNWR lining but many came to the LMS in plain black. The first locomotive to emerge from Crewe carrying LMS livery was No. 5971, which ex-works in July 1923 entered traffic carrying 18 inch

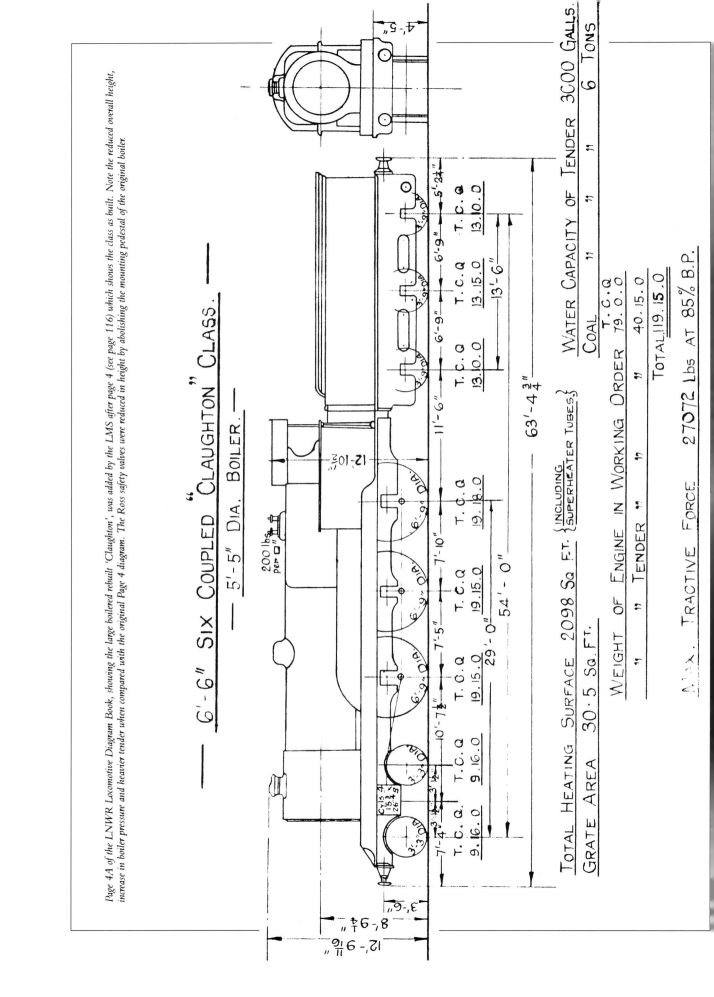

— 6'-6" SIX COUPLED "CLAUGHTON" CLASS. —

— 5'-5" DIA. BOILER. —

Page 4A of the LNWR Locomotive Diagram Book, showing the large boilered rebuilt 'Claughton', was added by the LMS after page 4 (see page 116) which shows the class as built. Note the reduced overall height, increase in boiler pressure and heavier tender when compared with the original Page 4 diagram. The Ross safety valves were reduced in height by abolishing the mounting pedestal of the original boiler.

TOTAL HEATING SURFACE 2098 SQ. FT. { INCLUDING SUPERHEATER TUBES }

GRATE AREA 30·5 SQ. FT.

WATER CAPACITY OF TENDER 3000 GALLS.

COAL " " " 6 TONS

WEIGHT OF ENGINE IN WORKING ORDER 79.0.0 T.C.Q

" " TENDER " " 40.15.0

TOTAL 119.15.0

MAX. TRACTIVE FORCE 27072 LBS AT 85% B.P.

numerals on the side of the tender with the small letters 'LMS' on the side of the cab. As previously mentioned, the reorganisation of Crewe works delayed repainting and renumbering and it was not until June 1928 that the final member of the class, No. 6020, was dealt with. Thereafter red with yellow lining remained the standard for the class with the stock number displayed on the cabside.

The first major change to the class came in 1926 when an attempt was made to try to reduce the high coal consumption by fitting Caprotti valve gear to a trial engine in the expectation that there would be a saving of 10% in coal consumption. The locomotive selected was No. 5908 and, as a result of the favourable performance, another nine were rebuilt in 1928 with Caprotti valve gear and a larger boiler; they were Nos. 5927, 5946, 5948, 5957, 5962, 5975, 6013, 6023 and 6029. Although it was not obvious at the time, the decision to order fifty new 4–6–0s, the 'Royal Scots', that were an improved and more powerful engine than the 'Claughtons', marked the beginning of the end for the 'Claughtons' in their original condition. The original design for the 'Claughtons' envisaged a larger boiler than was eventually used. The LNWR Chief Engineer would not allow locomotives with the increased axle load to run and, in order to reduce weight, a smaller boiler was designed, but by the mid 1920s, this requirement was relaxed somewhat, and in 1928 twenty 'Claughtons' were reboilered with what the LMS classified as Class G9S boilers, which were larger, 6 inch greater diameter, and thus heavier than the original boiler. The trial Caprotti valve gear engine No. 5908 was one of the twenty that were rebuilt with the new larger boiler, and the numbers of the other nine Caprotti valve gear engines, that were also reboilered, are given above. The other ten to be reboilered continued to retain their original Walschaerts valve gear and were Nos. 5906, 5910, 5953, 5970, 5972, 5986, 5993, 5999, 6004 and 6017.

The arrival of the 'Royal Scots' on the West Coast mainline meant the 'Claughtons' were displaced from working the most important expresses and, as was normal practice when new more powerful locomotives became available, there was a 'cascading down' and a number of 'Claughtons' were transferred to the Midland Division to work over the line from London St Pancras to Carlisle.

'Claughtons' on the Midland. Original allocation c.1928

Carlisle Durranhill (M.33)

5900	Sir Gilbert Claughton	Transferred to M.28 'later'
5923	Sir Guy Calthrop	Transferred to M.3 'later' (to work Carlisle Goods)
5932	Sir Thomas Williams	Transferred to M.28 'later'
5944	–	
5949	–	
5960	–	

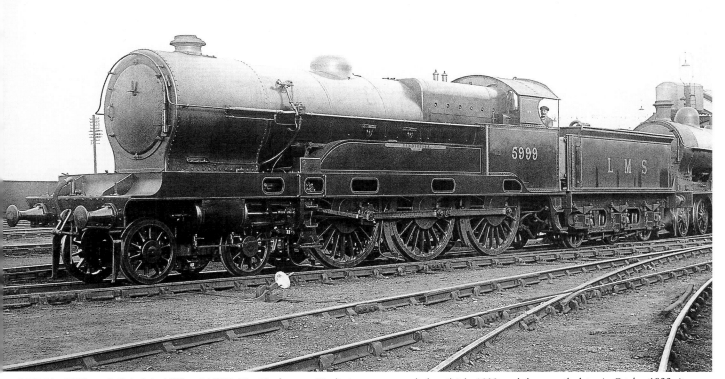

LMS No. 5999 was built in July 1920 as LNWR No. 13, the name Vindictive *was not applied until July 1922, and three months later, in October 1922, it was renumbered and ran as LNWR No. 2430 until March 1927 when the LMS stock number was applied. The following year, during April 1928, it was rebuilt with a 5ft 5in boiler and the cab altered to conform to the Midland loading gauge, as seen here, where it displayed livery code A8.* COLLECTION R. J. ESSERY

Leeds Holbeck (M.28)

5971	*Croxteth*	
5977	–	
5978	–	
5984	–	Transferred to M.3 'later' (to work Carlisle Goods)
6001	–	
6005	–	
6025	–	

Kentish Town (M.16)

5973	–	
5974	–	Later transferred to Sheffield

NB. These two engines may have spent part of their time at Holbeck.

The object was to reduce double-heading on the S&C and contemporary accounts say they did well; certainly Durranhill kept their allocation very clean and the enginemen liked them. All the Midland 'Claughtons' ran with ROD tenders of course. In 1930 a further batch arrived at Holbeck:

5905	*Lord Rathmore*	
5912	*Lord Faber*	Transferred to M33 11/33 and to M28 9/34
5933	–	
5940	*Columbus*	Transferred to Crewe just before withdrawal
5942	–	
5968	*John o'Gaunt*	
5976	*Private E. Sykes, V.C.*	Transferred to Upperby just before withdrawal

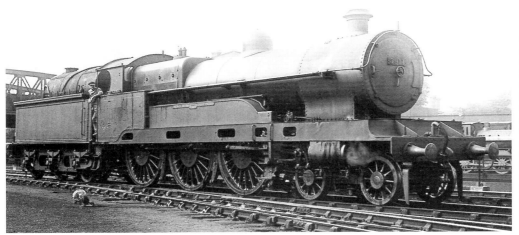

Over thirty locomotives were converted to burn oil during the miners' strike in 1926 when stocks of coal declined; however, the equipment was removed when the industrial problems in the coal mining industry were resolved. Various arrangements of oil tanks were used; here we show two on Nos. 5911 and 5926. 5911 was built in August 1914 as LNWR No. 260 W.E. Dorrington and its LMS stock number 5911 was applied in May 1926. As we can see, the engine and tender were painted black, there was no lining on them, and the stock number was carried on a smokebox numberplate. This picture was taken at Camden and the locomotive remained in service until March 1934 when it was withdrawn.

A. C. ROBERTS

This picture of LMS No. 5926 shows a twin tank mounted on the tender. Built in August 1916 as LNWR No. 2204 Sir Herbert Walker, it was renamed Sir Herbert Walker K.C.B. during April 1917. The allotted LMS stock number 5926 was applied in June 1926 but only displayed on the smokebox door numberplate. This locomotive remained in traffic until January 1933 when it was withdrawn from service.

COLLECTION R.J. ESSERY

Short term loans: No. 5955 transferred from Crewe to Holbeck (1934), No. 5964 *Patriot* at Kentish Town 1931, back at Rugby 7/32. All other engines withdrawn from the Midland Division.
(Ref. Bernard Roberts. 'Claughtons on the Midland', in *The Mancunian*, the bulletin of the Manchester Locomotive Society reprinted in *SLS Journal Vol. 51 No. 603. Oct. 1975*.)

Before they could run over the Midland Division, their cabs had to be altered to conform to the Midland loading gauge and the work entailed lowering the edge of the cab roof by 3 inches. A further change was required to enable 'Claughtons' to run north of Carlisle over the old GSWR and Caledonian lines. The Caledonian loading gauge maximum height was 12ft 11in which required a cut-down cab roof, chimney and dome. In addition, the engine whistle was removed from above the cab to be mounted in front of it in a horizontal position, and the pop safety valves were shorter than those normally used, and placed across the centre line rather than along it.

Besides the twenty large boilered engines listed above, a further eleven 'Claughtons' were altered to the Scottish loading gauge as well as the Midland cab profile. The seven members of the class transferred to the Midland Division in 1930 (see above) had been modified in this way so that they could take over Leeds Holbeck's Glasgow St. Enoch diagrams via the ex-Glasgow & South Western (Glasgow, Barrhead & Kilmarnock Joint) main line with its height limit of 12ft 11in. The remaining four 'Claughtons' in this category, Nos. 5915, 5917, 5926 and 5979, were, it is believed, at first allocated to Carlisle Kingmoor for operating over ex-Caledonian metals. Just why such a drastic cut down (see Diagram p. 120) was carried out in 1928, when the main line to Glasgow Central had been altered to a 13ft 3in height gauge in 1927 to accommodate the 'Royal Scot' class, must remain a mystery. Perhaps it was envisaged that 'Claughtons' might find employment on secondary ex-Caledonian routes such as the Callander & Oban! Within a few years the G&SW main line had also been brought up to the same height gauge as the Caledonian. The height limit on the Highland main line had always been a more generous 13ft 5in.

Including the large boiler engines, a total of sixty-three 'Claughtons' were altered to the Midland loading gauge. The *Claughtons and Patriots* monograph lists the numbers of forty-three of them, the others being Nos. 5905, 5912, 5926, 5927, 5933, 5940, 5942, 5946, 5953, 5957, 5962, 5968, 5972, 5976, 5986, 5999, 6004, 6013, 6017 and 6023.

Whilst it is known that 'Claughtons' worked into the Northern Division, no evidence has been found that any were allocated to Scottish sheds. One authority (Peter Tatlow, *LMS Journal*, 85th Anniversary edition) believes that Nos. 5905, 5912, 5915, 5917, 5933, 5940, 5942 and 5976 were all allocated to the Northern Division at various dates between 1928 and 1929. This, of course, could refer to Carlisle Kingmoor shed as previously mentioned. Tatlow omits No. 5926 from his list but includes No. 5997 – known to have been altered to the Midland loading gauge.

Another change to be noted was the conversion of some locomotives to burn oil during the 1926 miners strike. It was recorded by Yeadon's *Compendium of LNWR Locomotives Part 2* that thirty-seven 'Claughtons' were so equipped, but no numbers are given. *The Historical Monograph* lists thirty-two

A poor quality but rare view looking down onto LNWR No. 32 at Camden in 1923–4.   R. GRIEFFENHAGEN

and photographic evidence in the author's collection confirms the following: 5900, 5926, 5941, 5950, 5960 and LNW 208 (later LMS 6024), and Peter Davis has compiled the following list. Photographic evidence suggests that the first few conversions carried a single large tank on the tender, as No. 2221 had in 1921, but the later conversions were given two smaller tanks. A total of thirty-seven have been identified, namely:

Oil Fired 'Claughton' class

Engine number	Name	Number of tanks (from photos although it is likely that all 37 had two tanks)
5900	*Sir Gilbert Claughton*	2 (also 1 as 2222 in 1921)
5901	*Sir Robert Turnbull*	–
5907	*Sir Frederick Harrison*	–
163 and 5904	*Holand Hibbert*	–
2046	*Charles N. Lawrence*	–
5911	*W. E. Dorrington*	1
5912	*Lord Faber*	–
2239	*Frederick Baynes*	–
968	*Lord Kenyon*	–

Continued

This delightful picture was taken at Kenton in 1926 and shows the composition of a down express passenger train some three years after the grouping; note the mixture of carriages still in LNWR livery with others painted in LMS livery. The locomotive, LNWR No. 2179, was built in January 1920, and became LMS No. 5969, the LMS stock number being applied in January 1927. It had a short life, being withdrawn in September 1934.

T. S. STEEL COLLECTION

This undated picture shows LMS No. 5936, in red livery, code A7, at Tring heading a down express passenger train. Built as LNWR No. 1334 in April 1917, it received its LMS stock number in December 1926, having been converted to burn oil fuel earlier that year and was subsequently altered to burn coal again, as seen here. It was withdrawn in August 1932.

COLLECTION R.J. ESSERY

Oil-fired 'Claughton' class *continued*

Engine number	Name	Number of tanks (from photos although it is likely that all 37 had two tanks)	Engine number	Name	Number of tanks (from photos although it is likely that all 37 had two tanks)
1345	James Bishop	–	201 and 5983	–	–
2204 and 5926	Sir Herbert Walker K.C.B.	1, later 2	5984	–	–
5931	Captain Fryatt	–	5986	–	–
1334	–	–	5989	–	–
5939	Clio	–	1326	–	–
1335	–	–	5992	–	–
2373	Tennyson	–	5994	–	–
5947	–	–	6003	–	–
5950	–	2	63	–	–
2426 and 5959	–	–	119	–	–
1914 and 5964	Patriot	–	6012	–	–
5960	–	2	6015	Private E. Sykes VC	–
1726	–	–	208	–	2
5980	–	–	6028	–	–
			Total 37		

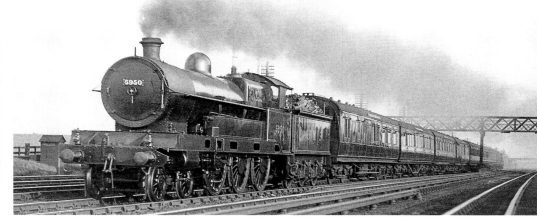

This early LMS period picture taken at Kenton on 28th April 1928 shows LNWR No. 116, which was built in August 1917, on a down Ulster express. The LMS stock number 5950 had been applied in September 1923. The engine, which was never named, had been converted to burn oil fuel during 1926 and was withdrawn in October 1934. COLLECTION R.J. ESSERY

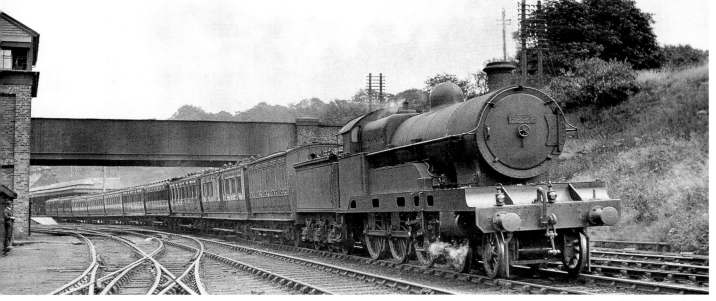

This picture, taken at Oxenholme sometime in the mid 1920s, appears in Yeadon's Compendium of LNWR Locomotives *wherein the engine, LNWR No. 2411 of June 1917 and renumbered 5944 when painted red in September 1923, is described as 'leaving . . . on an Edinburgh to Manchester train', presumably from a note on the back of the original print. This must have been an error because this train was composed of LNWR 50ft arc-roofed carriages fitted with vacuum brakes only and therefore, at that period, incapable of working north of Carlisle. As the engine was working on 'drifting steam' (the regulator was only cracked open in order to maintain lubrication), this train had run through the station without stopping and, judging by the headcode, was an empty stock train, the engine working to Crewe and its home shed Crewe North. 'Stock trains' were used to move surplus passenger vehicles from main stations to where they were next required. In this case the train is likely to have been the 'stock train' shown in the Lancaster & Carlisle District Working Timetable as leaving Carlisle Citadel at 10.15 a.m., stopping as required at Oxenholme at 11.47 a.m. These older vehicles (1895–1900) were probably destined for Wolverton Carriage Works for overhaul/disposal. This engine would have carried the code A2 livery, with small cabside letters when renumbered but had been given the LMS emblem, thus making it code A1, at a later date when the cab was altered to the Midland loading gauge as seen here.* COLLECTION R.J. ESSERY

Built in April 1920 as LNWR No. 201, this locomotive was not named. It was modified to burn oil during 1926 and the LMS stock number 5983 was applied in June of that year, but the date the cab was modified to conform to the Midland loading gauge does not appear to have been recorded. This picture, taken at Camden, shows a 'Claug*ton' in the most widely applied post-1928 livery, code A7, which it carried until withdrawn in October 1932.

COLLECTION R.J. ESSERY

At least three types of LNWR tender were coupled to the class, but generally the type with the single beaded coal guard was preferred; other variations are noted in the captions. From 1927 locomotives could be seen coupled to ROD tenders.

When compared to the original 'Claughton' tender, the increase in water capacity was most useful when working on the Midland Division where the distance between water troughs was much greater than on the Western Division.

The first 'Claughton' to be withdrawn was No. 5971. This was the result of an accident at Doe Hill, near Chesterfield, when there was a head-on collision at about midnight on 12th February 1929, and the locomotive was found to be beyond economic repair. Plans to rebuild the 'Claughtons' as three-cylinder engines were made and on 6th December 1929 an order was issued to rebuild two locomotives. Before work began, a second head-on collision on 6th March 1930 at Culgaith, which involved No. 5902, presented the opportunity to use the damaged engines and Nos. 5971 and 5902 became the basis for the 'Patriot' Class. A total of forty-two 'Claughtons' were withdrawn and replaced by 'Patriots', two in 1930 and forty during 1932/33. By 1935 the 'Claughtons' that retained their original boilers had all been withdrawn, leaving the reboilered locomotives to continue in service, but increasing numbers of new standard locomotives, Class 5 and 5XP, meant their days were numbered. In the same year No. 5986, the first of the of the rebuilt 'Claughtons', was taken out of service and in 1936 the last of the Caprotti engines was withdrawn, leaving just ten Walschaerts valve gear engines in traffic. At the outbreak of the Second World War, four were left, but one, 6017, was withdrawn in 1940 and two, Nos 5946 and 6023, the following year. The final survivor was No. 6004, which remained in service until April 1949 when it was withdrawn by British Railways still carrying its LMS stock number although its name *Princess Louise*, was removed in July 1935 and transferred to a new 'Princess Royal' Class 4–6–2.

LIVERY

From the beginning of the LMS period until the reorganisation of Crewe Works commenced, a number of locomotives were painted in the correct red livery style and some were correctly painted during 1924–26 when painting locomotives at Crewe Works largely ceased. Prior to the changes of livery styles that came into effect from 1928, a number of locomotives carried what has been described as 'assorted styles', for example, a red engine with 'LMS' on the tender side and an LMS coat of arms on the cabside with the number only displayed on the smokebox door. Others carried LNWR lined black livery with the LMS coat of arms on the cabside and stock number on the tender. Some were in LNWR lined black livery with the LMS coat of arms on the cabside, no number on the tender, but were fitted with a smokebox numberplate. Others merely had the LNWR numberplate removed and the new LMS stock number stencilled where the plate had been, whilst another variant was plain black livery with the LMS stock number stencilled on the cabside. Following the adoption of the 1928 livery style, the class still displayed a variety of styles, some still carrying plain black livery, whilst others displayed the correct post-1928 red livery style, which was carried by the survivors until they were withdrawn.

Built in October 1914 as LNWR No. 1567 Charles J. Cropper, *the LMS stock number 5917 was applied in August 1926 and the boiler mountings were altered to conform to the Northern Division loading gauge in September 1928 and the cab left unaltered as this engine was one of four believed to have been allocated to Carlisle Kingmoor for working over ex-Caledonian lines. The following year its cab was modified to suit the Midland Division loading gauge. The 'S' on the side of the cab indicated that the locomotive was, to use an engineman's expression, 'in good nick' and mechanically able to work top-link express trains. This information was most important and enabled the shed foremen to allocate suitable locomotives for the booked work. This locomotive remained in service until it was withdrawn in September 1934.* COLLECTION R.J. ESSERY

Photographed leaving Crewe North shed to work a southbound express sometime around 1930, LNWR No. 163 Holland Hibbert was the sixth 'Claughton' of the first production batch of nine, entering traffic in June 1913. The allotted LMS stock number was applied in July 1926 three months after it had been converted to burn oil. It was withdrawn in December 1934.

G. W. SHOTT

'Claughton' No. 5973 was probably photographed at its home shed Sheffield Grimesthorpe in 1930 – note the Midland '25' shed plate on the smokebox door. Built as LNWR No. 1741 in March 1920, renumbered as LMS No. 5973 in August 1926, it probably had its cab altered to the composite loading gauge at the time it was repainted in code A7 crimson lake and attached to an 'ROD' tender in preparation for its reallocation to Kentish Town in 1928. It was apparently transferred to Sheffield in or around 1930. This engine was only twelve years old when withdrawn in December 1932. However, its life was by no means the shortest (apart from the two accident victims) of the class; several members of the 1920–21 batches had considerably shorter lives. With a fully coaled tender, a crew on board and no lamps in place, it could be that the engine was in the hands of a shed duties link that would have either disposed of the engine or prepared it for its next turn of duty.

T. S. STEEL
COLLECTION

When the 'Royal Scots' displaced the 'Claughtons' from most top-link work on the west coast line, the latter were used elsewhere, in particular on the Midland Division. Three such 'Claughtons' are illustrated on this page. LNWR No 499 of May 1920, renumbered as 5984 in April 1926 (right) and converted to oil burning later that year, was later altered to the Midland loading gauge and allocated to Leeds Holbeck in 1928. Sometime around 1930, however, it was transferred to Saltley. This early 1930s picture shows it hauling what is described on the reverse of the print as the '4/35 Birmingham to Derby freight'. The train is likely to have been the Washwood Heath to Carlisle Goods, a known working for this engine and one for which the headcode shown here, Express freight or cattle train with the continuous brake on at least the first four vehicles, would apply. No. 5984 was withdrawn from service in October 1935.

COLLECTION I. KNIGHTON

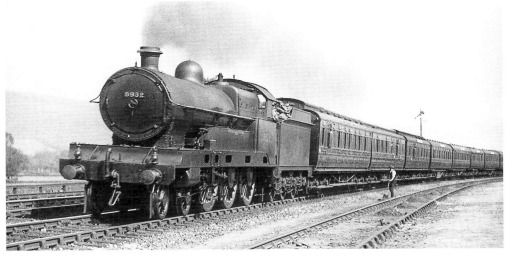

This delightful picture of LMS No. 5932 on a Down express was taken at Steeton and Silsden on the Bradford extension which runs between Keighley and Skipton. Built as LNWR No. 155 I.T. Williams in March 1917, it was renamed Sir Thomas Williams in December 1919, received its allotted LMS stock number in February 1927, and was altered to the Midland loading gauge at about the same time. It was withdrawn in April 1935.

REAL PHOTOGRAPHS

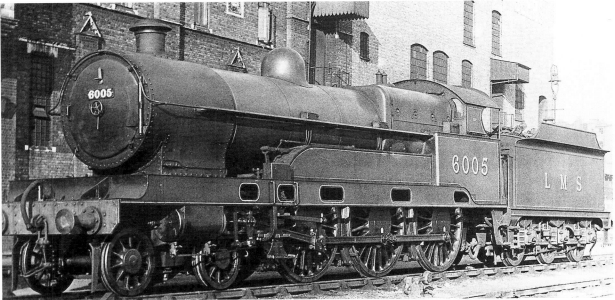

Built in August 1920 as LNWR No. 63, this locomotive became LMS No. 6005 in February having been converted to burn oil the previous year; the date the cab was altered to conform to the Midland loading gauge was probably 1926 and it was withdrawn in September 1932. This picture shows the locomotive at Kentish Town in red livery code A10.

COLLECTION R.J. ESSERY

Built in August 1917 as LNWR No. 986, the nameplates Buckingham were not applied until March 1922 and the LMS stock number 5953 in February 1927. In May 1928 it was rebuilt with a large boiler and the cab profile altered to the composite loading gauge, as seen in this picture, the locomotive remaining in traffic until September 1936 when it was withdrawn.

T. S. STEEL COLLECTION

Built in February 1920 as LNWR No. 2499, the name Patience was not applied until August 1922 and the LMS stock number in February 1927. This locomotive was rebuilt with a 5ft 5in boiler in July 1928, but although Baxter gives May 1928 for the date when the cab was altered to conform to the Midland loading gauge, I believe this work would have been undertaken when it was rebuilt. This picture of No. 5970 was taken at Camden shortly after it was ex-works when displaying the then new LMS 1928 livery.

W. L. REYNOLDS

LNWR No. 2095 was built in June 1920 and was not named. The allotted LMS stock number 5993 was applied in January 1927 and the following year, in May 1928, it was rebuilt with a 5ft 5in boiler and the cab altered to conform to the Midland loading gauge. The following year Baxter records the boiler fittings were altered to suit the Northern Division loading gauge, this work being undertaken in July 1929, but this is probably an error since the large boiler rebuilds were already within the Northern Division loading gauge (see diagram p.120). No. 5993 was withdrawn in May 1936. This picture was taken at Crewe where, judging by the coal in the tender, it was waiting to take over an express passenger train. W. POTTER

This picture of LMS No. 6017 in red, livery code A10, at the head of an Express passenger train, is a splendid sight and, as we can see, all the stock was in LMS livery. Built in April 1921 as LNWR No. 169, the name Bread-albane was not applied until March 1923 and the LMS stock number until November 1926. Rebuilding with a large boiler took place in August 1928 and this locomotive remained in service until October 1940 when it was withdrawn. T. S. STEEL COLLECTION

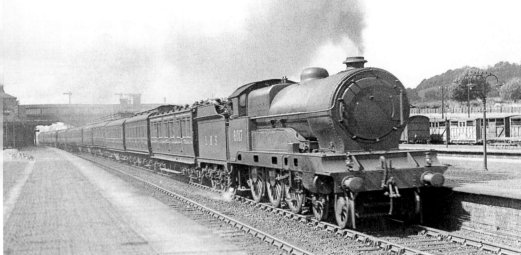

This picture of LMS No. 5957 was taken at Crewe c.1929. Built in September 1917 as LNWR No. 2368, it was rebuilt with Caprotti valve gear and a large boiler in September 1928 and when photographed it was in red livery code A10.
DON POWELL COLLECTION/KIDDERMINSTER RAILWAY MUSEUM

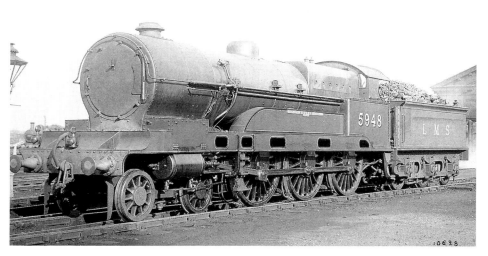

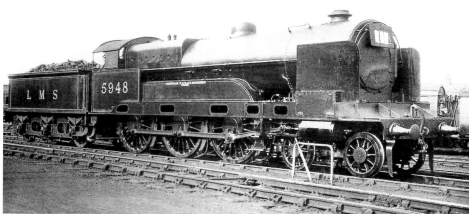

G. W. SHOTT

H. F. WHEELLER

On this page and the next we present four photographs of the same engine taken from different angles on occasions several years apart. The subject is 'Claughton' LNWR No. 2455 built in July 1917, one of only nine of the class to be named after the LMS was formed in January 1923. The name Baltic was bestowed in July 1923 and the LMS stock number applied in March 1927, and in June 1928 it was rebuilt with 5ft 5in diameter boiler and Caprotti valve gear. As shown in the diagram on page 118, the overall height of this design was slightly under 12ft 10in in order to suit the restricted Northern Division loading gauge, and although the top of the smokebox stood only $1\frac{3}{4}$ in above that of the small-boilered engine, there was insufficient headroom for a headlamp in the usual position. Therefore the large-boilered engines had the top lamp bracket on the smokebox door which was itself secured shut by eight radial clips or 'dogs' in the Deeley-Fowler manner while retaining the LNWR type of hinge. The top photograph shows the engine as turned out in 1928 painted in the code A7 livery. Note the large square cover above the outside cylinder housing the cam box of the Caprotti gear. The G9$\frac{1}{2}$S boiler with which these engines, and also the 'Baby Scots', were fitted, was a Derby design and hence all its fittings and controls were of the Midland pattern. An example of this concerns the replacement of the LNWR Beames oil reservoirs mounted on the handrail by standard shallow reservoirs of the Midland type and normally mounted below the handrail. The only exception, as seen here, concerned the Caprotti engines where the tubular reach rod, connecting the reversing wheel in the Cab, by means of a chain housed in a rectangular housing, with the reversing shafts, was positioned below the handrail instead of behind the splasher as in the Walschaerts gear 'Claughtons'. Hence the oil reservoirs on the left-hand side of these ten engines were mounted above the handrail. In the top picture their lids were, apparently, in the open position, suggesting that they were about to be refilled during the preparation of the engine. The middle view shows the right-hand side of the engine where the oil reservoirs were placed in the usual position below the boiler handrail. In this 1932 view the only perceptible differences from the top picture are the transfer of the shed plate from the cab roof to the smokebox door and the addition of smoke deflectors of the early straight pattern. The pipe emerging from the rear of the smokebox was seen on a number of these boilers, where the connection to the pyrometer originally ran, but its purpose here is obscure, possibly in connection with an atomiser for cylinder oil. The bottom photograph was taken at Camden on 29th June 1932 and shows the front end of a large boilered 'Claughton' to good effect. The arrangement of the pipework to the ejector is slightly different from that in the top picture. The picture at the top of the opposite page shows Baltic at Crewe on 19th July 1936 when allocated to Edge Hill shed (as shown on the LMS cast shed plate). The engine had been fitted with the improved smoke deflectors with inward bend at the top; these were introduced in 1933. Less than a year after this photograph was taken, Baltic was withdrawn – in April 1937.

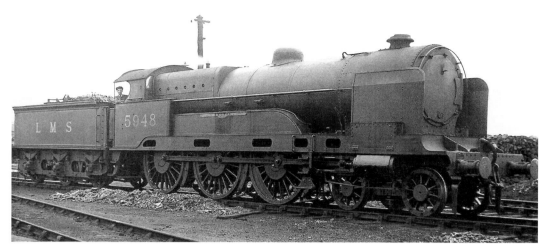

LNWR No. 2221 Sir Francis Dent was built in August 1916 and became LMS No. 5927 in June 1926 when the LMS stock number was applied. It was rebuilt with a larger 5ft 5in diameter boiler and Caprotti valve gear in July 1928 and remained in traffic until withdrawn in December 1936.
COLLECTION R.J. ESSERY

We have included this later picture of No. 5927 to show the slight inward bend of the deflector plate. A note on the reverse side of the print states that the location was Carlisle Upperby and the year 1935. COLLECTION R. J. ESSERY

This c.1932/3 picture was taken at Huddersfield and shows No. 5993 departing with an express passenger train for Liverpool. Built in June 1920 as LNWR No. 2095, it was never named; it received its allotted LMS stock number 5993 in January 1927. The following year, in May 1928, it was rebuilt with a larger boiler and remained in service until withdrawn in May 1936. In this picture we can see it had been fitted with straight smoke deflectors.

G. H. SOOLE

LNWR No. 1133 was built in May 1920 but not named; the LMS stock number 5989 had been applied in March 1926, the year it was also modified to burn oil. This picture was taken at Rugby in 1933 when stationed at Camden. The pipe at the rear of the smokebox connected the super heater header with the pyrometer in the cab. It was withdrawn in 1933.
H. J. STRETTON-WARD

This picture, taken at Bedford Engine Shed on 31st August 1932, shows an unidentified 'Claughton' on the wheeldrop. In addition to providing a close-up view of the valve gear, it is also most useful because it reveals the lining on a red engine.
COLLECTION
R.J. ESSERY

'Super power' in action, probably in 1931 or 1932, heading a Liverpool to Euston express of at least sixteen vehicles on Whitmore troughs. The train engine was almost certainly No. 5940 Columbus, the only one of the nine named 'Claughtons' cut down to the Northern loading gauge known to be allocated to Crewe at that period; it was being piloted by No. 5961 which was built in January 1920 as LNWR No. 178, receiving its LMS stock number in November 1923 and remaining in original condition until withdrawn in October 1934. Note the difference between the respective chimney and domes, necessary modifications to enable the train engine to run over the more restricted Northern Division lines. Other modifications were the safety valves placed across, rather than on, the firebox centreline and the cab roof. COLLECTION R. J. ESSERY

This train was almost certainly the daily 'Up Horse and Carriage Train' which ran from Crewe to Euston collecting surplus coaching stock such as horseboxes, parcels, newspaper, milk and other vans for redeployment at the London end of the line. Here it was running on the Up Slow line in Tring cutting at about midday and appears to have consisted of at least twenty-four vehicles. The engine, No. 5971, was built in February 1920 as LNWR No. 2511 and named Croxteth in July 1923 at the same time as the LMS stock number and crimson lake livery; code A2, was applied. It was the first 'Claughton' to be repainted in LMS colours and was nicknamed by the Crewe North men 'The Chocolate Soldier'. As seen here, Croxteth appears ex-works, so was probably running in on this rather slow train. It was a doubly unfortunate engine, suffering a fractured crank-axle at speed at Castlethorpe on 4th December 1922 and, after transfer to the Midland, collided head-on with a ballast train at Culgaith on 6th March 1930. Badly damaged, it was stored until withdrawn in December 1930, whereupon parts of it were re-used in 'rebuilding' it into a 'Patriot'.
H. L. SALMON/L&GRP 17053

On this page we illustrate three of the 'Claughtons' at work on the Midland Division. LMS No. 5984 was still allocated to Saltley when photographed at Water Orton on 14th September 1935 on a northbound train of empty coal wagons doubtless bound for collieries in the North Derbyshire and South Yorkshire areas. Built in May 1920 as LNWR No. 499, it was never named and the LMS stock number was applied in April 1926. The engine's days on the Carlisle Goods were over by this date, that train having been taken over by a new 'Black Five'; indeed No. 5984 was working out its last few turns as it was withdrawn in October 1935.

T. S. STEEL COLLECTION

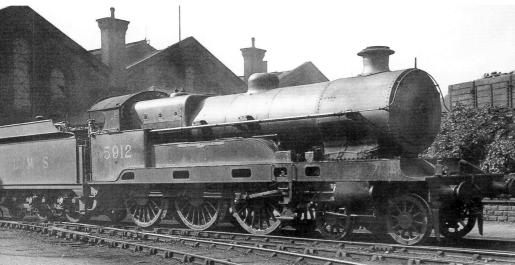

This picture of LNWR No. 1131 Lord Faber, built in August 1914, was taken at Holbeck on 28th July 1934. coupled to an ROD tender. The LMS stock number 5912 was applied in February 1926 and later that year the engine was converted to burn oil. In September 1928 the cab and boiler fittings were modified to conform to the Northern Division loading gauge but in 1932 it received this taller cast chimney, together with the Kylala blastpipe, from No. 6001, with which it was withdrawn in February 1935.

G. W. SHOTT

This picture of No. 5900 on the Down Thames Clyde express, one of the most important express trains on the Midland Division of the LMS, was taken at Leicester on 4th August 1934. Built in January 1913 as LNWR No. 2222 Sir Gilbert Claughton, it became LMS No. 5900 in June 1925, was converted to oil burning in 1926, and the cab was altered to suit the Midland loading gauge in April 1928. Seen here, it was fitted with a Deeley/Fowler smokebox door secured by eight 'dog' clips.

H. N. JAMES

Another picture of No. 5999 (see page 121), this time showing smoke deflectors which had been fitted at an unknown date. Later, in August 1936, the name plate still in place here was removed and the name transferred to a new 'Jubilee' Class 4-6-0 No. 5726. No. 5999 remained in traffic for another ten months before it was withdrawn in June 1937.

COLLECTION R. J. ESSERY

Built in April 1921 as LNWR No. 168, the name Breadalbane was not applied until March 1923 when the locomotive had become LMS stock, although the alloted number 6017 was not applied until November 1926. In August 1928 this locomotive was rebuilt with a 5ft 5in boiler and the cab altered to conform to the Midland loading gauge; this somewhat rear view shows this aspect rather well. No. 6017 was one of the

On the following two pages we have included views of the unique Caprotti 'Claughton' No. 5975 Talisman. Built in April 1920 as LNWR No. 12, the engine was named in January 1923 and acquired its LMS number in January 1927. In June 1928 it was rebuilt in the form seen here in a photograph taken probably in 1930. Of particular interest, positioned just above the first hole in the valance, is the end of a weigh-shaft of the usual type albeit mounted slightly further forward than normal on a 'Claughton'; the other nine Caprotti 'Claughtons' had no shaft in that position.

A. C. ROBERTS

Taken at Longsight on 29th May 1930, this view shows the engine in the same condition as the previous photograph. Note the holder on the back edge of the cab roof from which the shedplate had recently been transferred to the smokebox door.
COLLECTION R. J. ESSERY

Seen here at Aston shed on 9th October 1932, the engine had been fitted with a Kylala blastpipe and large diameter chimney as well as the first style of smoke deflectors – merely flat steel sheets edged with half-round beading.
COLLECTION R. J. ESSERY

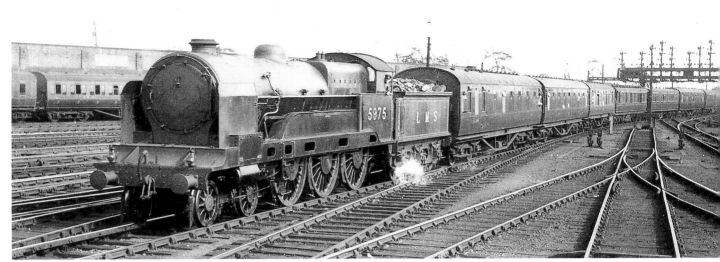

By 1934 or '35, when this photograph of a down express entering Crewe was taken, the engine had acquired the later type of smoke deflectors as fitted to the 'Royal Scot' and 'Patriot' classes. This view of the left-hand side of the engine shows how it differed from the rest of the Caprotti 'Claughtons'. This one retained the original screw reverser with a slightly longer reach rod in the usual position behind the splasher giving the normal seven or eight turns of the wheel from full forward to full reverse gear. The other engines had no screw, the reversing wheel moving slightly less than one full turn from forward to reverse and therefore needed more care on the part of the driver.   W. POTTER

Talisman was photographed waiting at Crewe on an up train on 16th August 1936.
                                                                                    L. HANSON

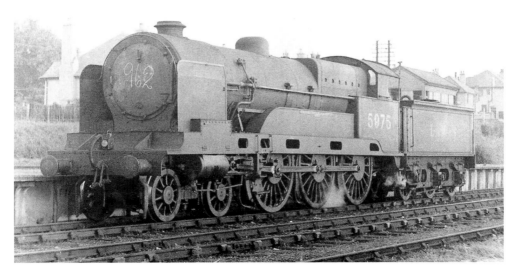

In this left-hand view of No. 5975 at Hest Bank in 1936, we can see the reach rod and arm more clearly. In this case the angular movement of the weigh shaft had to be geared up approximately four times to give the almost 120% on the reversing shafts to the cam boxes. Interestingly, although the oil reservoirs on the boiler could have been placed under the handrail, the position in the Walschaerts engines, they remained in the position above the handrail required by the other Caprotti engines. Talisman was withdrawn in June 1937.   J. A. G. H. COLTAS

During their final years, the surviving 'Claughtons' were often used to haul freight trains so we conclude the 'Claughton' story with a picture to show LMS No. 6004 on these duties. This locomotive was built in August 1920 as LNWR No. 42 and from February 1922 was named Princess Louise, but in June 1935 the name was removed and transferred to the new LMS locomotive, 'Princess Royal' class 4–6–2 No. 6204. In October 1926 the LMS stock number was applied and in April 1928 it was rebuilt with a large boiler. Following Nationalisation it was allotted the British Railways number 46004 but was withdrawn in April 1949 before it was applied. In this undated picture it was hauling a 'semi fitted' freight train, a railwayman's description of an express freight train where at least one third of the wagons in the train were fitted with an automatic vacuum brake connected to the engine. COLLECTION R.J. ESSERY

Allocations.

As we can see, the class was allocated to eight depots with the majority at Crewe North and smaller numbers at sheds that supplied motive power for long-distance workings, eg, Camden, Edge Hill, Longsight, Carlisle and Bangor. By September 1935 the number of 'Claughtons' still in service had been reduced to fourteen, with most stationed at either Liverpool Edge Hill or Carlisle, and the final survivor was still at Edge Hill in 1944.

Ultimate Allocations	1926	28th September 1935	8th April 1944	31st December 1947
Crewe North	5900–5954	5927, 5975		
Rugby	5955–5972			
Camden	5973–5991			
Edge Hill	5992–6009	5908, 5916, 5948, 6023, 6029	6004	6004
Longsight	6010–6020			
Preston	6021–6022			
Carlisle	6023–6025	5906, 5910, 5953, 5972, 6017		
Bangor	6026–6029			
Willesden		5999, 6004		

WEBB 1800 GALLON TENDER

This rear view of 1800 gallon tender No. 1776 (displayed on the cast-iron plate) shows that it was not equipped with vacuum brake as it was attached to a non-vacuum steam-braked 'Coal Engine'. LMS-type lamp holders had been fitted and the tender had a loose three-link coupling hanging on the rear coupling hook, probably because, by the date of the photograph, the engine was in use as a Crewe Works shunter.

J.P. RICHARDS HMRS

Although not much of this tender can be seen, the single row of bolts above the axleguards show that it was an 1800 gallon tender. Note that both the brake vacuum pipe and carriage heating pipe had been removed as redundant for another tender in use purely within Crewe Works, as this one was. Clearly shown here are the wooden spacers through which the buffer stocks were bolted to the buffer beam. Also visible are the ⅜in steel plate, with which the buffer beam was faced, and the 2in thick wooden apron above the buffer beam, which originally contained square holes to act as lamp sockets and hid the bottom line of tank rivets. .

G.H. PLATT

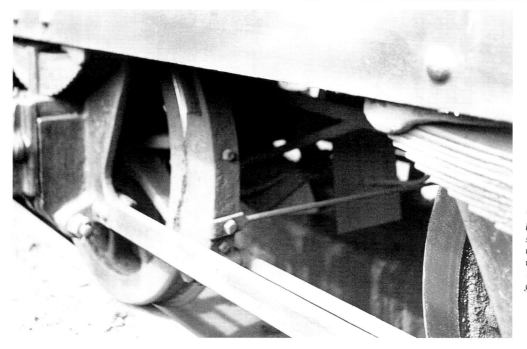

This picture has been selected to show a wooden brake block of the type that was still in use on some tenders into the LMS period. The flat tie-rods between the axleguards, as well as the much wider solebars, indicate that this tender was to Webb's final design whose capacity was 2500 gallons.

HMRS

TENDERS

The LMS inherited tenders of varying types from the LNWR. Three distinct types from the Webb era, one from the Whale years and no less than four from the Cooke period accounted for the stock at the time of the 'Great Amalgamation', as the grouping of 1923 was also known.

WEBB

A few dating back to 1882, about 700 of the standard Webb tenders with 1800 gallon water and 4 tons coal capacity, became LMS stock in 1923. A wooden underframe and 'U' shaped water tank were the main features of the design. In 1893 the slightly enlarged 2000 gallon tender was introduced. In those tenders the underframe had deeper solebars and the tank was wider than in the previous design. Finally, in 1902 the 2500 gallon design was introduced featuring wider solebars and a longer wheelbase as well as a slightly taller and wider tank.

This picture of 17in Coal Engine No. 28091 was taken after it had been renumbered in January 1937. In September 1948 it was renumbered by British Railways as No. 58321 and continued in service until withdrawal in August 1953. This picture shows it coupled to a Webb 1800-gallon tender, which can be identified by the single line of bolts above the springs on the axleguards.
COLLECTION
R. J. ESSERY

WEBB 2000 GALLON TENDER

Rear view of 2,000 gallon tender No. 603 showing the bottom line of tank rivets visible in this design because the wooden apron was attached under a $\frac{3}{8}$in steel plate inset into the top of the buffer beam. This arrangement was also used for the 2,500 gallon tender. Here the LMS lamp holders had replaced the LNWR lamp sockets. This tender retained the LNWR brackets that were used for storing fire-irons. These were removed during the LMS period. The pipe hanging below the brake vacuum pipe was the steam heating pipe.
COLLECTION
R.S. CARPENTER

WEBB 2000 GALLON TENDER

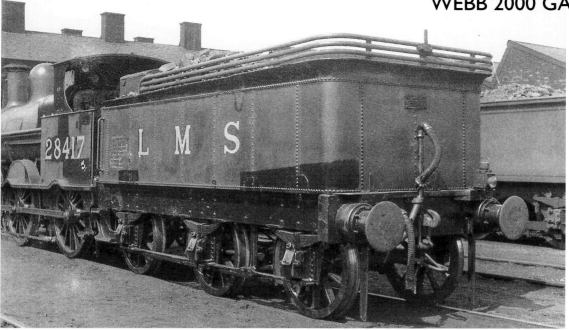

This picture shows a Webb 2000 gallon tender coupled to 'Cauliflower' No. 28417. The tank was the same height as the 1800 gallon one, but 6in wider, hence the increased overhang of the solebars. This was Webb's intermediate design of tender, the underframe of which was identical to the 1800 gallon type except for 15in deep solebars instead of 11in. Thus we see two rows of bolts attaching the axleguard instead of one. No. 28417's cab floor would have been built up by 4in to correspond with the higher footplate of the tender. The LNWR lamp sockets had been replaced by LMS type and a carriage warming pipe had been fitted. Note the retention of the Webb buffers.   G.H. PLATT

In this view of 2000-gallon tender No. 467 we see that the original sockets had been replaced by LMS lamp holders; also evident is the steel plate capping the wooden apron above the buffer beam.   COLLECTION R. J. ESSERY

A rear corner view of part of a Webb 2000 gallon tender providing a good view of the Webb buffer, wooden apron and method of attaching the guard-irons to the buffer beam and the vacuum brake pipe. As a locomotive that could work 'fitted' trains, the rear draw-hook had a screw rather than a three-link coupling.   G.H. PLATT

WEBB 2500 GALLON TENDER

The object of the photographer's attention was the 2500 gallon Webb tender. When turned, the wheel on the left-hand side applied the tender brakes, and the ring handle on the end of the pull rod used to lower the water scoop can just be seen above the raised fall-plate. The treadle lever pivoted on the handbrake screw box, used to raise the scoop, is obscured by the fall-plate. Note the two tool boxes, one probably contained the driver and fireman's 'traps' and the other various tools, oil cans, etc. G.H. PLATT

Previous page and above: A 2000 gallon tender attached to an 0–8–0, probably a 'C' or 'C1'. Note the patch riveted to the tank. On the original print the LNWR lining can be seen together with LMS on the side of the tank. COLLECTION R. J. ESSERY

This shows part of a Webb 2500 gallon tender, in particular the second pattern of oil axlebox which dated from 1902 and replaced the earlier type on almost all Webb tenders by the time of the grouping. Note the rough end of the wooden buffer plank. G.H. PLATT

The left-hand front axlebox of a 2500 gallon tender, showing the rear edge of the footstep. COLLECTION R. J. ESSERY

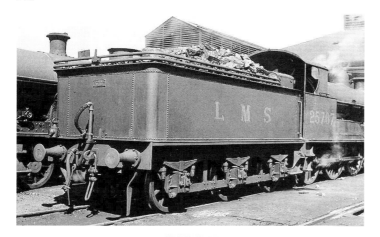

WHALE

The 3000 gallon tender attached to *Precursor* in 1904 was similar to the later Webb design as far as the 'U' shaped tank and tool boxes were concerned, but the historic wooden underframe of the Trevithick/Ramsbottom/ Webb era was replaced with a steel plate frame and the coal rails were reduced from three to two. This design was used for all the Whale classes and the only modifications they received were iron brake blocks from 1908 and, in most cases, vacuum braking from 1913 as well as the replacement of the original curved plate road springs with straight springs of the Cooke pattern.

These two pictures show the side and rear view of a 3000 gallon Whale tender No. 655 coupled to No. 25767 'Prince of Wales' class 4–6–0. These pictures were taken between May 1934 when the engine was renumbered and June 1937 when it was withdrawn. The presence of the steam heating pipe suggests that it was between September when it was fitted and May when it was removed. G.H. PLATT

This Whale tender had been fitted with coal doors. Note the LNWR fire-irons; LMS ones had a different shape handle so that the fireman could identify them when he could not see the other end. The small handle on the top of the tank controlled the water running into the steam injector and then into the boiler. The wheel was the fireman's hand brake. HMRS

COOKE

A new 3000 gallon tender was designed for *George the Fifth* based upon the Whale underframe but the time-honoured 'U' shaped tank was replaced by one which continued under a self-trimming coal bunker, giving, to the relief of hard-pressed firemen, a raised shovelling plate. The separate tool boxes were replaced by cupboards built into the tank on either side of the coal space. Coal doors were fitted in the centre of a forward bulkhead. A single coal rail 'all round' set above the tank coping was provided in place of the two on Whale's tenders.

The second type of Cooke tender was attached to *Prince of Wales* and was a revised version of the 'George V' tender

BOWEN COOKE 1ST DESIGN

The first type of Bowen Cooke tender, seen here coupled to 'George the Fifth' No. 5356 Gibraltar, had a single coal rail above the top of the tender side but, unlike the earlier Whale tenders, the toolboxes were not on the top of the tender front. There were D slots in the frames and the axlebox springs were straight. This picture was taken at Crewe Works on 16th August 1936, the following month the engine was renumbered, becoming No. 25356, and five years later, in August 1941, it was withdrawn.
L. HANSON

BOWEN COOKE 2ND DESIGN

This is a Bowen Cooke tender of the second design with the second type of numberplate, but it is not clear. It appears to read '1077'. This picture also provides a view of a Midland loading gauge cab on this 'George V'. Note the shunter on the footplate and his pole on the tender held in place by the vacuum brake pipe and left-hand lamp iron; this was common practice for shunters. This view-point shows that the ⅜in apron plate followed the same shape as it did in Webb's tenders. Stanier buffers had been fitted.
COLLECTION R.J. ESSERY

The second type of Bowen Cooke tender can be identified by the two small beads at the top of the tender side. They did not have any coal rails but they usually had straight springs, with D slots in the frames. This example is seen coupled to 'George the Fifth' No. 5343 Otterhound *sometime between April 1926 when it was renumbered and April 1936 when it was withdrawn.*

COLLECTION R. J. ESSERY

Second type of Bowen Cooke tender. Note the double coal rails without a space between them. This was Tender No. 1877 photographed at Warwick Milverton in 1930 while attached to 'George V' No. 5373.

COLLECTION R.J. ESSERY

with a double bead attached to the flared coping round the tank top, making a solid top in place of the coal rail. Road springs of thicker plate with a much flatter camber than the previous type were another feature of this design. In due course all Whale and Cooke tenders were fitted with these springs.

The Cooke third type appeared with the 'Claughton' design in 1913. The main difference lay in the underframe that looked the same as the other types but was vacuum braked to suit the engine, the blocks being hung behind the wheels instead of in front as in all the previous (steam-braked) LNWR tenders. All later tenders were built with vacuum brakes and as all the Whale and Cooke tender engines were gradually converted to vacuum brakes, so were

their tenders. Most had been converted by the time of the LMS takeover. The other, more easily spotted, difference concerned a further revision of the tank top coping. In place of the double bead top riveted onto the flared coping, the new design had the coping extended vertically upwards with a single half-round bead attached outside at the top. All three of these Cooke designs retained the Whale feature of 'D' shaped slots in the side frames between the axleboxes. The final design, introduced in 1916 carried the same tank with single bead on a redesigned underframe with oval slots between the axleboxes and a rear square-ended extension as far as the buffer beam with short guard-irons and a circular hole.

BOWEN COOKE
3RD DESIGN

This view of No. 5364 Nubian, taken at Chester in March 1934, shows it with the third type of Bowen Cooke tender. Note the single bead on the top of the tender side, and D slots in the frames. Built as LNWR No. 1623 in August 1911, it was renumbered by the LMS in October 1927 and remained in service until February 1926 when it was withdrawn. KIDDERMINSTER RAILWAY MUSEUM

This view of No. 25322 F. S. Wolferstan, taken at Chester on 8th August 1936, also shows the third type of Bowen Cooke tender. Note the single bead on the top of the tender side, D slots in the frames with straight springs. The 2xxxx series number on the engine was applied in July 1936, just prior to the picture being taken, and it remained in service for just over two years before it was withdrawn in December 1938. L. HANSON

BOWEN COOKE 4TH DESIGN

This broadside view of one of the final series of Bowen Cooke tenders coupled to 'Claughton' class No. 5983 was taken after the livery change to the post-1928 style, but before October 1932 when the engine was withdrawn. This series of tenders had oval slots in the frames, springs with a straight top and the rear end of the frame was 'squared off' in a very distinctive manner.

*Two details views of part of the front of a 'Claughton'
tender – see side door. The handwheel this side raised
and lowered the water scoop.*
J.P. RICHARDS/HMRS

The fourth style was usually coupled to 'Claughton' 4–6–0s but the others could be coupled to almost any Whale or Bowen Cooke class. These five designs, one by Whale plus four from Bowen Cooke, were regarded by those responsible for locomotive and train working as being totally interchangeable on the Whale and Bowen Cooke engines, except the 'Claughtons'.

'Claughton' tenders were non-standard because the floor of a 'Claughton' cab was 9in higher than the other classes, meaning that the tender floor was also built up, and for this reason only Cooke tenders were suitable because they had raised shovelling plates whereas the Whale tenders had shovelling plates at the usual footplate level of 4ft 5in above rail level. Also side doors and stanchion-type handrails were fitted on the early batches to match those on the engines; the handrails were fitted in front of the panel plates, which were set further out than usual, in line with the tank sides. Later

'Claughtons' had whichever style of tender was current when they were built, but always with these modifications. No. 2222's tender as built was unique – the only 'Claughton' tender with double-bead coping.

Reference to the engine diagrams confirms the following types: however, it should be pointed out that coal and water capacity were what was important from the standpoint of railway operation, and minor detail variations, which are important for modellers, were not recorded.

1. Wheelbase 6ft 6 inches × 6ft. Water 1800 gallons. Coal $4\frac{1}{2}$ tons.
2. Wheelbase 6ft 6 inches × 6ft. Water 2000 gallons Coal 5 tons.
3. Wheelbase 6ft 6 inches × 6ft 6 inches. Water 2500 gallons. Coal 5 tons.
4. Wheelbase 6ft 9 inches × 6ft 9 inches. Water 3000 gallons. Coal 5 tons.
5. Wheelbase 6ft 9 inches × 6ft 9 inches. Water 3000 gallons. Coal 6 tons.
6. Wheelbase 6ft 6 inches × 6ft 6 inches. Water 4000 gallons. Coal 7 tons. (This tender was coupled to the 2–8–0 'MM' Class but they were also coupled to certain LNWR locomotives to provide more water capacity.)

Bowen Cooke fourth type tender No. 298 attached to a 'George V' outside Chester shed in 1935.   G. H. PLATT

Bowen Cooke fourth type of tender coupled to No. 25718.

G.H. PLATT

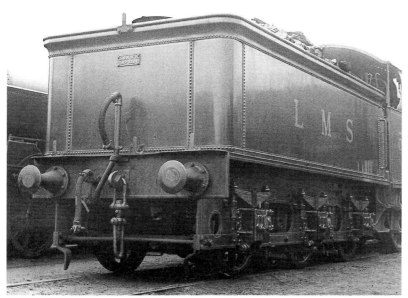

Bowen Cooke fourth type of tender No. 1114, with oval slots in the frames and LMS type buffers. It is seen coupled to 'Claughton' No. 5988.

J.A.G.H. COLTAS

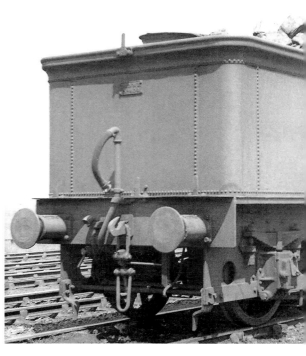

This is the Bowen Cooke fourth type of tender (No. 409) coupled to No. 25798 when photographed on 27th June 1939. Note LMS style of buffers, and the oval slots in the frames. COLLECTION R.J. ESSERY

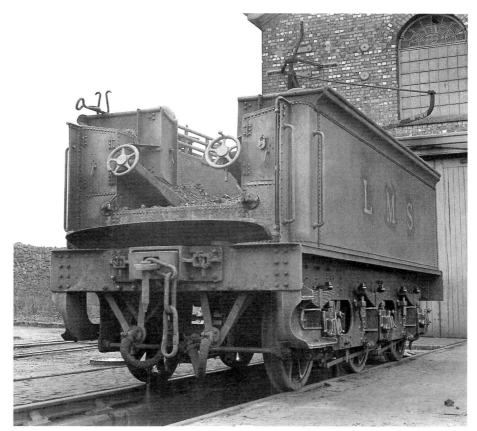

A Cooke tender of the fourth type outside Rugby repair shop, showing the taps allowing water to flow from the tank into the injectors positioned on either side just above the fallplate. They were both in the closed position when the photograph was taken. They were usually operated by the toe of the fireman's boot! HMRS

Bowen Cooke tender with 1916 frames, fallplate raised and showing the water taps on either side, peeping over the plate, to allow water to run into the injectors. HMRS

'ROD' TENDERS

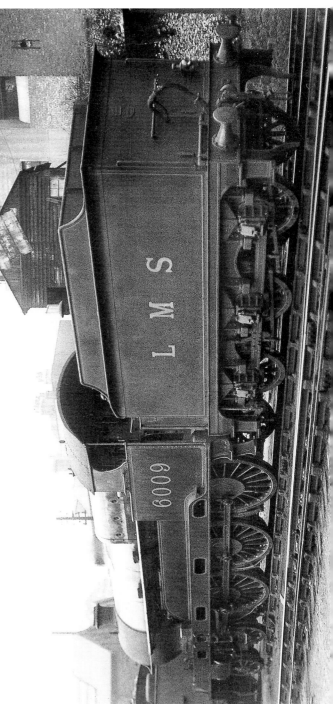

This picture shows an ROD tender coupled to No. 9462, which was LNWR No. 2093 when it became LMS stock in 1923. It was renumbered as LMS No. 9629 in March 1928, and again in September 1931 when it became No. 9462 as seen here. It was withdrawn in November 1932.

COLLECTION R. J. ESSERY

This view shows Claughton Class No. 6009 at Kentish Town on 18th May 1932 coupled to an ROD tender. Built as LNWR No. 119 in September 1920, it became LMS No. 6009 in June 1927 and remained in service until withdrawn in May 1934.

COLLECTION R. J. ESSERY

Surplus ROD tenders from the purchases of 4ft 8in Eight Coupled Consolidation Engine 'MM' Class (see Volume 3) were coupled to a number of LNWR classes. Their value was that the 7-ton coal and 4000-gallons water capacity was greater than any LNWR tender and enabled some LNWR classes to be used on the Midland Division where the water troughs were further apart than on the LNWR lines that had become the Western Division of the LMS. L. W. PERKINS

BIBLIOGRAPHY

Locomotive Liveries of the LMS. D. Jenkinson & R.J. Essery. Roundhouse Books 1967. Ian Allan.

An Illustrated History of LMS Locomotives Volume 2. R.J. Essery and David Jenkinson. OPC 1985.

A Compendium of LNWR Locomotives Part One Passenger Tender Locomotives. Willie B. Yeadon. Book Law/Railbus 1995.

A Compendium of LNWR Locomotives Part Two – Freight Tender Locomotives. Willie B. Yeadon. Book Law/Railbus 1996.

Claughton & Patriot 4–6–0s. G. Toms and R.J. Essery. Wild Swan Publications Ltd 2006.

The Locomotives of the LNWR. H.E.F. Livesey. The Railway Publishing Co. Ltd. 1948.

British Locomotive Catalogue 1825–1923 Volume 2A and 2B Compiled by Bertram Baxter. Edited by David Baxter. Published by Moorland Publishing Co. 1978 & 1979. (Note, some errors were found and caution is recommended)

An Illustrated History of LNWR Engines. Edward Talbot. Oxford Publishing Co. 1985.

The London & North Western Railway Eight-Coupled Goods Engines. Edward Talbot. Published by Edward Talbot 2002.

The L.N.W.R. Eight Coupled Goods Engines. J.R.Gregory, The Railway Correspondence and Travel Society.

The Journal of the Stephenson Locomotive Society.

Railway Observer, The Journal of the Railway Correspondence and Travel Society.

National Archive Rail Files.

LNWR Society Journal.

The allocation lists for 1926, 28th September 1935 and 8th April 1944 are published LMS documents and the 31st December 1947 allocations are taken from *Locomotive Allocations, The Last Day 1947* compiled by John Hooper.

Reflections on a Railway Career. LNWR to B.R. J.M. Dunn. Ian Allan Ltd 1966.

Steam Locomotives Compared. Terry Essery. Atlantic Transport Publishers. 1996.

Bashers, Gadgets and Mourners. Peter W. Skellon. Bahamas Locomotive Society 2011.

North Western Steam. W.A. Tuplin. George Allen and Unwin 1963.

The LNWR Precursor Family. O.S. Nock. David & Charles 1966.

West Coast 4–6–0s at Work. C.P. Atkins. Ian Allan 1981.

Locomotives Illustrated published by Ian Allan:

No. 27 *Claughtons and Patriots*

No. 54 *LNWR 4–4–0s*

Locomotives Illustrated published by RAS Publishing: (Some errors were found and caution is recommended)

No. 97 L&NWR Inside-Cylinder 4–6–0s

No. 107 Pre-Grouping Eight-Coupled Locomotives

No. 121 The LNWR 2–4–0s and Three Cylinder Compound 2–2–2–0

No. 141 London & North Western Railway 0–6–0s

No. 158 The LNWR 0–6–0 'Special Tanks' and 0–6–2T 'Coal Tanks'

Various editions of the *Railway Magazine*.

The LNWR Society Journal contains numerous references to particular classes, and membership of this Society is recommended to anyone with an interest in any aspect of the Company's affairs.

Membership Secretary: Alan Shepherd, 19 Totternhoe Road, Dunstable, Bedfordshire, LU6 2AF.

membership@lnwrs.org.uk. Tel. 01582 603 238.